D1522387

POLITICAL SYMBOLISM AND EUROPEAN INTEGRATION

MANCHESTER
1824

Manchester University Press

EUROPE IN CHANGE
SERIES EDITORS: Thomas Christiansen and Emil Kirchner

Tobias Theiler

POLITICAL SYMBOLISM AND EUROPEAN INTEGRATION

MANCHESTER UNIVERSITY PRESS
Manchester and New York

distributed exclusively in the USA by Palgrave

Copyright © Tobias Theiler 2005

The right of Tobias Theiler to be identified as the author of this work has been asserted
by him in accordance with the Copyright, Designs and Patents Act 1988.

Published by Manchester University Press
Oxford Road, Manchester M13 9NR, UK
and Room 400, 175 Fifth Avenue, New York, NY 10010, USA
www.manchesteruniversitypress.co.uk

Distributed exclusively in the USA by
Palgrave, 175 Fifth Avenue, New York,
NY 10010, USA

Distributed exclusively in Canada by
UBC Press, University of British Columbia, 2029 West Mall,
Vancouver, BC, Canada V6T 1Z2

British Library Cataloguing-in-Publication Data
A catalogue record for this book is available from the British Library

Library of Congress Cataloging-in-Publication Data applied for

ISBN   0 7190 6994 7 *hardback*
EAN   978 0 7190 6994 9

First published 2005

14 13 12 11 10 09 08 07 06 05   10 9 8 7 6 5 4 3 2 1

Typeset in Minion with Lithos
by Action Publishing Technology Ltd, Gloucester
Printed in Great Britain
by Biddles, King's Lynn

Hatch/grad
500110966
polsc
1-24-06

CONTENTS

*A*CKNOWLEDGEMENTS

This book has been a long time in the making and numerous people helped me along the way. Thanks to Lars-Erik Cederman, Anne Deighton, Jean Laponce and William Wallace for helping me frame the topic and for their feedback and encouragement at various stages. I am also grateful to the editors of the Europe in Change series, Thomas Christiansen and Emil Kirchner for their many helpful suggestions, to Tony Mason at Manchester University Press for his kind and patient support, and to all his colleagues at MUP who helped bring this book into being.

Many more people supported this book directly and indirectly. They include Stefan Auer, John Baker, Jean Brennan, John Coakley, Heather Cooper, Daniel Dunne, Kevin Farrell, Tom Garvin, David Glass, Dietmar Grypa, Jean de Lannoy, René Gorenflo, Lesley Hay, Katy Hayward, Susan Henders, Kevin Howard, Salvo Laudani, Jennifer Jackson-Preece and Steven Preece, Fraser MacDonald, Claire Mitchell, Diane Morgan, Cornelia Navari, Turlogh O'Riordan, Don Pittis and Christa Salamandra. I am also indebted to my colleagues in the Politics Department at University College Dublin and to my family back in Switzerland.

My research benefited from the help of many current and former European Union officials who agreed to be interviewed and to give me access to documents. While they must remain anonymous I thank them all for their time and cooperation.

I would like to acknowledge an Overseas Research Scholarship from the British government, an Oxford Overseas Bursary and various conference grants from the University of Oxford, a scholarship from the Canton of Bern and travel and conference money from the European Consortium for Political Research, the British International Studies Association, Linacre College Oxford and the European Union.

Introduction

29 May 1986 was an important day in the history of European integration. Such at least is the impression conveyed in an official account by the European Commission of what happened on that day. It reports a 'solemn ceremony' outside its headquarters in Brussels, staged to mark the official inauguration of the newly adopted Community flag. The ceremony, according to the Commission,

> took place in an atmosphere of festivity and youth: schoolchildren waving small European flags, Community civil servants in relaxed mood, astonished passers-by and Sandra Kim, the young Belgian singer from an Italian family, performing her song 'J'aime la vie', which won the 1986 Eurovision song contest. (Commission 1987a: 4; see also *Bulletin* 1986 [No. 4], point 2.1.81)

There was more music. While the Community flag (whose circle of twelve golden stars was similar to that on the much older Council of Europe flag) was being raised for the first time, the Communities' Choir sang Beethoven's 'Ode to Joy', the Community anthem. In his speech to mark the occasion, Commission president Jacques Delors 'expressed the wish that the blue and gold flag "might be a symbol for Europeans of endless hope nurtured by our ideal and our struggle"'. And Pierre Pflimlin, president of the European Parliament, 'proclaimed the wish that this emblem be "the symbol of peaceful struggle for European Union"' (Commission 1987a: 4).

Yet the story of the Community flag had many facets that went unmentioned in the Commission's cheerful rendering. For instance, strictly speaking the item raised at the flag-raising ceremony was not, after all, a flag. Rather, it was a Community 'logo' – or 'emblem' – that was eligible to be reproduced on rectangular pieces of fabric, among other objects. Such was the semantic compromise that had emerged when the Council of Permanent Representatives approved the quasi-flag on behalf of the member states, after years of intense lobbying by the European Parliament and the Commission and a series of reports partially devoted to the issue.[1] Furthermore, the formal inauguration of the Community logo led to acrimonious wrangles about its use. Was it to be displayed mainly on Europe Day alongside national 'logos' or on national holidays as well? Should European athletes wear it at the Olympic Games, either in conjunction with their national emblems or even in their place? Should public works projects acknowledge Community subsidies by displaying the Community logo? Should the British government be reprimanded for refusing to display it on car licence plates and on most public buildings on Europe Day? Should the logo find its way into classrooms, airports, train stations and onto postage stamps, as the European Commission and Parliament have frequently advocated since?

This study examines the events surrounding the adoption of the European logo and it probes into many other initiatives aimed at shoring up popular support for European integration. From the early 1970s there was a growing perception, mainly within the European Parliament and the Commission, that popular support for European integration was not solid and that this threatened the future development and even the survival of the Community.[2] This stimulated various attempts to enhance the Community's image through 'identity policies' (de Witte 1987: 135) in areas such as culture, education and audiovisual policy. In addition to plans for a European flag and anthem this included efforts to promote a European lottery, 'European rooms' in national museums, student and youth exchanges, a European television channel, the 'correction' of history textbooks, a 'European dimension' in national school curricula and many similar measures.

Yet these initiatives were neither uncontroversial nor unanimously successful. Some, such as proposals for a European flag, were eventually adopted and at least partially implemented. Others were accepted by the member states in the form of non-binding resolutions or declarations but were never put into practice. The third and largest category of 'identity policy' proposals stumbled from the outset over resistance mounted by shifting configurations of national governments, despite their skilful promotion by the Commission and the EP. By the late 1990s, both bodies had bowed to the limits of the politically possible and reneged on their more far-reaching cultural and educational ambitions. What remained were a raft of exchange programmes and public relations-style measures aimed at strengthening public support for specific EU policies such as enlargement and the single currency.

The Union's cultural and educational policy record reflects the continued determination by national elites to defend social and cultural boundaries and their near-monopoly over the creation and dissemination of political symbols. This determination grew all the while they allowed economic and to some extent also political integration to deepen. Such findings in turn open up an important perspective on contemporary European integration in that they highlight the potential staying power of the European nation-state as a bounded cultural, psychological and 'identitive' unit. Beyond this, they illustrate the difficulties the EU faces in trying to cultivate popular identifications beyond the state and the limits this could impose on further political integration in Europe.

The study falls broadly into what Joseph Weiler (1996) has called the 'third debate' in European integration studies – a debate about legitimacy, identity and popular consent in the European Union.[3] These questions have attracted much interest in recent years. Theoretically, this is due to several constructivist turns in integration studies (which in turn reflected broader developments in the social sciences at large), and their concern with concepts such as identity, subjectivity and the symbolic construction of political reality. Empirically, it was stimulated by phenomena such as a steadily diminishing turnout for elections to the European Parliament and the groundswell of popular opposition to the Maastricht Treaty in the early 1990s. Against the backdrop of dwindling popular support for European integration, many observers started to contemplate how the Union could improve its public image and whether policies in areas with high symbolic and 'identitive' potential such as culture and education could contribute to this.

All the same, as far as its treatment of political symbolism is concerned the 'third debate' literature has important shortcomings. For in contemplating whether policies in culture, education and related areas could boost popular support for the Union, many 'third debate' writings pay only the most cursory attention to what the Union has already done or attempted to do in these fields.[4] Since, as this study shows, the Union does in fact have a relatively long record of actual and attempted 'identity policies', this empirical neglect in the 'third debate' literature is not warranted. It is not unlike writing a treatise on the theory of agricultural subsidies in the EU that makes no reference to the Common Agricultural Policy.

Yet even those writers who *have* considered EU political symbolism at an empirical level often have done so in an incomplete fashion. As with many other areas of European integration, there is a tendency to focus on 'where the action is', i.e. on those parts of culture and education where the Union made some inroads (such as student exchanges). Typically, such accounts tell of a relatively smooth and progressive supranational expansion into culture and education, broadly in step with integration in some other areas. However, this study shows that such conclusions are not justified. The Union did expand its activities into some cultural and educational areas such as language learning, university exchanges and the free movement of 'cultural goods and services'. This involvement was often justified on broadly economic grounds and involved neither the dissemination of political symbols nor significant interference with existing national cultural and educational policies. By contrast, the Union made almost no progress in other, more symbolically and psychologically charged areas of culture and education – areas that ranged from

'European civics' in schools and EU-related public rituals to attempts to set up a publicly funded pan-European television channel in charge of airing 'denationalised' programmes. National governments remained unwilling to open these areas to Union interference even as they allowed integration in many other areas to develop. By bringing these developments to the fore, the present study adds a badly needed empirical dimension to the literature on legitimacy, identity and popular support in the EU, and thereby tells of an important chapter in the history of European integration.

The book is organised as follows. Chapter 1 draws on the broader social constructivist literature to work out the key concepts of the study: political symbols, political symbolism, symbolic power and their link to communal identifications, political legitimacy and institutional 'entity processes'. In brief, social constructivism treats symbols as markers that signify and foster the internalisation and thereby the legitimisation of political practices and institutions. This supports the assertion by many post-national theorists that the EU would not need to culturally homogenise its member populations in order to become seen as politically legitimate. Rather, it could follow the example of some multicultural domestic systems and opt for a 'thin' and largely 'civic' symbolic repertoire. Yet as the example of 'civic' multicultural states also suggests, political legitimacy is not likely to emerge as a mere 'reflex' to the establishment of EU-wide democratic institutions or as a mere by-product of intensified transnational communication and interaction. Instead, fostering political legitimacy always has a 'top-down' symbolic dimension. This entails the elite-driven construction and dissemination of symbolic categories which, if successful, stimulates more 'bottom-up'-type communicative and deliberative processes. A political system's reliance on political symbolism of this kind increases in proportion to it becoming more visible and penetrating more deeply into the everyday lives of its subjects, constituting a necessary balance between 'material' (i.e. political and economic) power on the one hand and symbolic power on the other.

Chapter 2 further develops and illustrates this argument. Drawing on historical examples of political legitimisation in state- and nation-building contexts, it explores the techniques, themes and mechanisms that characterised domestic political symbolism campaigns. Despite the obvious limitations of the analogy these examples are relevant for the EU. For one thing, they bear out the claim that institutional legitimacy does not result simply from interaction and exchanges but instead requires an elite-driven, 'top-down' symbolic dimension. For another, they show that such 'top-down' symbolism tends to centre on cultural and educational policy broadly defined, which merits a focus on those areas in the context of the present study. The chapter concludes by showing that competing approaches to European integration lead to diametrically opposed inferences regarding the Union's symbolic policy-making potential.

Chapter 3 begins the main empirical section of the book by examining cultural policy in the European Union. Its founding treaties denied the Union a cultural mandate, which helps account for why it stayed out of this domain until the early 1970s. That decade, however, saw cautious attempts to carve out a cultural role for the Union, most of which were spearheaded by the European Commission. What drove the Commission was a concern that popular support for the Union was fragile, and the belief that cultural policy could foster among its citizens what became variously referred to as a sense of belonging to the Community, a European consciousness or a European identity. Yet these early initiatives came to little. They were either vetoed by shifting alliances of national governments or, even if approved in principle, not implemented. An exception were some cultural exchange programmes and, especially after the Maastricht ratification crisis, various information and communication initiatives by the Commission. These centred on events sponsorship, promotional campaigns in the media and the distribution of public relations literature and involved a plethora of PR consultants, pollsters and focus group experts. Rather than seeking to shore up a broader overarching sense of community among Europeans, these campaigns try to foster support for specific policies (such as the common currency) by highlighting their supposed economic utility. Yet even though Union PR has become much more sophisticated over the years, its overall scope and funding has remained modest and its actual impact on public attitudes ambiguous.

Chapter 4 turns to audiovisual policy. The first part of the chapter looks at Commission and EP-driven attempts to promote a pan-European television channel, intended to confront its audience with non-national and thus supposedly European and Europeanising programmes. Yet a pan-European channel established with Commission support in 1985 faltered over a widespread audience aversion to its attempted non-national programming format and the refusal by many national governments to secure the Union-wide distribution of its signals. Similarly, member state governments vetoed most proposals by the Commission and the EP to help Europeanise the audiovisual productions sector by subsidising multinational coproductions, despite the Commission's increasingly vociferous warnings that boosting European audiovisual output was essential to protect Europeans and 'European culture' from an inflow of US films and television programmes. What audiovisual measures the Union did adopt in the end consisted mainly of attempts to boost the production of domestic output and its circulation throughout the Union, which did little to overcome the cultural and linguistic obstacles that tie many producers to their national markets. By the turn of the century, the Commission's audiovisual initiatives had become dominated by economic and technological objectives, gradually dropping both its earlier ambitions to use broadcasting as a European identity forger and to solidify the concept of 'European culture' by setting it up against the United States.

Chapter 5 deals with educational policy, the third major focus of the study. In the mid-1970s, the same concerns for the Union's popular standing led the Commission and the EP to advocate the introduction of a 'European dimension' into the school curricula of the member states. This would encompass the teaching of 'European civics', the 'correction' of history textbooks, the display of Union paraphernalia in classrooms and the celebration of Europe Day in schools. Yet these proposals quickly became entangled in a dispute about legal competences and ran up against fervent opposition by some member states. Throughout the 1980s, the Union did manage to initiate a range of tangible educational measures on the coattails of the Single Market programme, yet these were mostly limited to various educational exchanges and language learning schemes. Such 'horizontal' measures could in part be justified on economic grounds and they did not threaten the member states' monopoly in shaping educational structure and content. Here, too, an exception was the Commission's attempt to use schools as an outlet for its 'information and communication' campaigns. Yet this soon backfired as it provoked widespread accusations that the Union was targeting political propaganda at children. This chapter ends by reviewing a range of empirical studies which suggest that the 'European dimension' in national school curricula has remained largely elusive.

Chapter 6 assesses the wider significance of the Union's far-reaching failure to extend its reach into key areas of political symbolism. On the one hand, this does not imply that its public standing is set for an inevitable slide. For at least in the short and medium term political symbolism is not the only means of sustaining institutional legitimacy and legitimacy is at any rate not the only source of popular consent. In fact, the mid-1990s saw the return of a kind of 'instrumental acceptance' of the EU among national mass publics which seems to have remained relatively stable in the years since. On the other hand, the observation that many national governments did not cease to protect their cultural and educational prerogatives jealously against Union encroachment all the while they allowed for marked progress in economic and to some extent also political integration contains one of the most important lessons of European integration to date. It points to the continued determination of national elites to protect their near-monopoly over the tools of political identity creation from supranational interference. To the extent that, in the long-run, institutional legitimacy depends on a balance between political and symbolic power, it highlights the possible limits of European integration as a political and institutional project.

Notes

1 Though admittedly not a compromise that the Commission itself cared much to abide by: from the outset, it generally used the terms 'Community flag' or, bolder still, 'European flag'.
2 With the coming into force of the Maastricht Treaty, what had commonly been referred to as the 'European Community' (EC) or the 'Common Market' became part

of the newly established 'European Union' (EU). Throughout the book, I will generally use the term 'Community' when referring to pre-Maastricht events and 'Union' when talking about developments thereafter. When discussing the Community/ Union in a non-time-specific context, I use the two terms more or less interchangeably.

3 For good examples of third debate contributions see Beetham and Lord (2001), Thaa (2001), Kostakopoulou (1997), Laffan (1996), Obradovic (1996), Howe (1995) and Habermas (1991). The first debate, according to Weiler, bore on the formal legality of the Community's constitutional premises, whereas the second debate revolved around 'deontological' questions, related to democratic decision-making procedures (or the lack thereof) in the EU.

4 To the extent that they do have an empirical focus, this often centres on public opinion poll data. An important book-length exception is Shore (2000).

1

Political symbolism and the social construction of the European Union

The belief that political symbolism fosters popular support for political institutions is widely shared. Much of the literature on nationalism and state-building singles out museums, 'civics' textbooks, memorial day celebrations, public monuments and the like as critical tools of national identity construction. And some observers of the European Union (e.g. Baras 1989) have been quick to draw an analogy. They argue that for the EU to acquire lasting popular legitimacy it, too, would need to leave its imprint on the school curricula, memorial day calendars and television screens of its citizens.

All this raises many questions. What, precisely, is political symbolism and how and under what conditions can it foster institutional legitimacy? By extension, what does one need to look out for when trying to analyse political symbolism in an empirical setting such as the European Union?

To address these questions this chapter turns to the broader literature on social constructivism. This literature provides the theoretical backdrop against which political symbolism can best be understood and out of which much of the recent interest in it has grown. Moreover, constructivist scholars have long focused on some of the very issues that are central to the study of political symbolism and institutional legitimisation: norms, identity, institutional 'entity processes' and social categories, to name but a few.

This chapter thus ascertains both the contribution of social constructivist scholarship to understanding political symbolism and, by implication, the significance of political symbolism for the social construction of the European Union. To do so at some length is important. While terms such as 'political symbolism' and 'symbolic deficit' are now commonplace throughout much of the literature on the EU (to the point where many writers use the terms 'social construction' and 'symbolic construction' almost interchangeably), they have nonetheless remained underdefined and undertheorised. There is a need to work out in some detail what, precisely, symbols are, what they do, and how they are related to concepts such as political identification and institutional legitimacy. In turn, this provides a theoretical template to analyse historical examples of domestic political symbolism in Chapter 2 and, in the main part of this book, political symbolism in the EU from the Treaties of Rome to the present.

Social constructivism

What does it mean to say that the European Union is socially constructed? At first glance perhaps not all that much. After all, considering that at present the European Union exists whereas a few decades ago it did not, some kind of construction process must have taken place in the meantime. And further accepting that the EU is neither divinely ordained nor implanted in the genetic makeup of its inhabitants, this process could only have been social. In this broad sense, then, the claim that all aspects of social reality – states, armies, political science departments, supranational unions and so on – are socially constructed is as obviously correct as it is banal. Every analyst of European integration is at some level a 'constructivist'.[1]

All the same, in the recent literature on the EU the term 'social constructivism' has narrower connotations. Drawing on social constructivist work in disciplines such as sociology, anthropology and, more recently, political science and international relations, constructivist scholars of European integration share a range of core assumptions.[2] These can be condensed into seven propositions.

The first proposition is implicit in the term itself. All social institutions are socially constructed, i.e. they emerge through human interaction. Unlike 'brute facts' (such as cats, broccoli and asteroids) whose existence does not depend on human action and perception, social facts are rooted in particular intersubjective understandings about the world. This does not imply that the social world is always fickle: once constructed, many social institutions, practices and beliefs become deeply sedimented and thereby congeal and change only very slowly. Nonetheless, in principle social facts remain historically contingent and are thus subject to change, however slowly. During our lifetime the social world may be very sticky, but in the very long-run all that is social always changes beyond recognition (Searle 1995; Berger and Luckmann 1991).

Second, in tracing the construction of social reality constructivists privilege ideational over material factors. Material constellations and 'substances' (economic resources, territory, geographical distance etc.) 'are given meaning only by the social context through which they are interpreted' (Jupille, Caporaso and Checkel 2002: 7; also Chekel 1999; Adler 1997; Searle 1995). For instance, Finnish voters seem more concerned about immigration than their counterparts in Luxembourg, even though immigration levels are much higher in Luxembourg than in Finland; French elites are more worried by the spread of the English language than are Dutch elites, even though English has spread much further in the Netherlands than it has in France, and so on. In short, material facts acquire different meanings and elicit different forms of behaviour in different social circumstances. Social and political behaviour is, in the first instance, determined by socially produced ideas about the material world, not by the material world itself.

For social constructivists this has important theoretical implications. It leads them to reject approaches that overemphasise the impact of material forces on social outcomes while neglecting the social processes that give meaning to them. These include the more 'vulgar' strands of Marxism in the general social sciences (along with liberal and other types of economic determinism), neorealism in International Relations and neoliberal institutionalism in the study of international integration.[3] Moreover, it means that the various properties and laws often attributed to the social world are themselves ideational. Notions such as 'the structural logic of the international system', 'the inevitable trajectory of historical progress', the 'functional imperatives of the social system' or whatever may appear natural and self-evident to their exponents, akin to laws of physics or biology. In part this is due to the self-confirming character of social expectations: once a critical mass of actors behaves based on the expectation that social reality operates in a certain way, it *will* operate in this way, thus lending credence to the initial expectations and so on. Ultimately, however, these concepts, too, are ideational and therefore socially contingent. For instance, the material condition of international anarchy (defined as absence of world government) may at present be largely associated with self-help, threats and security dilemmas, but one day it might come to signify, say, unconstrained opportunities for cooperation and collective security. Likewise, cultural diversity may invoke (often self-fulfilling) expectations of friction and clashes in some settings, but in others it may breed expectations of peaceful cultural coexistence and mutual enrichment. The point here is that only for as long as humans intersubjectively believe that something has a certain meaning does it retain that particular meaning and shape social reality in a corresponding way (Theiler 2003; Wæver 1996; Wæver, Buzan, Kelstrup and Lemaitre 1993, Chapter 4; Wendt 1992).

The third aspect of social constructivism pertains to the relationship between actors and their identities and interests on the one hand, and the social structures and institutions within which they operate on the other. 'Rationalist' approaches throughout the social sciences typically postulate (sometimes only in the form of an 'as if' assumption) that actors have fixed preferences. These may include objectives such as security, economic welfare, prestige or any other good that actors subjectively value. If they interact and build social institutions, this reflects above all their attempt to maximise their preferences. Institutions remain 'thin' intervening variables that regulate how actors interact in the pursuit of their preferences (by enforcing rules, distributing externalities, solving commitment problems and so on) but they do not affect these preferences themselves (Chekel 1999, 1998).

Social constructivists, by contrast, suggest that social interaction in general and social institutions in particular may have 'thicker' effects upon the participants, affecting their preferences and social identities. Individuals and institutions, social agents and social structures are mutually constitutive and dialectically intertwined. Agents interact and build institutions, but in the process institutions act back upon agents and affect their interests and identities, which in turn shapes their social interaction patterns and institutional outcomes and so forth. What this amounts to is an attempt to come to terms with the basic chicken-and-egg-problem that overshadows all social analysis: humans *make* their social world as much as they are *made by* it. To conceptually puncture this circle analysts need to assume a process of ongoing mutual constitution, thereby endogenising individual interests and identities in their analysis (Wacquant 1996; Berger and Luckmann 1991; Giddens 1984).

A fourth aspect of social constructivism (though one that is 'bracketed' by some constructivist scholars especially in IR [e.g. Wendt 1999, 1992]) hinges on the distinction between social identities and corporate identities:

> Social identity captures the group's defining characteristics (type identity) or the members' collective conception of the group's mission or role within a given social setting. Corporate identity ... constitutes a group's very existence and its extension in time and space. ... Unlike social identities, then, corporate identities are configurations rather than mere properties of otherwise given actors. As such, they can undergo 'entity processes' with respect to both their existence and extent. (Cederman and Daase 2003: 7–8; also Jackson and Nexon 1999)

A statement such as 'Germany today sees itself as a European country' has thus both a social identity and a corporate identity dimension: the former because it attributes aims and identifications to a presumed social actor; the latter because it postulates the existence of an actor called 'Germany', able to develop identities and preferences and to 'see itself' in a certain way.

Neither social nor corporate identities are ontologically real, of course: they are social constructs and as such their survival depends on the social reproduction of the particular intersubjective understandings that sustain them. For social researchers, in turn, this means that their analysis must endogenise not only social identities (i.e. interests and preferences) but also corporate identities (i.e. the making and unmaking of collective actors which 'hold' such interests and preferences). In other words, they must treat corporate entities as dependent rather than independent variables, as 'categories of practice' rather than as 'categories of analysis' and as socially emergent rather than fixed (Brubaker 1996). Institutions and other corporate actors (countries, supranational unions, ethnic groups and so on) may change 'their' social identities and thereby acquire different interests and preferences.

Alternatively, they may become caught in reverse 'entity processes' and disappear: recent examples include Yugoslavia, the Soviet Union and the Geology Department at Queen's University Belfast.

Fifth, for social constructivists the process by which actors acquire social as well as corporate identities is one of social learning. Social learning involves internalisation. Following Durkheim's famous postulate, to internalise means to incorporate the social world into the self, leading towards a 'symmetry between objective and subjective reality' (Berger and Luckmann 1991: 183) and a 'correspondence between the objective classes and the internalised classes, social structures and mental structures' (Bourdieu 1995: 164). The closer this fit between external and internal reality becomes, the more natural and self-evident the social world appears to its inhabitants, and the more do they take its existence and functioning for granted.

If acceptance of the social world is a function of its internalisation, it becomes clear why throughout time and space many different types of social arrangements have managed to procure social legitimacy. For such legitimacy is not intrinsic or immanent to these arrangements (depending on qualities such as, say, democratic procedures, commitment to social equality or respect for divine law), but instead results from its internalisation. *Any* type of social order has the potential to become socially legitimate (i.e. subjectively perceived as legitimate) among those subjected to it provided they internalise it sufficiently.

Sixth, for social constructivists the transmission and reproduction of social reality is symbolic – so much so that many writers use the terms 'social construction' and 'symbolic construction' more or less interchangeably. At the same time, the concept of 'symbol' has remained elusive and lacks a universally accepted definition. Given that symbolism is central to this study it makes sense to dwell on its definition for a moment, starting with a distinction between primary and secondary symbols.

Primary symbols are the basic objectified and reified categories of social life – the very identity-assuming corporate entities discussed earlier: 'Switzerland', 'the European Union', 'University College Dublin', 'the Republican Party', 'the Catholic Church' and so on. Condensing the social world into objectified and bounded categories that are 'entity-fied' if not anthromorphised is a cognitive necessity for human beings. Social and political reality is too complex, too fluid, too abstract, too fuzzy and too remote from our everyday experience ever to be apprehended in its totality. 'Living in a society that extends well beyond our direct observation, we can relate to the large political entity only through abstract symbolic means' (Kertzer 1988: 8; Cohen 1989). But subjectively these representations 'are not viewed as symbolic constructions. Rather, they are thought of as objects that exist independently of people and their symbolic universe' (Kertzer 1988: 6).

If France is thus a primary symbol, the French flag and anthem are secondary symbols. They represent and signify the symbolic category called

'France' and, by extension, the multitude of social relationships and under-standings which 'France' encapsulates and signifies. Secondary symbols (which can include objects, practices, gestures, words, images and music) are important in several ways. At the most rudimentary level they serve as markers and 'mnemotechnic aids' (Berger and Luckmann 1991: 88) which fa-cilitate individuals' apprehension and internalisation of the social categories to which they are tied. Second, while a given symbol is typically linked to a particular referent it cannot simply be reduced to that referent; a symbol does not just 'stand for something else'. If it did, as Anthony Cohen (1989: 14) has pointed out, it would in many ways be redundant.

Instead, it is precisely to their ambiguity that symbols owe much of their significance. The same symbol can convey to different people (or even to the same person in different contexts) different associations and induce different emotions. This ambiguity makes symbols psychologically and socially impor-tant. Psychologically, it allows symbols to aggregate meaning and gives individuals leeway to interpret and thereby mould representations of the social structures which these symbols symbolise (and which they are to inter-nalise) so as to make them compatible with what they have previously internalised. Socially, it enables different people to subscribe to the same symbol without necessarily having to subscribe to identical norms. This facil-itates social solidarity and cohesion even in the absence of complete normative agreement (Kertzer 1988: 11; Firth 1973).

Much more remains to be said about the role of symbols and, above all, about their creation and transmission. Chapter 2 returns to these issues in greater detail. But for now I turn to the final aspect of social constructivism, which is its concern with power.

Power, like symbolism, is difficult to conceptualise and the social science literature offers many competing and overlapping definitions. What unites all of them is a notion of inequality. In every society, the ability to define social reality – social power – is distributed unevenly. Social power in turn has two components: material and symbolic.

Material power refers to the ability of a given agent to shape the material world: to affect the distribution of resources, institutional relationships of obedience and control, physical force and so on. Symbolic power, by contrast, pertains to one's ability to shape the 'subjective' side of the social world – beliefs, perceptions, representations and intersubjective understandings. Wielding symbolic power means generating and transmitting symbols that for their part ensure the internalisation of a given social order. In other words, it involves

> not only the resources required to impose one's view on others, but also the authority to determine the shared meanings that constitute ... identities, inter-ests and practices ... and to be able to get other actors to commit themselves to those rules because they are now part of their self-understandings ... In this reading, power is primarily institutional power to include and exclude, to legit-imise and authorise. (Adler 1997: 336 [emphasis omitted]).

What such a rendering also suggests is that material power and symbolic power go together and mutually sustain and reinforce each other in some measure – a claim that accords with a central tenet of social constructivism as discussed earlier: large parts of the material world are themselves socially determined, in that they are rooted in particular intersubjective understandings about what the material world *is*, which in turn elicits social behaviour of a kind that gives social reality a shape that conforms to those very understandings, and thereby further reproduces and entrenches them. Therefore, affecting material reality by implication means affecting the ideas that shape it and the social mechanisms which in turn shape those ideas but which themselves depend on a material infrastructure. Accordingly, to every viable social and political order attaches a symbolic apparatus, just as, conversely, symbolic power presupposes power over material resources: schools, churches, museums and the like. In some measure, material power *is* symbolic power and vice versa.

Material and symbolic power are not simply two names for the same thing, however; wielding power in one field does not inevitably confer a corresponding degree of power in the other. Even where elites have almost total control over formal outlets of political symbolism (schools, the media, public rituals etc.), they may nonetheless fail to have much of a legitimising impact. This happened in Central and Eastern Europe throughout the 1970s and 80s as elite-controlled socialisation mechanisms gradually ceased to function. In social constructivist terminology, the result was a growing gap between objective and subjective reality, the rise of alternative symbolic spheres (linked to independent churches, trade unions, civil rights movements and so on), and ultimately, the collapse of the regimes in question (Havel 1985).

Its partial autonomy from material power makes political symbolism interesting and the social construction of reality complex. In any given instance, the capacity of socially dominant agents to symbolically transmit the prevailing social and political order needs to be investigated rather than simply assumed. Moreover, where different social agents have competing political and material interests they will have different socialisation agendas, turning political symbolism into an arena of conflict and contestation. The frequent clashes in many countries between, say, secular state and church authorities about control of the school system and between different political parties about the ritual calendar bear this out (Green 1990; Kertzer 1988).

All the same, while symbolic power must thus be at the forefront of any constructivism-inspired research agenda it should not monopolise it. Social meanings, normative understandings and symbolic categories are not always the product of socially powerful agents imposing their definition of social reality on the subordinate. Instead, from Habermas to the Stanford School in sociology, many broadly defined constructivist approaches emphasise the potential for non-hierarchical, communicative and deliberative roads to shared social understandings (but note the caveat below). Likewise, many analysts point to more voluntaristic, cognitively driven forms of norm diffusion and internalisation (Meyer, Boli, Thomas and Ramirez 1997; Habermas 1984; see Cederman 2001a and Finnemore 1996 for a critique). Beyond this, social constructivists must be careful not to overestimate systemic needs for legitimacy in the first place, i.e. the extent to which social conformity hinges on shared internalised meanings. Instead, they must factor in the role of pragmatic acquiescence, apathy, instrumental consent and various forms of coercion in generating social and political compliance. To return to the earlier example, a breakdown in symbolic transmission mechanisms and a growing 'discongruence between objective and subjective reality' choked off the symbolic effectiveness of the Central and East European dictatorships in the late 1980s. All the same, it was Gorbachev's refusal to prop up their rule with Soviet tanks that spelled their ultimate demise. Legitimacy – defined as the symbolic apprehension of a given social order – matters, but it is not the *only* factor that determines the survival of this order.[4]

These caveats, however, do not obliterate the core insights of social constructivism: ideational rather than material forces shape the social world in the first instance; agents and structures are mutually constitutive; internalisation and social learning legitimise and reproduce social reality; and symbols and symbolic power are central to this. What, then, does all that imply for the study of European integration?

Social constructivism and European integration

One important clarification at the outset: social constructivism is not a theory of European integration. In and of itself it says nothing about its origins and future potential and about the factors that are driving or impeding it. Instead, the best way to view constructivism is as a broader social scientific paradigm, a conceptual prism through which more 'middle range' approaches to particular empirical phenomena such as European integration can be developed and assessed (see Christiansen, Jørgensen and Wiener 1999).

Trying to apply constructivist insights to European integration in this way is both promising and difficult. It is promising because, in principle, it helps us theorise underlying social and normative transformations which conventional perspectives cannot adequately capture. For example, while it is now common (far beyond the constructivism-inspired literature) to depict the Union as an 'emerging actor' and thus to imply an unfolding 'entity process', capturing such a process requires constructivist tools by definition. Since, as was argued, corporate actorhood is rooted in social norms, an approach that postulates fixed norms cannot explain the emergence (or the demise) of corporate actors – be they states, supranational unions or whatever.

The same is true for the *social* identities of the various actors implicated in the European integration process. In so far as European integration induces social learning and thereby alters norms and preferences among state elites and other actors, and in so far as these changes feed back into the integration process itself (thereby constituting an 'agent-structure dialectic'), we cannot assume fixed preferences. Instead, our analysis must endogenise changing interests and evolving social identities.

All this is of course easier to assert in theory than to apply in practice. The central challenge lies with the two 'in so far' clauses in the preceding paragraph. To argue that identities, preferences, norms, symbolic meanings and so on change is one thing, but to show that these changes actually stem from a particular social process (European integration, say) is quite another. What is still harder to demonstrate is that these changes *matter* in the sense of producing tangible political consequences that then feed back into the European integration process and influence its speed and direction. Critics of constructivism-inspired EU scholarship often make this their main complaint (e.g. Moravcsik 1999). In the EU as elsewhere, not all changes in norms, interests and identifications have the same origin and not all are politically relevant. Conversely, not all that is politically relevant thrives on underlying normative changes. In some respects, European integration probably *is* mainly about the pursuit of economic self-interest by national governments. The challenge for social constructivists is to separate those situations from others where 'deeper', 'thicker' and more constitutive dynamics are at work. This is clearly not an easy task.[5] To gain some handle on it, it makes sense to distinguish between three strands of social constructivism-inspired research on European integration.

Elite-centred constructivism

The oldest and best-established constructivist take on the EU focuses on social learning among decision-makers. As political elites (mainly within European institutions, but also to some extent within national bureaucracies and non-governmental organisations) become involved in the daily management of European integration, they can acquire new, more Europeanised loyalties, identifications and normative orientations. This in turn strengthens their normative commitment to European integration and their determination to advance it.

Investigating norm change among elites has a long tradition in the literature on European integration which anticipates the recent constructivist turn by many decades. A good example is the neofunctionalist concept of 'political spillover' and its notion of integration as a 'process whereby political actors in several distinct national settings are persuaded to shift their loyalties, expectations and political activities towards a new center' (Tranholm-Mikkelsen 1991; E. Haas 1958: 16; Chapter 2 in this volume). More recently, social-anthropological studies inside the European

Commission and other international agencies claim to detect similar processes (e.g. Shore 2000; Zabusky 1995). Among political scientists, Peter Haas' (1992) concept of 'epistemic communities' and Chekel's (2002) work of norm-diffusion in the Council of Europe are part of the same tradition.

For students of European integration a focus on elite learning is promising in many respects. Given that it pertains to political decision-makers its findings prima facie are politically relevant (but note the caveat below). Moreover, the underlying assumptions which guide this research, namely that social interaction and shared group situations can promote new social and corporate identities, find support from across the social sciences, above all from social-psychology (Hogg and Abrams 1988; Tajfel 1981). Finally, since elite-centred studies focus on a relatively small number of individuals (e.g. Commission officials) they are able to conduct in-depth personal interviews and engage in participant observation. That makes them less prone to the fallacy of wanting to infer norms and identities purely from behaviour and behavioural outcomes and tends to produce more empirically nuanced and sophisticated findings.

At the same time, to be theoretically interesting and empirically relevant, elite-centred constructivists must do more than demonstrate that integration affects elite identifications. Instead, they must also show that elites are actually able to pursue their Europeanised preferences to the point where this has political consequences. This brings them into overlap with more established debates in the integration literature, revolving around the relative power of various actors in the EU, the potential for political engineering by supranational officials and so forth (see Chapter 2 in this volume). All the same, even if normative changes at the elite level were found to occur, and even if these were found to promote integration, this would still say little about the EU's impact at the mass level. This is the focus of the second strand of constructivism-inspired scholarship on the EU, to which I turn next.

Transactionalist constructivism

Exploring the normative dimensions of international integration at the popular level, too, is deeply rooted in the literature, predating the emergence of a self-consciously constructivist strand of EU scholarship by many decades. By far the greatest credit goes to the pioneering studies by Karl Deutsch and his associates throughout the 1950s and 60s (e.g. Deutsch et al. 1957; Deutsch 1954; see also Puchala 1981; Pentland 1973).

For Deutsch, integration (both domestically and internationally) entails a growing volume of interaction and 'social communication' between the societies involved: trade, telephone calls, letters, tourism, cross-marriages, railway journeys, exposure to each other's media, music, languages and lifestyles and so forth. Such mutual exposure and interaction in turn can induce social learning (Deutsch used this very term), and a gradual change of attitudes between the affected populations. These may become marked by a growing mutual responsiveness and trust and by a reduction in negative stereotypes. According to Deutsch, psychological transformations of this kind can carry political changes in their wake. Initially they may lead to the formation of a 'pluralistic security community', characterised by some overarching 'we-feeling' and the elimination of all expectations of violence but no significant merger of institutions. Ultimately, a 'pluralistic security community' may evolve into an 'amalgamated' one, i.e. a supranational federation or some other type of unified or partially unified overarching political system.

Yet neither outcome is inevitable, according to Deutsch. On the one hand, the overall volume of transactions may remain too low to generate sufficient psychological and political momentum. On the other hand, too *much* interaction at too rapidly growing a rate can be disintegrative. Since interaction always has the potential to generate friction, it can overburden capacities for psychological and institutional adjustment.[6] Therein, for Deutsch, lie the relative merits of 'pluralistic' as opposed to 'amalgamated' security communities. A premature leap into political integration may backfire, since the very high volume of interaction this presupposes as well as generates may overload the system at large and thereby erode its very foundations.

Deutschian transactionalism has attracted many criticisms: notably for failing to differentiate more sharply between cause and effect, for its difficulties in measuring and quantifying transactions and for its fixation on behaviourist methodology (Adler and Barnett 1998; Puchala 1981; Connor 1972). However, in what follows I put these criticisms to one side, showing instead that Deutschian thinking has influenced the contemporary constructivist literature on the EU in two distinct ways.

A first group of transactionalism-inspired scholars detects a growing cultural homogenisation among the EU's member populations – a gradual levelling of lifestyles, social attitudes, consumption patterns, commercial cultures and so on. This includes national 'morality regimes' in areas such as drugs, sex and abortion (Kurzer 2001), practices on citizenship, multiculturalism and immigration (Soysal 1994) and a gamut of tastes, habits and social preferences (Borneman and Fowler 1997; Kaelble 1987). Following Deutsch, these writers all suggest that such levelling processes somehow thrive on 'interaction', though they typically cast their theoretical nets more widely. Some incorporate parts of the norm diffusion model developed by the Stanford School in sociology, while others focus on common market-induced regulatory arbitrage and its corrosive effect on national cultural particularities. Whatever their precise angle, these approaches share the belief that interaction ultimately fosters cultural sameness.

This raises several issues. First, while national norms and policies on, say, gay marriage and cannabis use might be converging, the same does not apply to many other issue areas (such as language and media consumption) where almost no levelling has occurred (see Collins 2002; Chapter 4 below). Second, even where cultural and institutional homogenisation is clearly evident this often represents a more general Western phenomenon rather than a specifically European one. Spain and Finland may be adopting similar norms on cannabis consumption and animal rights and they might be building increasingly similar-looking airports and shopping malls; but the same is also happening in places far beyond Europe's shores. Therefore, even those who claim to witness a 'European society' in the making (Kaelble 1987) would have to recognise that much of what it contains is not specifically European. By extension, more global, as opposed to just European, processes of cultural diffusion are bound to generate much of it.

The final objection is the most important one: the homogenisation of cultural form in some areas does not necessarily equate to a homogenisation of meaning, much less to the growth of overarching European identifications and political loyalties. After all, some of the most vicious conflicts of recent times have involved populations that share a great deal of cultural similarity – Rwanda, ex-Yugoslavia and Northern Ireland illustrate the point. Conversely, theorists of consociational democracy have long shown that continued cultural fragmentation does not necessarily preclude the development of shared political identifications (Theiler 2004b; McRae 1983; Lijphart 1977, 1968). Underpinning such observations is a key postulate of social constructivism as discussed earlier: ideas, not material forces shape the social world in the first instance, and whatever meaning attaches to the material world is itself socially determined. Against this backdrop, the wider political significance of the various transactionalism-inspired cultural Europeanisation accounts is far from obvious.

Post-nationalism and the 'tandem' hypothesis

The second strand of mass-centred constructivism takes such objections on board. Often termed (somewhat confusingly in the context of European integration studies) 'post-nationalism', it is not primarily concerned with the homogenisation of material culture or of relatively narrow social norms. Instead, it focuses on what it sees as the emergence of a broader normative and symbolic space among Europeans and of an overarching 'civic' identity to accompany it. This shared ideational realm is seen to include adherence to political and constitutional principles (liberal democracy, rule of law, human rights, separation of powers, etc.), together with values such as social tolerance, multiculturalism and the welfare state. For post-nationalist scholars, such values can develop even in the *absence* of cultural and linguistic homogeneity and indeed dissolve the need to bring about such homogeneity in order to sustain an emerging pan-European democratic system. Jürgen Habermas's well-known concept of 'constitutional patriotism' encapsulates such a faith in the viability of shared 'civic' identifications and democratic practices in the EU, drawing inspiration from multicultural democracies such as Switzerland, Canada and the United States (Fine and Smith 2003; Habermas 1991).

Communicative action and constructivist dialectics are at work all through the post-national story. Social and institutional linkages in EU-Europe drive the evolution and diffusion of liberal democratic norms and practices, leading to a shared European public space. Over time, this enables a supranational democratic process to take root, which strengthens and legitimises the EU's institutional and constitutional framework. This in turn helps to further consolidate EU-wide democratic and deliberative processes, further solidifying shared norms and symbolic meanings and so forth. These mutually reinforcing developments help transcend Rousseau's famous chicken-and-egg dilemma according to which democracy strengthens a sense of community but also *presupposes* it (see Cederman and Kraus 2002). For post-nationalists, democracy, community and demos beget and gradually strengthen each other.

Different post-national accounts have different nuances, discussion of which would go beyond the scope of this chapter (see Kostakopoulou 1997; Weiler 1996; Delanty 1995; Howe 1995). Yet the underlying assertion informing all of them has both normative and analytical appeal. In most normative readings, an EU signified by liberal democratic principles would be preferable to one predicated upon, say, claims to racial homogeneity, cultural similarity or a belief in the intrinsic supremacy of the Judeo-Christian heritage. From an analytical perspective, the central claim of post-national approaches is equally well taken, if seen against the backdrop of core constructivist assumptions as outlined earlier. Since symbols are markers that signify, transmit and thereby foster the internalisation of political structures and institutions, nothing in principle stands in the way of purely 'civic' themes becoming the defining markers of an overarching European polity. It is the degree to which symbols are disseminated and internalised, not the nature of those symbols, which determines the social legitimacy of a political system in the first instance (see Chapter 2 below).[7]

All the same, one central question overshadows all post-national approaches to the EU. Even if one accepts that transnational communication and democratic deliberation strengthen transnational identifications and demos-formation, this does not imply that the latter are a mere reflex to the former. Otherwise, democratic systems *ipso facto* could never face any legitimacy problems in the first place. Instead, for some otherwise sympathetic critics of post-national blueprints, transnational political legitimacy does not result from democratic interaction alone, but instead requires 'specific identity-building mechanisms that are at least partly independent of democratic decision-making' (Cederman and Kraus 2002: 7). More specifically, it requires a cultural and symbolic infrastructure to support, channel and mould communicative and deliberative processes and to cultivate among citizens the competences they need to participate in such processes in the first place as well as the communal identifications that make them *want* to participate. Such an infrastructure, in turn, requires the involvement of political elites and the use of symbols and symbolic power in the ways discussed earlier. In short, in this rendering an interplay involving 'top-down' and 'bottom-up' processes generates viable political identities. It alone produces 'communicative capacity that enables deliberation and generates a sufficiently strong we-feeling that can carry the weight of effective and democratic governance' (Cederman 2001a: 157).

Theoretically, this 'tandem' hypothesis reflects the earlier point that the social world is the product of seemingly spontaneous and uncoordinated social interaction *and* of reality-defining symbolic impositions by elites which help structure this interaction. Historically, most accounts of political legitimisation in domestic settings make much the same point: broad-based political mobilisation and democratic participation grew alongside the creation and dissemination of symbolic categories by state elites. Typically, this entailed a large measure of outright cultural and linguistic homogenisation, even in many states that are officially defined in largely 'civic' terms – France is a good example (Brubaker 1999; Calhoun 1997; Hobsbawm 1994; Weber 1976). But even where state elites renounced cultural assimilation they nonetheless fostered overarching communal sentiments and political loyalties by other means: they created shared myths and symbols, and used schools, the mass media, military conscription, public rituals and many similar devices to disseminate them. Even Switzerland, the empirical jewel in the crown of almost every post-nationalism theorist, was no exception. More recent historical accounts of Swiss state-building emphasise its elite-driven aspects, in opposition to more traditional conceptions of Switzerland as a purely voluntaristic 'nation of will' that to some extent still permeates the country's official national ethos (Altermatt, Bosshart-Pfluger and Tanner 1998; Hettling 1998).

What does all this mean for a constructivist take on European integration? Regardless of how close an analogy between state-building and European integration one is prepared to accept (more on this in the next chapter), the basic theoretical point remains: as did the former, the legitimisation of the EU requires the 'top-down' cultivation of symbolic categories and communicative capacities which, if successful, enables more 'bottom-up' processes of communicative action and democratic deliberation to take root and thereby lead to the formation of overarching political loyalties and political identifications. For this to be effective, the symbolic categories in question would have to become

> so internalised that they become part of the fabric of subjectivity and the individual's sense of self [. . .] They] include notions like 'European citizen, a 'good European', a 'European problem', 'common European values', 'European culture' and 'Europeanness' itself. . . . Constructing Europe requires the creation of 'Europeans', not simply as an objectified category of EU passport-holders and 'citizens' but, more fundamentally, as a category of subjectivity. (Shore 2000: 29–30)

This raises many questions, to be sure: 'How much' in the way of a shared 'European subjectivity' is needed to sustain the EU? And what, precisely, would it need to 'consist of'? The next chapter returns to these issues. But first, it is useful to take a conceptual step back by differentiating between three potential sources of legitimacy and levels of legitimisation in the European Union.

Three roads to legitimacy

The first type of legitimisation relies on the concept of 'utilitarian support' that reverberates throughout much of the literature on European integration. Utilitarian support grows when national publics become convinced that their interests are best served by membership of the European Union and/or by the pursuit or expansion of particular EU policies. There are no a priori restrictions as to what these interests may consist of, although most analysts assume that economic welfare concerns take centre stage. Moreover, individuals may either focus on their own personal welfare, or on that of a corporate category they identify with and whose perceived interests thus partially become their own (such as a state, region or interest group).

For some analysts utilitarian support can be captured outside a constructivist framework. After all, material welfare is often seen to constitute a fixed preference which requires no social construction and which does not change due to participation in the EU. Regardless of whether or not one accepts this, utilitarian gains (especially future ones) are often a matter of perception and as such they are subject to symbolic (re)definition. Take recent EU campaigns to promote public support for enlargement. Frequently, these revolve around attempts to dissociate the new members in Central and Eastern Europe from perceptions of threat (e.g. 'organised crime', 'immigration flood', 'not fully civilised') in order to link them to notions of benefit and opportunity ('new export markets', 'rich cultural heritage' 'youthful new democracies' and so on). As shown in later chapters, the same logic informs the EU's perennial efforts to make its public image appear less technocratic and more caring and in tune with the practical concerns of ordinary citizens.

The second mechanism capable of enhancing the EU's popular legitimacy requires the rise of (a) *new* interests and preferences among national publics and (b) a belief that these are best served by the EU. In as far as the nation-state is the interest-referent, this involves redefining national interests in order to make them more compatible with European integration. Sustained efforts by Irish political elites over the past three decades to 'reimagine' Ireland as a mainstream European country are a good example, as are attempts by post-war West German elites to define their country as a Western democracy whose 'natural destiny' lies 'in Europe' (see Hayward 2002).

Exploring how interests become redefined in this way requires a broadly constructivist line of inquiry. It presupposes that social identities are fluid rather than fixed, and that their evolution is dialectically related to the European integration process. As a polity participates in this process its preferences change, which in turn affects its participation in the EU and so on.

At the same time, what is at stake at this level of legitimisation are changes in social identity, not corporate identity. In other words, while the social identities attributed to the member states may become more amenable to European integration, this does not in and of itself turn the EU into a perceived corporate actor and identity category in its own right. It does not entail a European 'entity process'. It is this latter development which, if it occurs, constitutes the third potential source of legitimacy for the EU.

As suggested earlier, a European 'entity process' would entail growing perceptions of the EU as a real existing unit and actor and the parallel reification of 'Europeans' as a community with needs, aspirations and the capacity for agency. It would turn 'Europe' (or the EU) into an objectified, reified and internalised category, and a shared point of reference around which overarching communicative and deliberative processes could revolve. As 'Europe' would enter into the self-definitions of its citizens, they would identify with it and make its perceived interests and aspirations their own. Moreover, since the overarching communal category would now be bound up with their identity they would value its preservation as an end in itself rather than just as a means to achieve other ends. This would give it a self-referential claim to survival and in some measure insulate it from calculations of utilitarian gain (Wæver 1996).

Eventually, the rise of 'Europe' as a corporate actor and overarching identity category could come to submerge the corporate actorhood of the member states. In a less far-reaching scenario, the EU would evolve into a complementary category of belonging, representing the outermost level of identification in a Russian dolls-type arrangement. Either development would entail the acquisition of a symbolic repertoire to signify and sustain an overarching European communal category as well as the boundaries that would separate a new inside from a new outside. Following the 'tandem' logic, this would need to have a 'top-down' as well as a 'bottom-up' dimension. It would require the construction of new symbolic categories by elites as well as more broad-based communicative and interactional patterns to consolidate and reproduce these categories and thereby place them on a self-sustaining basis.

As suggested, there are no a priori limits as to what type of symbols such third-level legitimisation processes might draw on. In most state- and nation-building settings they had some 'thicker' cultural or ethnic flavour, but in principle purely 'civic' symbols, too, could come to signify an overarching European communal and corporate category. The next chapter will elaborate further on this 'thick versus thin' distinction. In any case, several factors help determine what kinds of symbols are employed in a given setting. They include pre-existing social and cultural conditions (the greater the degree of existing cultural diversity, the stronger might be the temptation to resort to thinner, non-cultural symbols), prevailing normative orientations (e.g. whether cultural assimilation is deemed an acceptable option), as well as more general elite preferences (e.g. whether they conceive of the EU primarily as a 'civic' or also as a cultural project). Mechanisms of elite socialisation as captured by 'elite-centred constructivism' described earlier help account for these preferences.

Cultivating perceptions that institutions meet existing interests, changing these interests and fostering new corporate identities are thus the three possible routes to political legitimacy, in the EU as much as in any other institutional context. Historical accounts of state- and nation-building suggest that all three were involved in every instance, albeit in various proportions. States appealed to the (often material) self-interests of their citizens while also seeking to re-shape pre-existing local and regional communal identifications to make them more amenable to inclusion in an overarching political category. All the while the state itself acquired a corporate identity of its own, either submerging local and regional affiliations in the long term (as in many unitary states) or incorporating them into a co-centric circles of allegiance scheme (as in federal and consociational systems).

'Entitativity' and boundaries

But why not stop at the second, or even only at the first level of legitimisation, short of engendering an overarching sense of community, 'entitativity' and collective actorhood? Most theorists of European integration follow their 'domestic' counterparts and rule out this possibility.[8] They insist that ultimately the EU cannot acquire lasting legitimacy unless it evolves into an overarching European community. This claim is often defended on 'practical' as well as psychological grounds.

'Practical' explanations build on the earlier point that political systems (especially democratic ones) can only function if their members inhabit a framework of shared meanings – constituted by basic normative orientations, cognitive reference points and a common symbolic repertoire to express and disseminate them (Thaa 2001). Such meanings, the argument goes, can only emerge and be sustained in bounded communal settings, as these give shape to and protect stable communicative and interactional patterns that produce and reproduce shared meanings in the first place. Psychological explanations, by contrast, highlight the Rousseauvian point that legitimacy, and especially democratic legitimacy, rely on underlying psychological conditions which only community can foster. One important factor is the alienating potential of majority decisions on the overruled; but if 'the *majority* has decided' becomes '*we* have decided' a sense of being dominated by others disappears.

Similarly, communal sentiments can foster popular acceptance of redistributive policies and of various obligations which overarching institutions impose upon their subjects. If these perceive an obligation towards these institutions as a duty towards other community members or towards the internalised communal 'entity' at large, they are less likely to experience alienation and more likely to comply (Thaa 2001; Scharpf 1998; Etzioni 1968, 1965). Finally, as suggested, the 'end in itself'-status and self-referential claim to survival that flows from 'third-level' legitimacy helps insulate the institution in question from utilitarian cost-benefit calculations and thereby makes it less vulnerable to changes in underlying material conditions.

Underlying both accounts is a broader theoretical point regarding the function of communal boundaries. More specifically, boundaries are not simply the result of what is going on inside them; they do not just reflect shared communal sentiments, political commitments and 'entity perceptions' among those whom they enclose. Instead, just as social processes and 'entities' define boundaries, boundaries can promote internal cohesion and fuel 'entity processes' (Cederman and Daase 2003; Cederman 2001b; Brubaker 1996; Abbott 1995; Bourdieu 1994, 1980; Simmel 1955). Social 'things' constitute boundaries as much as boundaries make social 'things'.

Strengthening boundaries and making them more visible can promote 'entity processes' and thus third-level legitimacy in three ways. First, it makes a given social category more discernible and thus easier to internalise. Second, it makes that category more salient as boundary awareness promotes outgroup awareness, which in turn increases the salience of the ingroup. Finally, by accentuating perceptions of external difference, boundaries increase perceptions of internal similarity, thereby facilitating internal cohesion and the emergence of communal sentiments (Theiler 2003; Hogg and Abrams 1988). On account of this logic, then, political institutions are more likely to emerge and to survive if (a) they are embedded in a bounded communal 'entity' and (b) they manage to accentuate the boundaries of this entity, above all by differentiating it from outgroups. The extension of this claim is that political institutions will seek to preserve and, if necessary, cultivate boundary awareness among their subjects, and that those that succeed in doing so are more likely to prevail than those that do not.

Neither claim is theoretically invincible. In the first place, accentuating boundaries with outgroups is not the only conceivable way of fostering communal sentiments and overarching 'entitativity'.[9] More broadly, strong first- and second-level legitimacy might obliterate the need for moving to the third level in the first place. Nonetheless, to say that the rise of a bounded overarching European sense of community and corporate identity is not the only conceivable route to political legitimacy does not invalidate the notion that such third-level processes would be conducive to it. As indicated, all historical examples of state legitimisation point to the presence of third-level mechanisms, albeit to varying degrees (more on this in the next chapter).

Without third-level political legitimacy, the onus on the other two sources might well become unrealistically high.

To briefly sum up this chapter: social constructivism stresses the primacy of ideational over material factors, and the dialectical relationship between individual agents and institutions. Of the various ways of applying constructivist principles to European integration, those that centre on the potential emergence of a pan-European symbolic and communicative space are the most sophisticated. They reflect constructivism's emphasis on ideas. At the same time, these approaches must incorporate not just social communications-type 'bottom-up' dynamics but also 'top-down' ones that revolve around symbolic legitimisation strategies by political elites. Finally, the chapter identified three specific sources of political legitimacy. These are (1) a growth in perceptions that institutions meet existing interests; (2) a change in those interests; and (3) the emergence of a new overarching corporate identity. The next chapter seeks to put more empirical flesh on the relatively bare theoretical bones sketched so far before the second part of the book turns to actual and attempted political symbolism in the European Union.

Notes

1 The common French term 'la construction européenne' captures this much better.
2 Key constructivist texts in sociology include Bourdieu (1995), Searle (1995), Berger and Luckmann (1991) and Giddens (1984). For important theoretical additions see Emirbayer (1997) and Abbott (1995). For applications of constructivist thinking to International Relations see Cederman and Daase (2003), Guzzini (2000), Jackson and Nexon (1999), Wendt (1999, 1992), Chekel (1998), Adler (1997), Ringmar (1996), Wæver, Buzan, Kelstrup and Lemaitre (1993) and Onuf (1989).
3 Such criticism against materialistic approaches to the social world is nothing new, of course. As Émile Durkheim (1922) famously observed, every social fact can only be explained in terms of other social facts as opposed to underlying material or psychological factors. Otherwise, we could not account for the vast amount of cultural complexity and diversity across time and space.
4 On the wider issue see Held (1988, Chapter 4), Abercrombie and Turner (1978) and Mann (1970).
5 Reserving constructivist insights for long-term processes and 'rationalist' ones for the short-term cannot fully resolve this problem. It is true that identities (both social and corporate) are more likely to change over the long haul: very few of today's corporate actors existed a thousand years ago. At the same time, once constructed, many social practices, beliefs and institutions become deeply sedimented and thereby congeal over long periods of time (Cederman 2001a; Berger and Luckmann 1991). Conversely, when social and corporate identities do change, this often happens very rapidly, through sudden breaks and disjunctures rather than through incremental evolutionary transformations (Theiler 2003). In the end, both Yugoslavia and the Soviet Union died very quickly, just as, a few decades before, the political transformation of post-war Western Europe was as profound as it was rapid and in many ways unexpected.

6 Moreover, it may well depend on a range of contextual variables such as the 'themes' around which contacts revolve (Hogg and Abrams 1988; Connor 1972).

7 Though language in particular has an ambiguous status in this context. To the extent that it serves as communal signifier, linguistic homogenisation is not needed to promote political legitimacy as alternative, more 'civic' signifiers can do the job. However, language also has a more practical function in that it is linked to communicative and deliberative competence which for its part can facilitate the emergence and entrenchment of shared 'civic' values (see below). And while the Swiss example shows that overarching democratic processes can take root without a common language, most other states have tried to promote some measure of linguistic homogenisation, or at least an overarching lingua franca alongside local and regional languages.

8 An exception were the early Functionalist blueprints of integration. Elaborated in the inter-war period by David Mitrany and his collaborators, they advocated the gradual replacement of the states-system with an arrangement of de-territorialised, de-communalised and mutually disconnected institutions whose scope and powers would reflect solely their respective functional remit (McLaren 1985; Mitrany 1966). But the early Functionalism found few adherents. Its critics denounced it as overly technocratic and rationalistic, arguing that supranational institutions not rooted in a corresponding supranational community are either impossible to achieve or doomed to suffer from a chronic lack of legitimacy and popular identifications (see Pentland 1973).

9 For example, in his earlier work Habermas himself does not insist on community as a precondition for effective communicative action. In this rendering, communicative action can lead to shared meanings provided the participants share broadly commensurate cognitive and normative horizons. They do not, however, necessarily have to partake a bounded communal context in the sense defined above. Yet in at least some of his more recent writings on post-nationalism and 'constitutional patriotism' in the EU Habermas postulates more stringent conditions, depicting supranational communal sentiments as a prerequisite for a viable supranational political system. His aim is of course to show that these sentiments could be 'civic' as opposed to cultural or ethnic, but they would be communal all the same. Incidentally, very few critics of the 'constitutional patriotism' blueprint criticise it from this angle. Instead, most are preoccupied with doubts as to whether a 'thin' supranational community would be 'thick enough' (but see Kostakopoulou 1997; see Thaa 2001 for a differing interpretation of Habermas's concept of post-nationalism).

2

Political symbolism in practice

Whereas the last chapter dealt with political symbolism in theory, the present chapter analyses its practical workings. Drawing on examples of political legitimisation in domestic settings, it explores the tactics, techniques, themes and mechanisms that defined domestic political symbolism drives. How were political symbols developed, disseminated and maintained? What makes 'top-down' symbolic initiatives more likely to induce the kind of 'bottom-up' processes which in turn lead to shared political identifications and institutional legitimacy? Finally, what can we infer from this regarding political symbolism in the EU, bearing in mind the obvious limits of such an analogy?[1]

The last point is important. It calls for some preliminary remarks on the appropriateness of drawing limited parallels between domestic politics and contemporary European integration. Above all, there is a need to address potential objections to the effect that the very open-endedness and *sui generis* character of the EU rules out valid analogies with any other political system, the modern state included. Two arguments, however, help counter such objections.

First, a limited analogy between state-building and European integration does not imply that the two are qualitatively the same, either in terms of process or 'end product'. For example, it does not suggest that the EU will have to become a nation-state-type entity in order to acquire popular legitimacy. What it *does* presuppose is merely that in some aspects the two phenomena are sufficiently similar to make a comparison between them meaningful. This is the minimum condition for any kind of fruitful social comparison, and in the present case it is clearly satisfied. At both the state and the European level there is a need to foster popular consent for political institutions and practices. In both cases, moreover, there are three potential routes to legitimacy. As discussed in the last chapter, they range from a growth in perceptions that shared institutions meet existing interests to the emergence of new overarching corporate and communal identifications. Finally, in both cases the underlying mechanisms of political legitimisation would be comparable, including the role of symbols and the general means of their transmission. This being said, the specific *types* of symbols and transmission mechanisms liable to be used in the early twenty-first century EU might well be different from those used inside states (which of course strongly differed among themselves as well). Moreover, depending on the general political development of the EU, the intensity of their transmission and their overall salience might remain much lower without compromising their effectiveness – an issue I return to further below. In short, the examples discussed in this chapter serve to illustrate symbolic form and method rather than intensity and 'content'.

Culture, audiovisual policy and education, and the symbolic construction of political identities

Political symbolism is not a new concern in the literature on state legitimisation, nation-building and related subjects. In fact, much of this literature has become rather preoccupied with it, sometimes inspired by and sometimes preceding the various constructivist waves in recent years. Different writers capture the process by which political reality is symbolically transmitted and mediated under different headings: 'symbolic politics', 'political symbolism', 'political pedagogy', 'political ritual' and 'political aesthetics' are among the most frequently used (Dörner 1996; Kertzer 1988; Edelman 1967; also A. P. Cohen 1989; A. Cohen 1969).

Exploring political symbolism in action is difficult, however, bearing in mind the earlier point that every aspect of social reality has a symbolic dimension and that all social and political behaviour therefore has symbolic consequences. But if all politics is symbolic, political symbolism becomes synonymous with 'politics' and vanishes as a distinct field of inquiry. In order to overcome such definitional problems the present study concentrates on cultural, audiovisual and educational policy, taking them to be the most important outlets for political symbolism. These areas are broad and require definitional work in their own right, but they are nonetheless more circumscribed than is 'political symbolism' at large. As is argued below, cultural, audiovisual and educational policies typically reflect symbolic intent. Moreover, while not all such policies are designed to achieve political ends, the fit is relatively close the other way round. Most state- and nation-building drives concentrated heavily on cultural and educational (as well as, in later stages, audiovisual) policy, and those areas were often subjected to ferocious rivalry between different elites with competing political socialisation agendas (e.g. between church and secular authorities over school curricula). Likewise, as later chapters show, in the European Union most policies aimed at strengthening public support for integration fall under the responsibility of Commission departments in charge of culture, audiovisual policy and education. Before proceeding, it is helpful to briefly define these policy areas.

Cultural policy, to begin with, is a vague concept. Theoretically, this corresponds to the vagueness of the term 'culture'. Empirically, it is due to the fact that state practice has differed widely. Most Western democracies have ministries whose brief includes culture. Especially in Anglo-Saxon countries these are often in charge of 'heritage matters'. The powers of these ministries vary, however. Some enjoy extensive competences while others do little more than hand out a few subsidies. In many federal systems (such as Germany, Switzerland and the United States), culture – along with education – falls primarily under the competences of the federal sub-units. Many countries also channel public money into autonomous or semi-autonomous cultural organisations, such as Pro Helvetia in Switzerland and the National Endowment for the Arts in the United States. In the UK, lottery money has become a major source of cultural funding. What is more, governments often address cultural issues under other policy headings, such as sports, tourism, employment, regional policy and indeed education.

Throughout this study I adopt a definition of cultural policy whose underlying conception of 'culture' lies half-way between one that restricts it essentially to the arts and one that equates it with everything humans practice, produce and believe (as anthropologists and cultural theorists often do). More specifically, I take cultural policy to include every policy whose *primary aim* is to have some kind of aesthetic impact, be it through physical objects (e.g. museums, monuments, paintings), acoustics (music), language (e.g. literature, poetry, dictionaries, oratory) or aural/visual performance (theatre, dance, etc.). 'Aesthetic' in this context does not refer to beauty standards, but instead 'to sensuous perception, [to something] received by the senses' (*Oxford English Dictionary* 1989).

To give some examples, redesigning postage stamps qualifies as a cultural policy, as does the building of a museum, the restoration of a national monument, the sponsoring of a folklore festival and the change of rules on the use of the Irish language in the Irish civil service. The public commemoration of a historical event counts as a cultural policy as does the annual holding of a minute of silence to commemorate fallen soldiers, the hiring of a public relations firm to promote a particular government policy and the drawing up of contingency plans for the televised state funeral of the Duke of Edinburgh. All these policies have, and are intended to have, an aesthetic impact, in the sense of being 'received by the senses'. Moreover, given that they are mostly initiated by political elites they tend to have a political dimension, if only in the sense that some however diffuse and unarticulated political intent goes into their making. The extent to which this political dimension is overt and clearly detectable depends of course on the policy and on the political regime in question. Some cultural policies wear their political aspirations on their sleeve, while others are at least on the surface dominated by more apolitical features and objectives.

This definition of cultural policy is very broad yet conceptually it is precise. The key term is 'primary aim'. Building a new airport or a new prison, too, has a sensual and thus aesthetic (and, as was argued, by extension always also a symbolic) impact, as indeed does any conceivable policy in any conceivable policy area. But for the most part this is not the primary purpose of such projects. However, there are many mixed cases. Building a new parliament or a new capital city has a strong utilitarian element, but typically also a very much intended aesthetic and indeed political one. The same applies to the design of state-related artefacts such as money, border signs, passports, licence plates and uniforms.

Later chapters show that such a broad definition of cultural policy is not just conceptually useful but also corresponds rather neatly to actual practice in the EU. The Commission's Directorate-General whose brief includes culture is not merely responsible for the arts. Instead, it deals with a wide range of issues that include (or at various times have included) the graphic design of driving licences and passport covers, 'information and communication' campaigns, Europe Day celebrations, the organisation of 'European yacht races' and the building of 'European pavilions' at world exhibitions, to name but a few.

Audiovisual policy is a sub-field of cultural policy. It pertains to all areas of film and programme production and to the dissemination of audiovisual content through radio and television broadcasting, video cassettes, DVDs, CDs, the Internet and other means. Examples of audiovisual policies include organising a film festival, subsidising film and television productions, licensing radio stations, setting content quotas for broadcasters, amending censorship laws and so on. While audiovisual policies of this kind are often intended to have an aesthetic and indeed political impact, the economic and technological stakes in the audiovisual sector are higher than in many other areas of cultural policy, leading to more 'mixed motive' policies.

Educational policy, finally, pertains to all areas of formal and generally institutionalised learning: kindergartens, schools, universities, adult education, teacher training and the like. Particular educational policies may seek to regulate curricular content (through textbooks and teaching syllabuses), teaching methods, exams, school discipline, classroom decorations and school rituals such as pledges of allegiance and school prayer. This definition, too, is largely in line with that adopted by the EU itself, and it reflects the core competences of most national (and sub-national) ministries of education.

As does any policy in any given policy area, all educational policies have an aesthetic impact. To the extent that this is their primary aim they, too, could be treated under the broader heading of cultural policy as defined above. At the same time, some educational policies have other primary aims, which range from the transmission of utilitarian skills (such as reading and writing) to social selection and knowledge assessment. What is more, with regard to many educational policies it is impossible to separate utilitarian and aesthetic/symbolic objectives, since they are intended from the outset to meet both and thus represent 'mixed motive' cases. For example, a textbook might be designed to improve pupils' reading skills while at the same time present them with national imagery or particular ideological positions.

At this point, the question 'what can cultural, audiovisual and educational policies do to help generate political legitimacy?' can broadly be answered as follows: such policies can help legitimise political institutions and practices by designating and transmitting symbols that are tied to these institutions and practices and thereby promote their internalisation. The present section examines more closely what this can entail in practice, relying on examples drawn from the literature on domestic institutional legitimisation. These examples help to illustrate the theoretical argument outlined in the last chapter. They also render the actions of the European Commission and the European Parliament, as they are analysed in subsequent chapters, more intelligible. For in drawing up their cultural, audiovisual and educational policy proposals, both bodies were often inspired by similar policies at the national level and consciously sought to imitate and adapt them to an EU context. In what follows I begin with cultural policy and then turn to audiovisual policy and education.

As was argued, cultural policies have an aesthetic impact and as such are potential vehicles for political aesthetics and political symbolism. Political symbolism, to recall, refers to the creation and transmission of political symbols, i.e. symbols that are 'attached' to political institutions and practices and facilitate their internalisation. Applied to institutional legitimisation inside states two questions arise from this: First, what kinds of symbols were used? Second, how were they transmitted?

On the first question, the literature on state legitimisation[2] offers many examples of what political symbols can consist of: national flags, anthems, costumes, poems and landscapes, heroes and heroines, buildings and monuments, to name some of the most recurrent ones. Some of these were 'purpose built' and made as it were from scratch: designing a national flag, composing an anthem and inventing an architectural style for national monuments all represent symbol-making of this kind. Most symbols, however, are designated symbols. They consist of pre-existing objects, practices, myths, traditions, images and sentiments that at some point became politicised and attached to state-related political institutions and practices. Thus landscapes became national landscapes and real or imagined historical figures were posthumously turned into national heroes and heroines. The Hermann myth in Germany, the 'Gallic ancestors' in France, Wilhelm Tell in Switzerland and the lacustrian settlements on Swiss lakes all represent historical myths-cum-facts that states incorporated into their symbolic repertoire (Patman 1999; Kaeser 1998; Dörner 1996; Coakley 1992; Citron 1991). The fusion of political symbols with religious themes, gender conceptions, ethnic markers and the like is of course part of the same phenomenon (Smith 1992, 1991).

Political symbols can only be effective if their intended recipients regard them as credible and if they can relate to them. For this reason they must be targeted. Historically, this need arose especially where groups with different cultural, religious or ethnic traditions merged into a single state. For instance, children from all Swiss cantons learn roughly the same national myths and historical events in their school textbooks, but these are adapted to suggest continuity and compatibility with their respective local and regional histories, myths and traditions (Schmid 1981). To the same end of maintaining symbolic continuity, local, cantonal and federal symbols often appear alongside each other.

The Swiss example is instructive in yet another regard, as it illustrates the distinction drawn in the previous chapter between three different levels of legitimisation. As was suggested, even the Swiss polity developed a shared sense of overarching community and 'entitativity', indicating third-level legitimacy mechanisms at work. Nonetheless, as Switzerland remained culturally and politically decentralised and as the different sub-units preserved their own corporate identities, the first two levels are more and the third level less significant compared to more centralised states. In fact, throughout the nineteenth century Swiss state-building revolved in large part around making regional (especially cantonal) interests appear to benefit from membership in the confederation (first-level legitimisation). In addition, it entailed some remoulding of local and regional identities, especially those of the Catholic cantons after their defeat in the civil war (second level legitimisation). For its part, the overarching Swiss 'entity' and communal category is marked by mainly 'civic' as opposed to ethnic or cultural signifiers. This does not come at the expense of its solidity (more on this below). However, it enables it to coexist more easily with the social and corporate identities of the cantons and localities, which for their part are often more 'thickly' textured. In Switzerland as in many other places, symbolic complementarity underpins political legitimacy.

If political symbols are to promote the internalisation of the norms and institutions for which they stand they must be transmitted. Here, too, the literature offers many insights into what this can entail and how cultural policy contributed to it.

One way to transmit symbols is by grafting them onto widely seen and circulated objects. These can include passport covers, postage stamps, coins and bank notes, educational certificates and the tails of aircraft. Political symbolism also became woven into more narrowly defined cultural output: films, poetry, paintings, songs, television serials, statues, novels, theatre plays, the work of linguists and historians and so forth. As suggested, the straightforwardness with which cultural policy is used in this way depends on the policy in question and on the nature of the regime that pursues it. For example, under Nazi rule German cultural policy openly dictated cultural content and severely punished transgressors (Mosse 1991). By contrast, contemporary cultural policy in established Western democracies mostly avoids overt interference. In such settings, efforts to infuse cultural output with political symbolism can at the most be subtle. As shown in later chapters, the EU's decision to commission a European history textbook from a team of sympathetic historians without, however, prescribing its content was an example of this, as is its sponsorship of various cultural and sporting events that return the favour by displaying the European flag.

Transmitting political symbols often relied on public events of various kinds: national exhibitions, athletic competitions, processions, folklore festivals, state funerals, remembrance day ceremonies, youth and women's gatherings and public parades are among the most recurrent examples (Houlihan 1999; Spillman 1997; Bendix 1992). At some of these events political symbolism took centre stage while at others it receded subtly into the background. With the advent of electronic mass media such events started to reach audiences beyond those who were physically present. The early BBC became famous for its diligent coverage of royal coronations, weddings and funerals (Morley and Robins 1989). Electronic media also allowed for 'virtual' mass events, such as royal Christmas broadcasts and presidential addresses to the nation (see below).

Internalising political institutions and practices is a form of learning, and learning benefits from doing as opposed to merely watching. Thus, many public events turned their audiences into active participants: they made them march, sing, run, pray, share a minute of silence, pledge allegiance, carry torches, wear national dress, stand up to salute the flag or join together in roaring applause or laughter. These participatory elements transformed such events into 'experiences', imbuing them with emotional significance and increasing the likelihood that the participants would absorb the political imagery presented to them (Hettling 1998, 1997; Shils and Young 1975).

Learning also benefits from repetition. Accordingly, many rituals and mass events took place regularly and, over time, evolved into traditions. Following Hobsbawm's classic definition, an invented tradition is 'a set of practices, normally governed by overtly or tacitly accepted rules and of a ritual or symbolic nature, which seek to inculcate certain values and norms of behaviour by repetition, which automatically implies a continuity with the past ... where possible ... with a suitable historic past' (Hobsbawm 1993a: 4; see also Hobsbawm 1993b). This notion of 'invented tradition' thus fits well into the present discussion, though the last point needs some elaboration. Repeating an event over an extended period by default establishes a 'tradition' and gives it a historical dimension. Yet, as Hobsbawm's own definition suggests, this does not necessarily imply that the themes and symbols in question connect to a real or imaginary past. Some invented traditions clearly do seek to establish such a link, but others do not, or even seek to signify a radical break with the past. Still others suggest break and continuity at once. For ex-ample, through their selection and presentation of artefacts, French museums in the immediate aftermath of the Revolution sought to root revolutionary ideals in a legacy of antiquity and the Enlightenment, but at once depicted them as a radical leap far beyond anything history had hitherto come up with (Poulot 1997; also Davis 1996). As is discussed in later chapters, the European Union designed many of its cultural policies to convey a similar set of mixed – or parallel – messages. While portraying the Union as the political embod-iment of Europeans' alleged cultural unity and shared roots in the past, they at once celebrate it as a radical break with European history to date and are drenched in allusions to the 'new age' for the 'new Europe'.

The last chapter suggested that fostering overarching communal identifi-cations and 'entity processes' entails the construction of boundaries which in turn involves self-differentiation from others. In state- and nation-building contexts cultural policy typically took centre stage in this. For example, from the outset German state-building had strong anti-French connotations, signi-fied by a barrage of anti-French songs, popular plays, poems and paintings. Likewise, attempted cultural emancipation from Britain defined Irish state-building after independence, with the cultural markers cultivated by political elites ranging from the Irish language and music to the Gaelic Athletics Association (Cronin 1999; Dörner 1996; Hobsbawm 1993a).

Switzerland, too, became internally more cohesive as a result of the isola-tion and danger it faced during both world wars. After the Nazi takeover in Germany, Swiss political elites adopted a series of cultural 'Swissification' policies to support the government's 'spiritual defence of the homeland' strategy and to encourage cultural self-differentiation from its northern neighbour. In the German-speaking part this included efforts to promote Swiss-German dialects as well as films, plays and exhibitions that adapted Swiss political mythologies (such as Wilhelm Tell) to the situation at the time. Incidentally, once these themes had become internalised they acted back upon Switzerland's stance towards the outside world, leading the Swiss electorate to opt for a reclusive foreign policy with regard to the EU and other international organisations (Theiler 2004a; Sciarini, Hug and Dupont 2001). Rather than just transmitting social reality, symbols always help to constitute it.

Still on the subject of boundaries, interaction across them has an ambigu-ous effect. As was argued, following Deutschian thinking it may (though not inevitably) help to improve mutual perceptions between the participating populations. Applied to cultural policy, the Franco-German cultural exchange programmes after the Second World War are often seen as a successful example of this (Letze 1986; Farquharson and Holt 1975). At the same time, interacting with others across group boundaries does not neces-sarily erode these boundaries, regardless of whether or not it improves mutual perceptions. Rather, by enabling people to *experience* them it can strengthen perceptions of social difference and the presence of the ingroup in the consciousness of its members, making it more salient in the process. Both as individuals and as groups, interacting with others can make us more aware of ourselves and of what divides us from others (Cohen 1989; Barth 1969). Consequently, even seemingly internationalist cultural policies – transnational youth exchanges, sports fixtures, theatre festivals, literary translations and so on may promote internal cohesion and, by extension, contribute third-level legitimisation processes (see Billig 1995).

Turning to audiovisual policy, its potential role in political symbolism is implicit in the discussion so far. Like other forms of cultural output, films, radio and television programmes can, in principle, generate and transmit symbolic meanings that promote the internalisation of social and political reality. Before illustrating this, two major caveats are in order.

First, modern liberal democracies typically establish relatively strong safeguards to insulate broadcasters – above all public service ones – from overt political interference. In such settings the symbolic role of the mass media can at the most be subtle and indirect, reminiscent of other cultural policies discussed above.

Second, research on mass media impact has undergone fundamental shifts in recent decades. This included a move away from basic 'transmission models' of communication to those that highlight the different ways in which audiences receive, interpret and 'decode' information. Influenced by various theoretical strands ranging from behaviourism to Marxist-inspired 'false consciousness' and 'hegemonic control' conceptions, earlier accounts postulated a relatively straightforward relationship between the intention of the transmitter of a message and its content on the one hand and its effect on the recipients on the other. By extension, they believed that the mass media had a crucial role in shaping social and political identifications, sometimes going as far as to depict it as a kind of 'hypodermic needle' with which meaning could be 'injected' into audiences, and their political identifications manipulated at will.

By contrast, newer theories of mass communication no longer see audiences as unprotected against manipulative ploys of electronic image providers. Often inspired by Stuart Hall's classic work on 'encoding' and 'decoding' (Hall 1980; also McQuail and Windahl 1993; Morley 1992; Ravault 1986), they postulate that viewers 'decode' and demystify mass media images in relation to other messages supplied to them through vernacular channels of communication. These channels link them to their own 'interpretative communities', provide a code of interpretation, and mediate between message transmitter, message content and message recipient. Especially if transmitted in a trans-cultural or trans-social context, the manner in which different audiences 'decode' mass media content may thus vary significantly and does not conform to a simple stimulus-response model.

As the 'status of the viewer has been upgraded regularly during the course of communications research' many analysts concluded that 'the media can be consumed oppositionally ... and not only hegemonically' (Liebes and Katz 1989: 204). Exposure to mass media messages can come to play a role of 'provocation rather than seduction' (Ravault 1986: 276) and induce a 'boomerang effect' which mobilises those at the receiving end against the messages relayed to them – and ultimately against the source of transmission itself. Similar doubts about the political effect of mass communication have long prevailed in political science. For example, as far back as the early 1970s, Walker Connor cautioned against attempts to 'telescope' ethnic assimilation in culturally fragmented states merely by augmenting inter-cultural communication (Connor 1972). In a similar vein, political sociologists have increasingly questioned the efficacy of the mass media in fostering consent for political institutions across different parts of the social spectrum (Held 1988).

Mass communication is thus unlikely to enjoy the almost magical powers of political persuasion that some earlier theorists had afforded it. However, this does not obliterate its potential contribution to political symbolism, merely making it less certain, less straightforward and more conditional upon other variables. Mindful of these caveats and drawing on the earlier discussion, this contribution can take three different forms.

A first factor is media content, i.e. the 'text' of the messages conveyed to audiences. Crucially, even seemingly apolitical content – such as coverage of national sports teams competing or archetypal 'national' characters in television serials – may affect (but, following the above argument, is never certain to affect) political identifications in a particular way. The role of the early BBC as discussed earlier illustrates this.

Second and related to this, films and, above all, radio and television broadcasts can facilitate communal experiences among viewers, strengthening the boundaries of their shared group category and its internal cohesion. In this rendering, the actual content of what is being consumed is less important than the act of consuming it in – albeit virtual – togetherness, often amplified by its subsequent discursive rehearsal in face-to-face social contexts (e.g. conversations at work about a television programme seen the previous night). Films and broadcasting may thus function akin to the print media in Benedict Anderson's well-known account of nationalism, creating shared experiences and allowing audiences to 'imagine' themselves as a community welded together on a shared journey through time (Anderson 1991).

Finally, a more Habermasian rendering highlights the role of the mass media as the cornerstone of the public sphere in modern societies, as a kind of node for broader communicative and deliberative processes. It is of course this very notion which serves as the main rationale for the continuation of public service broadcasting systems in many Western democracies. On this account, the mass media are a catalyst for political diversity and contention but also, potentially, for social cohesion and institutional legitimisation in their overall effect. As suggested in the last chapter, such more 'bottom-up' legitimising dynamics are especially strong if they interact with more 'top-down' symbolic elements as implicit, for instance, the other two forms of mass media use.

What is true for many cultural policies applies to education as well: the claim that educational policies can promote political legitimacy is almost undisputed. It reverberates throughout the historical state- and nation-building literature and is supported by many sociological accounts, from Durkheim (1922) onwards (see also Percheron 1985; Meyer 1977; Bourdieu 1971).

These accounts typically hold education to be an effective symbolic tool for several reasons. A first factor is the long period of time individuals normally spend passing through the school system. Also, their motivation to absorb school-transmitted knowledge tends to be strong as their prospects for social and economic advancement partially depend on it. What is more, in so far as the education system is directly subjugated to political power, educational content and method can be centrally steered and adapted quickly to meet the needs of particular socialisation agendas (e.g. through state-run curriculum development and assessment agencies, examination boards and the like).

A further important factor is that individuals start to undergo schooling at an early age. This is especially critical when the institutions and practices that are to be legitimised are themselves changing rapidly – situations brought about, for example, by political integration at the intra- and interstate levels alike. For in the case of adults who have been socialised in a pre-integrative setting, the most that can be achieved is their re-socialisation into a post-integrative context. Yet what has been acquired during childhood socialisation can rarely be completely 'de-internalised'. Adults thus remain a potential source of opposition to integration; pre-integrative 'memories' remain latent and may become, as it were, reactivated. Children, by contrast, have as yet acquired few political representations (but see Piaget and Weil 1951). This makes them more amenable to acquiring new political loyalties and identifications and these will be particularly stable and resistant to change.

The sociological emphasis on mass education as a tool to foster political identifications reverberates throughout the more historically oriented state- and nation-building literature. Their grip on emerging mass education systems – and especially elementary schooling – boosted the ability of national elites to pursue their national socialisation-cum-internalisation agenda against efforts by rivalling agents with competing agendas, such as the church or local feudal regimes. According to many accounts the rise of nationalism as a mass phenomenon was inexorably linked to the formation of universal schooling. As H. J. Graff, commenting on the role of popular education, observed:

> The 'greatest function' of the modern school was to teach a 'new patriotism' ...
> The school was first a socialising agent. The message was communicated most

effectively together with reading and writing. The school's task included not only national and patriotic sentiments but establishing unity in a nation long divided by region, culture, language, and persisting social divisions of class and wealth. Learning to read and write involved the constant repetition of the civic national catechism, in which the child was imbued with all the duties expected of him: from defending the state, to paying taxes, working, and obeying laws. (Quoted in Guibernau 1996: 69; see also Green 1990)

These observations also suggest that the utilitarian aspects of formal education do not make it less suitable as an outlet for political symbolism. Rather, they might well enhance it as they provide a basis to which political myths and symbols can be 'grafted'. While learning to read and write, pupils can at once internalise a given social and political order.

Yet the potential contribution of mass education to political legitimacy goes beyond its immediate socialising function. First, in many states universal mass education developed alongside notions of universal citizenship and universally held rights and obligations. In many ways the two went hand in hand.

Beyond defining and extending national culture, mass education defines almost the entire population as possessing this culture, as imbued with its meanings, and as having the rights implied by it. Mass education ... allocates persons to citizenship – establishing their membership in the nation over and above various subgroups. And it directly expands the definition of what citizenship and the nation mean and what obligations and rights are involved. (Meyer 1977: 70)

Second, formal education systems also help reify and exalt particular fields of knowledge bound up with the political legitimisation cause. 'National civics', 'national history' and the like are thus important not only because they help transmit symbolic meanings to pupils studying these subjects, but also because they are formal educational subjects in the first place, enjoying the social prestige and moral authority conferred upon officially sanctioned knowledge. In this sense, mass education can help socialise *all* members of society into a particular national framework, not just those who happen to attend schools at any given point in time.

At the same time, the basic principles that govern the effective use of cultural policy for political legitimisation purposes apply to education as well. To illustrate this, a focus on culturally plural and politically decentralised states is once more instructive. In those states, the political centre does not hold a monopoly on education policy. Instead, local and regional authorities retain important educational powers (e.g. near complete formal control over school curricula in Switzerland, Belgium, Canada, the United States and many other federal and quasi-federal systems). As suggested, the main challenge facing the political centre in those systems is not to weaken or discredit sub-unit symbolism, but instead to ensure that symbols pertaining to the different institutional levels are transmitted alongside each other in ways that suggest compatibility rather than competition.

Symbolism and legitimacy in the European Union

Overall these observations square well with what has been argued in the previous chapter. In domestic settings, political legitimacy did not emerge simply as a reflex to the creation of overarching political institutions and democratic practices, nor was it simply the product of interaction and exchanges. Instead, as the 'tandem' hypothesis suggests, successful state legitimisation always involved a measure of 'top-down' political symbolism by elites, for which cultural, educational and at later stages also audiovisual policies served as important outlets. Frequently, political elites aimed for and achieved cultural and linguistic homogenisation. But even in systems that remained culturally divided with only limited central institutions (such as Switzerland) it entailed a measure of 'cognitive homogenisation', leading to a shared awareness of and responsiveness to overarching myths and symbols among all population groups.

Furthermore, even in these culturally plural and politically decentralised states some third-level legitimisation occurred. This entailed the formation of an overarching sense of communal membership and 'entitativity', and, by implication, of boundaries separating insiders from outsiders. All the same, where the centre remained relatively weak such third-level processes could remain correspondingly modest, as could the salience of overarching communal identifications. The sub-units retained their own corporate identities and the symbolic repertoire to maintain them.

By keeping a balance between authority and legitimacy (or, to use the earlier terminology, between material power and symbolic power), these systems heed a critical postulate that reverberates throughout much of the comparative politics and political sociology literature: a political system needs to attract political loyalties in proportion to its perceived power and salience, i.e. in proportion to which its subjects are aware of its norms, institutions and policy outputs and consider them significant.[3] And herein precisely lies one of the 'secrets' of stable multicultural systems: since in those systems too aggressive a push by the political centre for third-level legitimacy could threaten the ability of the sub-units to maintain *their* respective corporate identities, they restrict the powers and visibility of the political centre to the point where it only requires a relatively limited amount of third-level legitimacy in the first place. The need for legitimacy is always relative to the salience of what is to be legitimised.

What does all this imply for the European Union, recalling once more the limits of an analogy between the EU and domestic political systems as discussed at the beginning of this chapter? First, it seems unlikely that in the EU political legitimacy could emerge as a mere by-product of transnational interaction and exchanges, or as a mere reflex to an expansion of supranational institutions or democratic procedures. Rather, as in domestic settings, it would involve a measure of 'top-down' symbolic construction, designed to stimulate 'bottom-up' communicative and deliberative processes. Cultural, audiovisual and educational policies could once more take centre stage in this, even though the precise themes and symbols liable to be employed successfully in the EU might bear little resemblance to those used in domestic contexts (more on this below).

Second, even if the EU remained politically weak and decentralised this would not prima facie exempt it from the need to acquire third-level legitimacy. It would not obliterate the necessity of an overarching 'entity process' and the emergence of some shared communal identifications among Europeans. However, the salience of this European corporate identity could remain relatively low, provided the scope and powers of supranational institutions remained correspondingly limited. The classic neofunctionalist concept of 'authority-legitimacy transfers' captures this well. As long as EU-related institutions and practices assume a low degree of authority and visibility in relation to their national counterparts, the latter can (and indeed must) remain the main focus of political loyalties and identifications. But as EU institutions become more politically salient the need for corresponding loyalty shifts also grows (Pentland 1973: 104; Haas 1970: 633–636). In the EU, too, material and symbolic power must grow together.

There are further potential parallels between plural domestic systems and the EU. As did the former, the EU would need to establish a symbolic continuity and compatibility between its own symbols and those used by its member states as part of their domestic political symbolisms. The diversity of national contexts in the EU would require a rigorous symbolic targeting, if not with regard to the actual symbols used, at least in respect of the means and intensity of their transmission. What is more, the EU, too, would need to weave its political symbols into the everyday lives of its citizens, yet without at the same time appearing to symbolically overpower them. And the transmission of EU-related symbols would again be more effective if it were linked to the creation of 'experiences', even if only in surrogate form through the mass media. Finally, in all this the underlying challenge for the EU would be one of finding a symbolic vocabulary to which all its member populations could relate – clearly not an easy task, given the wide range of different cultural contexts and historical experiences in EU-Europe (see Smith 1992, 1991).

'Thick' and 'thin' symbolism

At this point, the traditional distinction between 'thick' and 'thin' political symbols and identifications once more comes into view. It preoccupies much of the contemporary literature on the EU just as it interests many writers on nationalism and state legitimisation. Many older contributions to the state- and nation-building literature equated the presumed 'thickness' of particular national symbols (i.e. their degree of ethnic-cum-linguistic-cum-religious 'content') with their strength and persistence and with the durability of the communal identifications they sustain. Some writers on European integration echo these assumptions. They contend that the European Union, too, would have to predicate itself on some kind of 'thick' ethnic or cultural basis, though they disagree as to what, precisely, this would entail. 'Euro-essentialists' search for Europe's underlying 'meaning' and argue that Europeans need to 'rediscover' their shared cultural roots as a precondition for developing shared political commitments (e.g. de Rougemont 1985). Others adopt a more constructivist stance. They sense a need to make Europeans *believe* that they share a cultural heritage by inventing traditions and possibly fostering some cultural homogenisation in the process (see Cederman 2001a). Despite these differences, however, both groups agree that in the EU as elsewhere only 'thick' identifications can be strong.

More recently, many critics have come to question such claims. Relying on the examples of (once more) Switzerland and some other mainly 'civic nations', they point out that even though those systems have only 'thin' (i.e. mainly 'civic') overarching markers and even though they enjoy only limited salience, these markers are nonetheless very firmly entrenched and the communal identifications they sustain are equally stable – much more so in fact than in some more 'thickly' defined polities. As discussed in Chapter 1, this is the basic claim underpinning post-national approaches to European integration, and it stands on firm theoretical ground. Social psychologists and social anthropologists have long shown that the 'content' of particular group markers says little about the stability of corresponding group identifications. 'Everything', in this rendering, 'may be grist on the mill of symbolism' (Cohen 1989: 19; also Percheron 1985: 187). Likewise, the kinds of symbols appropriated by a given political system are not always a reliable guide to its character and workings. In short, reflecting the signifier-signified separation suggested by constructivist theory, symbols act, in the first instance, as conveyors of whatever meaning has been attached to them. In Clifford Geertz's useful definition, a symbol can be 'any object, act, event, quality or relation, which serves as a vehicle for a conception – the conception is the symbol's 'meaning' ...' (Geertz 1973: 91; see also Brubaker 1999; Kostakopoulou 1997).

Two qualifications are in order. The first pertains to the difference between solidity and salience. For example, I may have internalised the category 'Swiss' very firmly and thus identify consistently, unambiguously and solidly as Swiss. Nonetheless, my Swissness may not actually *matter* to me a great deal in everyday life and thus not be particularly salient to me. Some of my other social identities (ping-pong player, university lecturer, male, trade union member, etc.) may take up a greater share of my self and thus have greater salience in guiding my beliefs and behaviour. In other words, salience has more to do with the 'size of the share of the self' something occupies than with its 'stability of position in the self'. This brings salience into conceptual affinity with what some strands of social psychology refer to as 'attitude importance' (Krosnick 1988). More concretely, it means that political systems and communal identifications may be strong and stable yet not very salient at the same time. In fact, as was argued, in many decentralised and multicultural systems it is precisely the low salience of the political centre that helps account for its solidity and popular acceptance.[4]

Second, in the EU as elsewhere the signifier-signified separation may be very far-reaching but it is not infinite. For contrary to what some post-modern approaches assert, signifiers are not entirely 'empty'. Thus, if the EU became defined in, say, racial terms, it would be unlikely ever to constitute itself as a liberal democratic polity. But at the same time, their choice of 'ethnic' signifiers has not prevented many states in the EU and beyond from forming stable democratic systems – largely 'blood-based' citizenship laws in many Western democracies are a good example. Perhaps, symbols are more prone to rule in than to rule out: successful liberal democracies must have at least some 'civic' symbols pertaining to shared democratic values and prac-tices, but these may be embedded in a wide variety of non-'civic' themes without endangering their viability or credibility (see Auer 2004). The basic point, however, remains: within the limits defined by its overall liberal demo-cratic ethos, we should not, in the first instance, focus on the 'content' of whatever myths and symbols the EU manages to acquire – be they cultural or 'civic', 'thick' or 'thin'. Instead, what matters most is the intensity and tacti-cal skill with which these are being disseminated, as this determines their propensity to be internalised and to induce 'bottom-up' communicative processes on which the emergence of lasting political legitimacy ultimately hinges.

Yet, to take this logic one step further, the very need to make EU symbols compatible with those of its member states might call for a symbolic register very unlike that used in any existing domestic context. The more the Union succeeded in developing such an alternative symbolic vocabulary, the more might it prevent fears that it was treading on the symbolic territory of the member states and the insecurities and backlashes this could provoke. In the EU as in plural domestic settings, symbolic compatibility between different institutional levels is an important part of effective political symbolism.

The question of impact

The present discussion must end on a cautionary note. It touches on the earlier observation that the effectiveness of political symbolism ultimately de-pends on its reception. But reception-centred studies are difficult to carry out, on the living and still more so on the dead. For this reason, there is no sure way of knowing how well any given symbolic policy actually 'worked' in domestic contexts. Differently put, it is easier to detect the presence of 'top-down' symbolic strategies than it is to ascertain whether they stimulated the kind of 'bottom-up' responses through which political legitimacy ultimately emerges.

Indeed, mere presence of political symbolism strategies does not guarantee their effectiveness. There are many examples where political symbolism was pursued ferociously but nevertheless failed to produce political legitimacy. Many would-be states and nations never made it past the drawing board of a few ambitious elites and cultural entrepreneurs while many others disintegrated: Yugoslavia, the Soviet Union and Czechoslovakia are recent examples.

It is tempting to attribute such legitimisation failures to incompetent political symbolism. Yet even if political symbolism meets all the criteria spelled out in this chapter its effectiveness is never assured. Instead, it depends in part on what Hobsbawm refers to as a 'felt need'[5] among the populations at which these policies are directed – a need which is not open to unlimited 'top-down' manipulation. To put the same point more crudely, if the 'product' is unattractive the most sophisticated 'marketing' strategy will not make it popular. In part, then, the success of political symbolism in the EU would depend not only on how aptly it was designed and executed. Rather, it would hinge on the Union's general evolution in relation to the needs, interests and aspirations of its member populations.

To further complicate matters, the converse may also be true. Even where (a) a given political system enjoys popular compliance (or at least a lack of active popular resistance) and (b) symbolic policies in culture, the audiovisual sector, education and related areas are being pursued, this still does not demonstrate how much the former actually contributes to the latter. As was suggested, legitimacy is only one reason for political compliance. Coercion, apathy and ignorance are among the others, and these different motivations are often very difficult to disentangle. This does not mean that political systems can completely forgo legitimacy in the long term. Nor does it mean that such legitimacy can emerge in the total absence of 'top-down' symbolic strategies. What it does mean, however, is that the relationship between political symbolism and political compliance is subject to many social, economic and political variables. This is true domestically as much as it would apply to the European Union.

These caveats highlight the limits of what the present study can hope to achieve. On the one hand, the EU's record in instrumentalising culture, audiovisual policy and education for symbolic purposes may well be an important indication of its long-term viability and potential for political growth. But on the other hand, the presence of such 'top-down' symbolic policies would not guarantee their success, just as their absence would not inevitably spell the Union's demise. Like all other parts of social reality, European integration involves many tendencies and probabilities but few certainties and inevitabilities.

Symbolic policy-making

The literature reviewed in this chapter shows how cultural, audiovisual and educational policies became tools for political symbolism at a domestic level. Beyond this, it offers yet another important insight: before political elites could instrumentalise cultural, audiovisual and educational policy in this way they first had to gain control over it. Often this occurred in the face of strong opposition from competing elites. The many struggles between, for example, religious and secular authorities over school curricula and the ritual calendar illustrate this. In the European Union this would be no different. To become symbolically active the EU, too, would need to gain an effective foothold in the relevant policy areas, which in turn raises the question of whether and how it might be able to do so.

On the face of it this would not seem to be an easy task. As is discussed in later chapters, the Union was established as a largely economic entity and its founding treaties barred it from symbolically sensitive areas such as culture, audiovisual policy and education. Rather like foreign policy and defence, the power to employ legitimising and identity-conferring symbols was to remain a national prerogative.

However, the absence of an explicit legal mandate for EU involvement in a given area does not always constitute a barrier in practice. Initial prohibitions may weaken over time due to an interplay of formal and informal processes: EU practice stretches legal boundaries, which are then adjusted or reinterpreted only to be pushed outwards again by still more ambitious policies and so on. This process may be helped along by activist jurisprudence by the European Court of Justice, interest group pressure as well as conscious 'political engineering' by the Commission (more on this below).

Yet such an expansive process is far from automatic and many policy areas have proven relatively immune to it. In determining whether or not it occurs, elite preferences are clearly an important variable. Analysts of the EU from all periods and persuasions generally assume that supranational elites (mainly within the Commission) are, on average, keener on expanding the Union's remit than their national counterparts. Elite-centred constructivism as discussed in the last chapter seems to explain this well. Positioned at the centre of integration, supranational elites in this rendering become gradually 'denationalised', identify ever more strongly with the integrative cause and become ever more keen to promote it. In fact, such an account points to a central tenet of all constructivist approaches to integration, namely that preferences – both national and supranational – are not fixed. Instead, they are continuously moulded and re-moulded by the integrative process; they are endogenous rather than exogenous to it. Consequently, when judging the potential for integration in any given policy area it is not sufficient to take a snapshot impression of competing preferences at a given point in time, project these into the future, assess the balance of power between different actors and based on this infer likely policy developments. Instead, we need to ascertain how preferences might be *transformed* by integration, how this would affect the Union's policy prospects, and how this in turn would feed back into the integration process so as to once more affect the interests and preferences of various actors.

Given the very large number of variables involved and the uncertainty that comes with trying to predict human interests and behaviour this is clearly very difficult. At the same time it is not a new challenge. And of all approaches to European integration it is classical neofunctionalism that tries hardest to apply the endogenisation principle to the practice of integration, subsuming it under the well-known concept of 'spillover'. In what follows, I briefly discuss the three types of spillover postulated by neofunctionalists and then examine how these might conceivably apply to culture, audiovisual policy and education. To conclude, I turn to an alternative approach to European integration. It, too, seeks to endogenise preferences yet as far as the Union's political symbolism prospects go it turns neofunctionalist spillover predictions on their head.

Spillover versus 'countervailing pressures'
Neofunctionalism predates the constructivist turn in European integration studies by many decades and is thus not generally held to fall within the constructivist paradigm. All the same, neofunctionalists anticipated some of the key postulates of social constructivism, above all the claim that social identities, social behaviour and social structure interact in a dialectical fashion. This justifies some engagement with neofunctionalist theory, even for those who reject the economic and technological determinism of which (especially many earlier) neofunctionalists stand rightly accused. Central to neofunctionalist thinking is the concept of spillover, which comes in three variants.

The concept of *functional spillover* holds that integration in one policy sector generates pressures to take further integrative steps in that same or in related sectors in order to fully reap – or further augment – the welfare benefits that induced the initial integrative move. Welfare, in this context, is defined largely in economic terms. Further integration might also become necessary to alleviate strains, inefficiencies, or distributional distortions that result as an unintended consequence of an earlier integrative decision (Schmitter 1996; Harrison 1990; Pentland 1973; Haas 1967, 1961; Lindberg 1963).

Applied to political symbolism, functional spillover might promote the EU's policy prospects in several ways. Central is the notion of the 'authority-legitimacy balance' as discussed earlier: as the Union's salience and visibility increases, so does the need for corresponding 'legitimacy transfers' to maintain popular consent.

At the same time, reflecting the influence of behaviourism throughout the social sciences at the time, most neofunctionalists expected national publics to shift their political loyalties more or less automatically as they would come to realise that the European Union could meet their economic welfare needs more effectively than their national governments. By contrast, some later neofunctionalist writings suggested that this might not happen after all and that supranational institutions thus needed to acquire a measure of 'identitive power' in the form of legitimising myths and symbols (Pentland 1973, Chapter 4; Lindberg and Scheingold 1970). All other things being equal, this need is bound to increase during periods in which the Union's economic attractiveness is low, since this calls for alternative motivations for support. It is also likely to grow in response to or in anticipation of integrative 'leaps', such as the Union's expansion into new policy areas or the accession of new member states. What is more, according to this logic such pressures can be expected to operate not only at the EU level but inside the member states as well. European integration is, among other things, a policy pursued by national governments and as such it is subject to their desire to see support for it secured.

The neofunctionalist notion of *political spillover* has intellectual roots in liberal pluralist and 'group theory' approaches that became popular among many political scientists from the 1950s onwards. It focuses on the role of non-governmental interest groups with particular aims and policy agendas, such as trade unions, employer federations and consumer associations. For as long as the decisions they sought to influence were primarily taken at the national level most of these groups organised nationally and their political loyalties and expectations were focused on national institutions and decision-making processes. But once supranational institutions have started to acquire an initial amount of competences, interest groups start to shift their political activities to the supranational level as do their members' political expectations and, ultimately, their political loyalties. Likewise, they start to organise transnationally, for instance by forming pan-European umbrella organisations and by entering close formal and informal ties with the Commission and other supranational bodies (George 1991; Tranholm-Mikkelsen 1991; Pentland 1973, Chapter 4; Haas 1964, 1958).

Political spillover, too, would seem to have the potential to advance the Union's position in culture, the audiovisual sector and education. Not least, both policy areas depend heavily on public funding, which makes various cultural and educational interest groups more likely to engage in political lobbying. All the same, from a political symbolism perspective one obstacle to this might well be that those cultural and educational policies with the greatest symbolic potential – 'European civics' in school curricula, say – tend to be economically insignificant. Two factors would determine whether these would nonetheless attract interest group pressure on their behalf. The first is the extent to which interest groups with a strong and explicit pro-integration agenda – such as the Federal Trust in the UK – would come to champion an

EU involvement in culture and education to further their aims. The second factor is the Commission's ability to devise policy packages that 'smuggle' more symbolically oriented cultural, audiovisual and educational proposals in with those that are more economically charged and thus more likely to attract interest group support. This overlaps with cultivated spillover to which I turn next.

The concept of *cultivated spillover* centres on the idea that supranational elites – primarily within the Commission but also within the European Parliament, the Court of Justice and other bodies – consciously drive integration beyond its initial remit. As suggested, this has strong affinities to elite-centred constructivism. It assumes that supranational elites change their loyalties and are able to advance integration above all by 'interject[ing] ideas and programmes into the [integrative] process that cannot be reduced to the preferences of national or subnational groups' (Schmitter 1996: 6; also Pentland 1973, Chapter 4; Lindberg and Scheingold 1970; Haas 1961).

Cultivated spillover accounts emphasise the Commission's monopoly of issuing legislative proposals to the Council and its more or less informal role as bureaucratic facilitator, mediator and information provider. National officials are seen to rely on the Commission to reduce transaction costs and uncertainty associated with gathering and exchanging information amongst themselves. Commission information also helps them overcome 'information scarcity', for example as regards the preferences of other actors and policy consequences. For its part, the Commission can manipulate the information it provides to national decision-makers in a way that encourages them to take further integrative decisions. For instance, it might exaggerate the extent to which integration has created distortions and inefficiencies and to which further integration could correct these. Similarly, in this rendering the Commission can influence intergovernmental bargaining by working out package deals that link different issue areas, by engineering coalitions between different member states, by playing different governments against each other and by devising face-saving formulas and side-payments that enable more reluctant governments go along with integrative decisions.[6]

Of all three spillover types it is the cultivated variety that prima facie has the greatest potential to advance the Union's role in culture and education. Almost by definition, a committed and self-consciously expansive Commission would be keen to strengthen support for integration by increasing its symbolic presence at the mass level. In trying to obtain the necessary powers the Commission might adopt several of the strategies discussed above. More specifically, anticipating the potential sensitivity of the more symbolically charged parts of culture, audiovisual policy and education, the Commission might seek to 'package' proposals for policies in those areas in a way that de-emphasises their symbolic objectives in favour of economic ones. Alternatively – or parallel to this – it might represent the strengthening of popular support for the EU as a 'function' in need of being fulfilled in order to secure the survival and further development of the Union, and depict policies in culture, the audiovisual sector and education as necessary to accomplish this goal. In this sense, cultivated spillover and functional spillover are closely linked. For 'functional needs' to have behavioural consequences they must be *perceived* as such.

All three spillover concepts are vulnerable on several counts: functional spillover for overestimating the intrinsic 'connectivity' of different issue areas and the economic origins of political behaviour; political and cultivated spillover for exaggerating the importance of interest groups and of bureaucratic elites respectively. But in what follows I put these more general criticisms to one side in order to concentrate more specifically on the relevance of spillover accounts to political symbolism. The main objection is this: whether or not spillover occurs in other fields, culture, education and other symbolically charged areas are subjected to a different logic altogether: as 'material' integration advances, it releases countervailing pressures that make 'symbolic' integration less, not more, likely over time.

The best way to render this 'countervailing pressures' argument is by bringing together two distinct strands of thinking about the EU. So far these have mostly been treated in isolation, but they complement and reinforce each other. The first strand builds on the Deutschian idea that interaction between different population groups may produce an overarching identity but may also have the opposite effect. Even if it makes the participating societies 'objectively' more homogenous (e.g. in terms of consumption patterns) it may reinforce 'subjective' divisions and the psychological affirmation of communal boundaries. As suggested, this is not a new insight: in comparative politics and anthropology it informs various 'conflictual interaction' and 'symbolic boundary reconstitution' approaches (Cohen 1989; Connor 1972; Barth 1969), and many social psychologists have made broadly similar claims (Hogg and Abrams 1988; Tajfel 1981).

Applied to the EU, 'conflictual integration' accounts build on the notion that most West European nation-states have remained firmly entrenched. They continue to be reproduced through stable symbolic mechanisms, not least involving national policies in culture and education. Consequently, national identifications have become neither psychologically unfulfilling nor otherwise 'dysfunctional'. There is little 'demand' (or, in Hobsbawm's terms, little 'felt need') for adopting new, Europeanised political loyalties and communal allegiances, and there is strong resistance to surrendering existing national ones. With supranational identifications absent and national communal categories salient, electorates fear that further integration could undermine the viability of their national boundaries. This in turn triggers 'societal security' reflexes, signs of which range from anti-immigrant and anti-EU parties in many member states to a growing preoccupation with protecting national food standards, languages, music and television programming against foreign 'contamination' (Theiler 2003; Wæver 1996; Wæver,

Buzan, Kelstrup and Lemaitre 1993, Chapter 4). Relying on the concept of the 'authority-legitimacy balance', all this might simply be taken to bear out the urgency of giving the EU a greater symbolic role. But for 'conflictual integration' theorists this is not a feasible option. It would boost the Union's social and cultural intrusiveness which they see as the main cause of opposition to it in the first place. After all, even among otherwise EU-friendly electorates a large majority has consistently opposed a Union involvement in socially and culturally sensitive areas such as cultural policy and education (Theiler 1999a; *Eurobarometer* 1973 *et seq.*). In this rendering, as symbolic policies become more necessary in the EU they become less viable at the same time.

Turning to the elite level, some theorists claim to have identified a similar logic at work. Much of their argument stems from applying the principles of consociational democracy to the European Union, and the understanding of conflicting elite objectives to which this gives rise.

At the heart of 'Euro-consociational' approaches is the observation that, like domestic consociational systems, the European Union is a cartel of elites: it is managed and kept together by its member governments through continuous bargaining and compromise. National governmental elites are driven by two main objectives. First, they recognise the benefits of integration to their respective member states and must therefore, among other things, secure sufficient domestic support for it. But, second, they do not want integration to weaken their respective national constituencies to the point where it could threaten their own position. After all, 'the status and authority of the members of the cartel are dependent upon their capacity to identify segmental [i.e. member state] interests and to present themselves as leaders and agents of a distinct clearly defined community' (Taylor 1991: 114; also Chryssochoou 1994; Hix 1994).

Yet these two objectives are not easy to reconcile. On the one hand, national elites want to take part in integration out of economic and political self-interest. But on the other hand, this 'may generate within the elites an increasing anxiety about the implications of strengthening the horizontal links between the segments since that would also tend to weaken their constituencies' (Taylor 1991: 114). According to 'Euro-consociational' theorists, national elites try to break out of this dilemma in several ways. Above all, as economic and political integration proceeds they become more protective of social and cultural boundaries, trying to preserve the cultural distinctiveness of their member states in a Europe of weakening economic and to some extent also political boundaries. Likewise, they become more protective of their own symbolic power vis-à-vis their constituents and more sensitive to the prospect of having it usurped by supranational institutions. If popular support for integration becomes problematic they will choose other remedies, including potentially a reversal of certain integrative policies. Paradoxically, then, comprehensive international arrangements [such as the EU] may in some ways challenge rather than reinforce the process of developing a transnational socio-psychological community. They may release pressures that encourage the encapsulation of nations, and fundamentally alter ... the teleology of integration theory by indicating an end situation which has built into it pressures which preserve segmental autonomy within a cooperative system – a symbiotic arrangement. (Taylor 1991: 113)

Combining the two logics just discussed, a potentially powerful 'countervailing pressures' alternative to the earlier 'spillover' accounts emerges. Elite and mass preferences conjoin to make symbolic integration less likely as integration in other areas progresses. While the 'authority legitimacy balance' demands that growing material (i.e. political and economic) power must be matched by growing symbolic power, the 'countervailing pressures' logic suggests that the former may make the latter less likely.

The two lines of reasoning just outlined thus make opposing claims and lead to opposing predictions regarding the EU's symbolic policy-making potential. All the same, in practice they are not necessarily incompatible. Instead, they may work alongside, counteract and partially offset one another, producing partial solutions and compromise arrangements in the process.

To illustrate this it is helpful to return briefly to the domestic level, focusing on the very consociational systems from which 'Euro-consociationalists' draw their empirical inspiration. As indicated, in those states (with Switzerland usually serving as the paradigmatic example) the overarching centre did acquire a measure of symbolic power, albeit sometimes against strong initial objections by local and regional authorities and only to a limited extent. While the centre cultivated overarching myths and symbols, it left a great deal of symbolic autonomy to the sub-units. The different symbolic spheres are compatible or even symbiotic rather than competing and form a more or less stable equilibrium. Moreover, while processes of overarching community and corporate identity formation (i.e. third-level legitimisation) transpired in every stable consociational system, they remained relatively weak and did not usurp the corporate identities and communal boundaries of the sub-units. Finally, as interaction between their constituent populations grew, consociational systems protected the social and cultural boundaries dividing them, through minority language charters, linguistic territoriality rules, cultural subsidy schemes, decentralised school curricula and the like (Laponce 1988; McRae 1983; Lijphart 1977, 1968).

Perhaps, then, we should expect something along these lines to transpire in the EU as well: a partial 'sharing' of symbolic power, but accompanied by strong symbolic decentralisation and autonomy protection schemes. In this rendering national governments might accept the use of cultural, audiovisual and educational policies to shore up support for integration in areas where they want it to occur and find public acceptance as well as to accommodate pressure by the European Parliament and the Commission. But at the same time, they do not want integration to become a state-transcending undertaking and thus remain determined to preserve the bulk of their cultural and educational prerogatives and to protect the member states as the primary units of mass identification.

The policies emerging out of such a scenario would thus share a range of characteristics. First, they would be aimed at strengthening public support for specific and relatively narrowly circumscribed projects (e.g. the common currency) rather than at the creation of more diffuse and all-embracing feelings of Europeanness – in many ways they would be more like public relations measures than building blocks of a European 'nation-building' strategy.

Second, in such a scenario EU-pursued political symbolism would be complementary to rather than competing with existing national symbolisms. For instance, instead of replacing national 'civics' lessons or history textbooks it would involve the distribution of complementary European material in schools. And instead of leading to the replacement of national symbols with European ones, it would entail the dissemination of complementary symbols displayed alongside their national counterparts.

Finally, while in this scenario the Commission and the European Parliament might be able to carve out a role for themselves in designing and implementing particular cultural, audiovisual and educational measures, national governments would nonetheless insist on various safeguards and the ability to apply 'emergency breaks' to prevent supranational bodies from unilaterally expanding their cultural and educational remit beyond a level they deemed compatible with the continued role of the member states as the primary units of mass identification. To the same end, they might establish various mixed implementation bodies, insist on regular policy reviews, ensure that cultural and educational funding remained closely tied to specific, pre-approved projects, and so forth.

All this, of course, remains to be empirically investigated rather than just theoretically deduced. The next three chapters examine political symbolism in the European Union, from the Treaties of Rome to the present. In line with the argument so far they focus on cultural policy, the audiovisual sector and education. How did political elites in the EU at various levels seek to shore up support for European integration through cultural and educational policies? Did such initiatives have popular appeal? What resistance did they encounter, from national publics and/or from elites with competing symbolic agendas? Lastly, what conclusions can we draw from this regarding the relative significance of the two alternative logics just discussed and, more broadly, the future development of the European project?

Notes

1 I use the terms 'state legitimisation' and 'state- and nation-building' to depict situations in which state institutions sought to legitimise themselves in the eyes of their

subjects. In some instances this went hand in hand with, or followed closely in the wake of, state founding. Examples are the creation of Germany and Italy in the late nineteenth century. In Italy the task at hand was famously epitomised by Massimo d'Azeglio's exclamation 'We have made Italy: now we must make Italians' (quoted in Hobsbawm 1993a: 267). In other cases, political elites sought to attract mass loyalties in already well-established states, e.g. in nineteenth-century Britain or the French Third Republic. Some writers use terms such as 'national consciousness formation' or 'nationalisation of the masses' (Mosse 1991) to label this process. But in the present context 'state legitimisation' is more useful. It highlights the key variable at stake, namely the creation of popular consent for a given political order.

2 This literature has grown significantly in past years, generally subsumed under the heading of 'nationalism research'. Canonical works in the English language include Hobsbawm (1994), Anderson (1991), Smith (1991) and Gelllner (1983). For more specific case studies see also the excellent contributions in Gillis (1996). Also see Brubaker and Cooper (2000) and Billig (1995) for important critiques.

3 Habermas's (1976) influential account of what he terms 'legitimation crisis', for instance, rests in part precisely on this notion (also Held 1988, Chapter 4).

4 All this raises the question of whether there is an intrinsic link between salience (as opposed to strength and solidity) and the kinds of signifiers used in a given political system. In other words, could such a system rely on purely 'thin' signifiers yet at the same time be very centralised and enjoy a very high degree of salience and third-level legitimacy? From a social constructivist angle nothing would seem to prevent this in principle. Yet since very centralised democracies require a very high degree of system-wide interaction and communication and since there are no subordinate corporate identities to take into account, elites might be more tempted to press for linguistic and cultural assimilation. Self-styled 'civic' polities that are in reality culturally and linguistically homogenised (such as France) illustrate this. Applied to the EU, this calls for a slight qualification of the earlier point: if the EU were to evolve in such a way as to erode the political viability and corporate identities of its member states (that is, into a centralised European state), achieving some degree of cultural homogenisation which in turn would lead to 'thick' communal markers might become (or, at any rate, be perceived as) a practical necessity. However, at present this seems to be a very faint prospect at best.

5 Hobsbawm (1993b: 307). This stress on 'need' is implicit in numerous accounts which attribute the success of nationalist movements to individuals' search for meaning and belonging in the face of uprooting developments such as urbanisation, secularisation, and the breakdown of traditional local hierarchies and communities.

6 Not surprisingly, neofunctionalists typically link the effectiveness with which the Commission can 'cultivate' integration to the skill and determination of leading supranational officials of the day, above all Commission presidents. They attribute expansive periods in the EU's development in part to the calibre and ambition of the Commission leaders who presided over them (such as, most recently, Jacques Delors), whereas they partially blame weaker Commission presidents for periods of stagnation (Ross 1995; Sandholtz and Zysman 1989).

3

Cultural policy

Despite much enthusiasm in the early post-war European unification movement for bringing a 'cultural dimension' to European integration,[1] neither the
treaty that set up the European Coal and Steel Community nor the subsequent Rome Treaties gave the Community any powers in cultural policy. The
only direct reference to culture in the original EEC Treaty resides in Article
36. It stipulates that, in exceptional cases, the Community may suspend its
free trade provisions to assure the 'protection of national treasures possessing
artistic, historic or archaeological value'. This provision thus established a
cultural exemption clause liable to be invoked by national governments, not
a legal basis for a cultural involvement by the Community.

There was one actual and one potential exception to the Community's
exclusion from the cultural field. First, according to standard legal interpretation Article 36 never amounted to a wholesale exception of cultural 'goods
and services' from the Community's free trade and freedom of movement
provisions. In principle, these were to apply to culture as much as to any other
economic activity. Second, in some renderings a conceivable way of involving
the Community in culture was through Article 235 of the EEC Treaty. It
authorised the Council of Ministers, acting unanimously, to initiate 'action
by the Community' in areas not explicitly mentioned in the treaty, if this
'should prove necessary to attain ... one of the objectives of the Community
and [the EEC Treaty]'. The significance of Article 235 for cultural policy
remained disputed, however. Some argued that the EEC Treaty's call for an
'ever closer Union' contains an 'allusion to European culture' (Massart-
Piérard 1986: 34), yet for many others this far exceeded the limits of
permissible treaty interpretation (e.g. Blanke 1994; Faroux 1993).

In any case, during its first two decades the Community had no broader
cultural or public relations ambitions, save for a small 'information unit'
attached to the Commission (mainly in charge of liasing with journalists) and

the occasional publishing of brochures and leaflets aimed at schools or a wider public. It was only in the late 1960s that the Community's far-reaching cultural abstinence became questioned: in Community rhetoric first, and subsequently through tangible policy initiatives.

The rise of 'European culture' and 'European identity' in Community discourse

The late 1960s saw the launch of a series of official pronouncements – some by the Commission, some emanating from intergovernmental gatherings – which suggested a growing concern with public attitudes towards European integration. These pronouncements had a common theme: if the Community was to thrive in the long term and possibly move into new areas such as foreign and monetary policy or direct elections to the European Parliament, it would need to do more than demonstrate its economic utility. Instead, it would need to generate a new quality of popular commitment, described variously with terms such as 'awareness of the non-material values of European unity', 'European consciousness', 'European values' and 'European identity'.

Among the first examples of such rhetoric is the 'Declaration by the European Commission on the occasion of the Achievement of the Customs Union on 1 July 1968':

> But Europe is not only of customs tariffs. Europe does not belong only to the manufacturers, the farmers or the technocrats ... Europe is not only the Europe of the Governments, of the Parliaments or of the administrators. It must also be the Europe of the peoples, of the workers, of youth, of man himself. All – or nearly all – still remains to be done. (Commission 1972 [1968]: 69)

Of a similar bent was the declaration issued at the Paris Summit some three years later, this time by the heads of state and government themselves. It proclaimed that 'economic expansion ... is not an end in itself. ... It must emerge in an improved quality as well as an improved standard of life. In the European spirit special attention will be paid to non-material values ...' (Bulletin 1972 [No. 10]: 15–16).

Of all such pronouncements, however, it was the 'Declaration on European identity', issued at the Copenhagen Summit in 1973 which signifies the most forceful entry of this type of rhetoric into the Community's official vocabulary. In many ways a 'woolly and confusing text' (de Witte 1987: 135; also Delahaye 1979) it refers to the 'framework of common European civilisation, the attachment to common values and principles, the increasing convergence of attitudes to life', which would give the 'European Identity [sic] its originality and its own dynamism'. Moreover,

the European Identity [*sic*] will evolve as a function of the dynamic of the construction of a united Europe. In their external relations, the Nine propose
progressively to undertake the definition of their identity in relation to other
countries or groups of countries.

In some respects these various declarations seemed like rhetorical window
dressing. They lacked tangible proposals on how the envisioned European
identity should be promoted, and their grandiloquence often seemed little
more than a rhetorical compensation for their lack of policy substance. All the
same, for the Commission, the European Parliament and at least some
member state governments they reflected a genuine concern for the
Community's public standing. This reverberated throughout a series of internal Commission documents and working papers, which blamed the
Community's stagnation at the time in part on its technocratic image and lack
of emotional mass appeal.[2] Most visibly, these concerns led to the creation of
the Eurobarometer research unit in 1973. Funded by the Commission,
Eurobarometer's task was to conduct regular opinion polls throughout the
Community, providing the Commission and national policy makers with
scientifically compiled time-series data on public perceptions of the
Community and particular policies in different member states (see Reif and
Inglehart 1991; de Witte 1987). In short, by the early 1970s, many policy-
makers believed that popular attitudes towards European integration had
become a problem, and that European culture, European values and
European identity could offer a solution. The various identity declarations at
the time were one manifestation of this belief.

But what was the actual policy impact of these declarations, given that
they lacked tangible proposals? With hindsight two factors seem relevant
above all. First, at the level of elite discourse these pronouncements marked
an incipient European 'entity process', helping to gradually solidify the idea
of the Community as a real existing corporate actor and carrier of particular
European meanings and values. Throughout all these declarations, European
identity, European values, European culture and the like were depicted as
self-evident facts, merely in need of being 'rediscovered' or 'strengthened'
rather than constructed or invented. This in turn became a rhetorical underpinning of most subsequent cultural policy proposals by the EP and the
Commission, heralding a broader trend whereby 'the notion of "European
identity" ... became progressively transformed and reified, and then
presented as a fixed, bounded and "natural" category, through successive
policy initiatives' (Shore 1993: 788; Perriaux 1990). As will be shown, by the
1980s this had led to the appearance in Commission and EP discourse not
only of a shared European heritage, a European identity and European values,
but also, in places, of a European culture and a European people. Making
Europeans more aware of these became the foremost declared aim of
Community cultural policy.

Second, by acknowledging European identity, European culture and the

like as something at least in principle worth promoting, national governments provided the Commission and the European Parliament with a general
heading under which they could place their subsequent initiatives for a
cultural (and also, as discussed in Chapter 5, educational) involvement by the
Community. It allowed them to portray these initiatives as merely giving
substance to an objective whose widespread recognition was already on the
record. For a long time to come, almost every cultural proposal by the
Commission and the EP referred to the Copenhagen Declaration and to its
theme of European identity promotion. As is shown next, this process took a
long time to build up critical momentum. Nonetheless, by the late 1980s it
had led to some tangible cultural involvement by the Community for the first
time.

From the Tindemans to the Adonnino Report

Throughout the 1970s and 1980s attempts to involve the Community in
culture had two components. First were the various grandiloquent but vague
'European identity' declarations just discussed, rapidly making their way into
more and more pronouncements by the Commission and the EP while also
becoming a set-piece feature of many Council and European summit statements. These declarations had no direct policy impact but, as suggested, their
depiction of European identity, European culture and European values as
both self-evident facts and problem areas (because not yet sufficiently 'rediscovered', 'affirmed', or 'brought to the fore') established a basis on which
more tangible cultural proposals could be predicated. These in turn came in
two varieties: first, comprehensive cultural 'package initiatives', unambiguously aimed at increasing the Community's symbolic visibility and mass
appeal; second, more low-key proposals that concentrated on cultural
exchanges and other circulation-enhancing measures and were often justified
on economic rather than identity-centred grounds.

   The first comprehensive cultural policy initiative formed part of the
'Report on European Union', submitted by the Belgian Prime Minister Leo
Tindemans to his European Council colleagues in 1976. Tindemans had been
given the task of drafting a wide-ranging blueprint for the Community's
future development and for its progression towards what was vaguely termed
'political union'. While the bulk of his report dealt with the Community's
expansion into foreign and monetary policy and a broadening of EP and
Commission powers, one section, titled 'A citizen's Europe', suggested ways
of broadening the Community's popular appeal.

   Tindemans's stated logic was clear: to overcome the prevailing
'Eurosclerosis' at the time and to expand into new policy areas the
Community would have to shed its technocratic image and attract popular
loyalties and commitment of a kind that had hitherto proven elusive. These,

in turn, would not simply emerge as an automatic by-product of economic and political integration but instead would require carefully devised policies. Some of Tindemans's proposals to this end had a strong utilitarian flavour (e.g. improving consumer rights in the Community) whereas others were mainly circulation and exchange-centred (e.g. improved communication links, cultural and educational exchanges and a 'European Foundation' in charge of organising them). A third category of proposals sought to enhance the Community's symbolic presence in the everyday lives of its citizens through what Tindemans called 'external signs of our solidarity'. Suggestions under this rubric were relatively sparse, however, centring on proposals for a common European passport cover design and a range of additional symbols whose nature was to be decided at a later stage.

Other than bringing the heads of state and government to profess their 'very great interest' in its recommendations at the Hague Summit in November 1976 (Bulletin 1976 [No. 11], point 2501), the Tindemans Report led to no tangible cultural or symbolic measures. It did, however, prompt the Commission to submit a range of follow-up proposals to the member states, the most comprehensive of which was its 1977 initiative for 'Community action in the cultural sector' (Commission 1977). The bulk of it concentrated on better freedom of movement provisions for 'cultural goods and services' and 'cultural workers', both of which were justified largely on economic grounds and depicted to fall squarely within the Community's existing economic mandate. Complementing this, the Commission also proposed more symbolically charged measures that went further than those suggested by Tindemans. So it called for 'European rooms' in national museums (to highlight works 'which form part of the Community's heritage'), 'Community cultural institutes', and a series of '365 broadcasts, each of which will last five minutes and be devoted to a great European of the past or present'. In addition, the Commission proposed 'Europiades' broadcast on Eurovision throughout the Community. Their impact on viewers, along with that of similar Community-sponsored mass events, should be assessed through 'high level scientific studies' in order to maximise their Europeanising effect on popular attitudes.

Yet the Commission's 1977 initiative, too, came to nothing. Despite an almost desperate sounding supporting resolution by the European Parliament in 1979 (EP 1979: 50–51), the Council refused even to debate it. Overt resistance was spearheaded by Denmark and the UK, but with the tacit support of other member states. France had generally been open to classic inter-governmental cooperation in culture (along the lines of the many Franco-German programmes pursued since the end of the Second World War) but rejected a cultural involvement by the Community. The British government broadly shared this position. Germany, for its part, was driven by Länder fears of an erosion of their cultural prerogatives, which became steadily stronger over the years.[3]

The failure of these early cultural initiatives carried several lessons. First, it highlighted the crippling effect of the Community's lacking legal mandate in culture and the 'fundamental lack of legality and legitimacy' (Sandell 1996: 268) that overshadowed all cultural initiatives as a result. The Commission's attempts to use proposals for the better application of freedom of trade and movement stipulations to culture (where it did have a legal mandate) as a 'cover' for more proactive and symbolically charged cultural initiatives (where it had no legal mandate) ultimately proved ineffective. The delicate balance of power between the Commission and the Council of Ministers – which governs decision-making in areas where the Community does have real treaty-based powers – was tilted almost completely in favour of the latter as far as culture was concerned. Without a legal mandate, the Commission was forced to submit its cultural proposals in the form of 'communications' and 'draft resolutions', neither of which had a clear legal standing. As for the member states, they were free to ignore these at will, simply pleading legal objections.

In this sense, Britain and Denmark's accession to the Community in 1973 had an ambiguous effect. On the one hand, in both countries popular support for the Community was much lower than in the original six. This gave an additional sense of urgency to the Commission's calls for measures to improve the Community's public standing. But on the other hand, those two countries also became the staunchest sceptics of any cultural involvement by the Community. Other countries that were more favourable and thus could to some extent counterbalance British and Danish obstructionism – namely Greece, Spain and Portugal – did not join the Community until the 1980s.

Beyond this, the rhetorical framing of the Commission's 1977 initiative might well have been a tactical mistake. Proposals for 'European cultural institutes', 'European showrooms' in museums and the like reeked too much of self-conscious attempts at European 'nation-building' to be acceptable even to those governments that might not have opposed less grandiloquent initiatives. As one former Commission official put it, the 1977 initiative and the rhetoric that accompanied it reflected more the uncompromising 'commitment to the European ideal' by the Commission officials who drafted them than pragmatic policy considerations (interview, February 2001).

After the defeat of the Tindemans Report and the Commission's 1977 proposals it took almost a decade for another comprehensive cultural initiative to emerge. It originated with a decision taken at the Fontainebleau Summit in June 1984 to appoint a committee chaired by the Italian MEP Pietro Adonnino to examine ways in which the Community could, in the words of the European Council, 'strengthen and promote its identity and its image both for its citizens and for the rest of the world' (Bulletin 1984 [No. 6], point 1.1.9 [subheading 6]). The Adonnino Committee was to deliberate parallel to the Dooge Committee on institutional reform that was to prepare the impending overhaul of the founding treaties in the Single European Act.

Two factors helped bring the Adonnino Committee into being. The first was the unexpectedly low popular turnout at the European Parliament elections in June 1984. Many Commission officials as well as some of their colleagues inside the member states took this as a warning sign that the impending Single Market programme might encounter unexpectedly high levels of public resistance (interviews European Commission, June and September 2000; Janssen 1985). At the very least, it suggested that democratising the Community and making it more visible might not, in and of itself, enhance its popular appeal. The notion that popular support for the EU had once more become a 'problem' strengthened the hand of the Commission, the EP and some member state governments (led this time by Italy) in convincing more sceptical governments to accept the Adonnino Committee.

Second, in part the Adonnino Committee was also a consolation prize, compensating the European Parliament, the Commission and the more culture-ambitious member states for the absence of cultural policy from the upcoming Single European Act. This became an increasingly likely prospect at the time, despite vigorous lobbying by the European Parliament (especially in its Draft Treaty Establishing the European Union [EP 1984]).[4] Since Britain and Denmark had already signalled that they would veto attempts to give the Community legal powers in culture, the Commission itself had largely given up on pursuing the issue. Instead, it concentrated on trying to use the Single Act to expand into less controversial areas such as environmental policy (interview European Commission, June 2001; Delors 1985).[5] The Adonnino Committee, by contrast, was much easier to swallow for even the most sceptical member state governments. Its recommendations would not be legally binding and could thus be ignored more or less at will if they were deemed to be legally or substantially offensive – the fate of the Tindemans Report had amply demonstrated this.

The Adonnino Committee presented two reports to the member states (both in 'A People's Europe' 1985). Following the by then customary division, the first report concentrated on 'utilitarian' support measures, especially the 'easing of rules and practices which cause irritation to Community citizens and undermine the credibility of the Community'. Among other things, it suggested an increase in customs allowances for travellers within the Community, the relaxation of internal border controls and better social security and taxation provisions for intra-Community migrants.

The second report, by contrast, dealt with cultural policy and education. While many of its proposals centred on exchanges, others sought to increase the Community's symbolic visibility in the everyday lives of its citizens – measures the report deemed 'essential to European identity and the Community's image in the minds of its people, [... and where] support for the advancement of Europe can and must be sought'. They included suggestions for the Community to sponsor transnational audiovisual coproductions, European postage stamps, a 'European academy of science, technology and art' ('Europe needs an institution with international influence to highlight the achievements of European science and the originality of European civilisation') and a Euro-lottery. Its weekly draw would be televised throughout the Community and the prize money paid out in ECU. By being 'an event with popular appeal', such a lottery could 'make Europe come alive for the Europeans' and thereby 'help promote the European idea'. Under the heading 'information policy', the Adonnino report recommended that the Community and national governments cooperate more closely to, among other things, 'point out to people what the costs would be if the Community did not exist'. It also demanded the replacement of 'inadequate and obsolete signs' at internal borders with 'border signs of a common design' and the introduction of a European flag. It would be used 'without of course affecting the use of national flags' and accompany the frequent playing of Beethoven's 'Ode to Joy' which was to be designated as the official Community anthem.

The two Adonnino reports were approved in principle by the heads of state and government at the Brussels and Milan Summits respectively (European Council 1985: 31). Many Commission officials, however, doubted the member state governments' real intentions, recalling the similarly warm formal welcome they had extended to Tindemans's 'citizen's Europe' agenda a decade earlier (interviews European Commission, June 2000). And the wider reception of the Adonnino Report was sceptical at best. Many commentators likened it to a hastily assembled collection of uncoordinated brainstorming sessions; and suggestions such as those for a European lottery and postage stamps quickly attracted widespread ridicule and comments to the effect that they 'are easily to be deemed dysfunctional' (Janssen 1986: 212, my translation[6]; also Janssen 1985).

Nonetheless, circumstances had changed from the previous decade. One factor was the general revival of the integrative process in the mid-1980s. It was one thing to argue, as had Tindemans and the Commission in the 1970s, that a boost in popular commitment was needed to lead the Community out of stagnation, if this stagnation could ultimately be blamed on the very governments at which these pleas were directed; it was quite another to argue that measures already implemented or about to be implemented (i.e. direct elections to the EP and the Single Act) needed to be made more popular. The accession of Greece, Spain and Portugal in the 1980s gave added momentum to Adonnino's cultural policy drive. Together with Italy and (on occasion) the Socialist government in France, these were more receptive to a Community involvement in culture and less worried about legal transgressions and ambiguities. This helped counterbalance the more sceptical members led, as always, by Denmark and the UK.

Most importantly perhaps, this time round the Commission acted much more skilfully than in the wake of the Tindemans Report. Rather than issuing yet another comprehensive cultural package initiative, it used the momentum generated by the Adonnino Report to put forward a steady flow of relatively narrowly circumscribed follow-up initiatives. And to ensure that these would be debated in an appropriate forum, it managed to bring about regular meetings of the national ministers of culture.

The 'small steps' approach to culture

Some three years prior to the Adonnino Report the Commission had scored a major success when the national ministers of culture met for the first time. To alleviate concerns by Denmark, the UK and Germany (the latter driven by the habitual Länder fears), they first met informally and then under a 'mixed' semi-Community-related, semi-intergovernmental label 'Ministers of culture meeting within the Council' (Ryngaert 1987; Polaczek 1982).

Many of the initial meetings were dominated by French culture minister Jack Lang's incessant but ultimately futile calls for mandatory quotas on foreign audiovisual imports (further discussed in the next chapter). But after the Adonnino Report and under sustained lobbying by the European Parliament and the Commission they nonetheless led to a cascade of concrete cultural initiatives. For example, in 1985 the culture ministers agreed on a programme to market European films outside the Community and on a European sculpture competition (Bulletin 1985 [No. 5], point 2.1.59 et seq.). In 1986 they adopted a programme for 'transnational cultural itineraries' (Bulletin 1986 [No. 2], point 2.1.89; Ministers responsible for Cultural Affairs 1986a). In 1986 there followed three resolutions pertaining to the private sponsoring of 'cultural events' and cooperation in architectural heritage protection and art conservation (Ministers with responsibility for Cultural Affairs 1986a, 1986b, 1986c). Furthermore, the culture ministers agreed to sponsor a 'European film and television year' (Ministers responsible for Cultural Affairs 1986b), literary translations (Council 1987a), and to enhance promotional activities organised by the Commission (see further below). There followed the creation of a 'European cultural month', held in addition to the annual designation of a 'European city of culture' (Bulletin 1990 [No. 11], point 1.3.193) and various resolutions on the training and exchange of 'arts administrators' and on transnational theatre promotion (Council 1991a, 1991b). Lastly, the Community helped sponsor a growing number of cultural prizes for architects, film producers, writers, literary translators, town twinning organisers and the like. They ranged from the 'European prize for literature' and the 'European prize for translation', to the 'gold stars of town twinning' prize (Bulletin 1990 [No. 11], point 1.3.12; Bulletin 1993 [No. 10], point 1.2.176; Commission 1990b, 1990c).

Apart from some Community-sponsored events and prizes that fell under the direct auspices of the Commission, most of these initiatives amounted to little more than intergovernmental declarations of intent. They were legally non-binding and implemented by the member states alone with the Commission obtaining at the most some form of observer status (Ryngaert 1987: 586). What is more, while most of these measures were justified in part with the need to foster support for the Community, they had, on the face of it, only a limited potential to actually do so. Some, such as Community-sponsored restoration schemes for national monuments, had little in the way of a tangible 'European dimension' to begin with. Even the 'European city of culture' programme involved (and still involves) above all the use of Community funds to support local cultural projects, garnished with some Europe-wide tourism promotion. It lacks a strong conceptual link to European integration, let alone to specific Community policies and institutions. Other measures did feature a – however embryonically conceived – 'European dimension', but mainly in the sense of boosting transnational cultural exchanges. Also, most of them focused so strongly on 'high culture' (classical music, sculpture exhibitions, literary translations) that their mass appeal was limited from the outset – aggravated by their minuscule funding in relation to the Community's population size.

Nonetheless, placed in the overall context of the development of Community cultural policy these initiatives were significant. Within a few years they had led to the actual initiation of a number of concrete cultural policies, the Community's continued lack of a legal mandate in culture notwithstanding. And while they were mostly initiated at an intergovernmental level, this occurred nevertheless within a notional Community context: most were initially proposed by the Commission, participation was restricted to the member states of the Community, all Community members participated in them, and most gave the Commission some nominal (though often largely observer status-type) role in their implementation. Finally, though all these initiatives started out with only very modest funding, this, too, had the potential to grow. After all, once the Community begins to fund a given project in any given area, demand almost inevitably comes to outstrip supply. Its supporters can then use this as evidence that the project in question meets an underlying 'need' and lobby for its expansion. As is shown below, this is precisely what the Commission sought to do with many of its cultural actions in subsequent years, albeit with mixed success.

How to account for these post-Adonnino programmes? A first factor was the Commission's cleverness in 'packaging' and rhetorically justifying them. On the one hand, it 'economised' many of these initiatives. Its main declared cultural objective became the creation of a borderless 'cultural space' in which 'cultural goods and services' could be exchanged freely. This fit in well with the mobility-centredness of the Single Market programme and it pushed back the conceptual boundary between cultural policy (where the Community had no mandate) and economic and social policy (where it did have a mandate) in favour of the latter. On the other hand, together with the EP the Commission continued to invoke identity-related arguments, maintaining that cultural policies were needed to shore up support for European integration and that the member states had acknowledged as much by approving the Adonnino Report. In the 1970s, the Commission had portrayed this as neces-sary to catapult the Community out of its stagnation; in the 1980s, it depicted it as indispensable to sustain the Community's rising fortunes at the time.

The joining of Greece and later Spain and Portugal in the early to mid-1980s further boosted the Commission's cultural clout. First, as suggested, together with Italy these countries soon became the most ardent supporters of a Community involvement in culture. Second, a disproportionate number of new Commission staff recruited from these three countries joined the administrative units in charge of culture and education, thereby raising the profile and relative status of these policy areas within the Commission and leading to their growing professionalisation.[7] Throughout the 1980s the Commission accumulated specialised expertise in areas ranging from the taxation of 'cultural workers' to the economics of the audiovisual productions sector, and it compiled a steady stream of internal briefs, assessments, memo-randums and draft reports in part concerned with these areas. This in turn prepared the ground for a cascade of cultural proposals put forward in the second part of the 1980s. These achieved, at the very least, a kind of 'nagging effect' upon the member states, making it more difficult for them to simply ignore the Commission's cultural initiatives or to dismiss them out of hand as they had done throughout the preceding decade.

The first Community symbols and public relations campaigns

If the Adonnino Report boosted the Community's standing in cultural policy, its greatest impact was in the area of political symbols and public relations. For instance, even though demands for a fully-fledged European flag re-mained unacceptable to some member states (the British government led the objectors[8]), the Commission and the EP ultimately managed to obtain approval for a 'European logo'. It featured a design of twelve stars arranged in a circle, similar to that already used by the Council of Europe. 'Once adopted, [... the European logo] was of course used on flags – but these lacked official status' (Wallace 1990: 122). What is more, the prelude to Beethoven's 'Ode to Joy' was declared the Community's official anthem, this time without much visible opposition from the member states (Bulletin 1986 [No. 4], point 2.1.81).

Following Adonnino's recommendations the Commission also expanded its public relations activities. Most were funded by the Commission's infor-mation budget under the auspices of its Directorate-General X. In addition to its traditional brief of 'information', DG X had by then also been given responsibility for cultural policy and, in recognition of the Adonnino Report, for 'people's Europe' issues. And it was in this latter field that DG X soon developed a flurry of activities. For example, advised by a public relations firm it stocked up 'EC-shops' in Brussels with pencils and mugs engraved with the European logo and with 'I love Europe' T-shirts. For added effect it decorated its own Brussels headquarters with 'Europe, my country' posters and commissioned promotional videos for general distribution. Titles to choose from included 'A European Journey', 'Jean Monnet, Father of Europe', 'The Tree of Europe' ('an original feature which will make all Europeans aware of the common roots of their past') and 'After Twenty Centuries'. This video, proclaimed the Commission, could teach Europeans about their 'shared experiences at political, intellectual and cultural level' over the past 2000 years (quoted in Shore 1996: 485). In addition, the Commission sponsored a European yacht race, a festival for European car collectors, various bicycle races, a 'walk for Europe' and many similar events (Commission 1987b).

The corporate feel inherent to many of the Commission's public relations activities did not meet with unanimous approval, not even by the normally very sympathetic European Parliament. One telling incident occurred in 1986, when a group of MEPs was given a preview of a promotional video produced by a French public relations firm for the Commission.

> What followed was a pastiche of advertising images, holiday brochure-type depictions of European places and peoples ... These supposedly positive and 'up-beat' images were set to music; a synthesised pop remix of a Mozart symphony. The video culminated in a scene of American tennis star John McEnroe winning a European Tennis tournament, but instead of holding up to the cheering crowd a cup or trophy, the champion's hands were clutching an enormous plastic eurocheque, announcing in ECU the value of his prize-money. At the end of the presentation, there was a stunned silence followed by some angry exchanges which later culminated in at least one MEP tabling a formal complaint to the Commission for squandering public money. (Shore 1993: 790)

All the same, their homespun quality did not reduce the importance of these early measures for the development of public relations policy in the European Community. Like parallel forays into more conventional areas of cultural policy at the time, they established precedents and paved the way for a much more extensive involvement in the 1990s and beyond. In fact, in 1990 'information and communication' received, for the first time, a separate entry in the Community's budget, and its funding grew rapidly in the years thereafter to an annual average of around forty million ECU in the first few years of the 1990s (see the budget section in the Commission's annual *General Report on the Activities of the European Union*).

Parallel to this grew the Commission's eagerness to define and implement a coherent information strategy. From the late 1980s, and against the backdrop of the impending end-of-1992 Single Market deadline, the Commission released annual 'Priority information' and 'Priority publications' programmes' into which it channelled the bulk of its 'information and communication' budget (e.g. *Bulletin* 1990 [No. 3], point 1.1.190; *Bulletin* 1990 [No. 7–8], point 1.3.304). In 1989–1990 the three – somewhat vaguely defined – 'priority themes' about which the Commission sought to 'inform' its citizens were 'making a success of 1992', 'enhancing 1992', and 'preparing for post-1992' (*Bulletin* 1989 [No. 2], point 2.1.84). The year after they were 'the building of a new Europe', 'Europe at the service of its citizens' and 'Europe: a world partner'. For each of these themes the Commission produced leaflets, newspaper advertisements, 'information events', and various exhibitions in the member states as discussed further below.

A significant proportion of the Commission's PR budget at the time went into sponsorship of large-scale public events. For instance, in July 1991 a Commission subsidy of 300.000 ECU helped launch the first 'European Youth Olympic Games' (*Bulletin* 1991 [No. 4], point 1.2.146). One year later, the Commission sponsored a 'Community pavilion' at the world exposition in Seville. It housed a display titled 'from Renaissance Europe to the renaissance of Europe' which attracted around two million visitors (Commission 1992a: 391; *Bulletin* 1992 [No. 3], point 1.2.221). But by far the most significant event sponsored by the Commission at the time were the Olympic summer and winter games in 1992.

DG X at the Olympics
To both Olympic games the Commission made a sizeable contribution: four million ECU to the winter Olympics in Albertville and six million to the summer games in Barcelona.[9] In return, the Community obtained a substantial symbolic presence at the games. The Community logo was displayed at their televised opening and closing ceremonies and these also featured 'choreographed scenes devoted to the Community'. In addition, the Commission sought to have a direct impact on location. The Community press service distributed information material aimed primarily at 'opinion leaders' who attended the games, and the Community logo featured on '300 banners at Albertville and 1800 banners in the streets of Barcelona'. A travelling Community exhibition, called 'Euromobile', attended both games, handing out information leaflets and Community paraphernalia.

Parallel to all this the Commission pursued several accompanying measures 'with a view to making the Community message more explicit and more effective' and to ensure that 'the opportunities for communication offered by the sponsoring of [... the Olympic Games] could be exploited to optimum effect'. On these the Commission spent a further 4.5 million ECU. This publicity drive entailed 'Euromobile's' tour of seventy European cities. Members of the public were lured into the exhibition with video footage from the Olympics on high definition television screens. Once they had entered they received information literature and small European flags. Complementing this the Commission ran a newspaper advertising campaign throughout the Community. It highlighted the Community's Olympic involvement and compared the Community to winning sports teams ('A thousand faces, a single force'; 'The European Community: More is possible when you pursue the same idea').

All the while it was planning, implementing and assessing the impact of its Olympic campaign, the Commission was clearly worried that it could backfire in public opinion. In its own words, it saw a 'danger that the exercise might be interpreted as "political propaganda" ... or as a "waste of taxpayer's [*sic*] money"'. When accusations of precisely this kind did surface, notably in the UK and Denmark (coupled with complaints that the use of the Olympics for political advertising violated the Olympic Charter), the Commission launched a strategy of trying to 'counteract these accusations or at least attenuate their impact and pre-empt any chain reaction throughout the Community press'. This included meetings with journalists attending the Olympics, in order, among other things, 'to convey the notion of an investment useful to the organisers [of the games]'.

The Commission's involvement with the Olympic games had several aspects that gave it a pioneering role in the general development of the Union's public relations campaigns. Remarkable, in the first place, was its scope and financial backing. It exceeded that of any comparable measure the Commission had hitherto undertaken. Moreover, the fact that in designing, implementing and assessing its Olympic offensive the Commission was assisted by a plethora of external experts and PR consultants heralded a growing professionalisation of Community public relations. This shone through not least in a hitherto unprecedented degree of reflexivity, leading the Commission to expect that some citizens could reject its Olympics campaign as political propaganda and to draw up contingency plans for rebutting such criticisms.

Certainly by the standards of most commercial mass-media-based advertising and public relations campaigns such an anticipation of potential 'oppositional reading' outcomes is nothing out of the ordinary (see Chapter 2 above). Yet for the Commission it represented a leap in sophistication over many of its previous attempts to shore up popular support, especially those launched under the 'people's Europe' heading in the late 1980s. In particular, it bore witness to a growing understanding by the Commission's information strategists that even if they conveyed seemingly positive images and messages about the Community this would not *ipso facto* improve its public standing. Though its Olympic campaign, too, ultimately sought to increase the Community's visibility and symbolic presence, the Commission's anticipation that this might backfire represented a departure from the crude 'the more the Community makes itself felt in the consciousness of its citizens the more these will inevitably come to support it' assumption that had dominated its earlier approach.

At the same time, with hindsight Commission officials concede that their Olympics campaign did not sufficiently heed these principles and that this caused it to backfire in some member states. They criticise the campaign for having been overly 'propagandist' and having led to the Community's 'over-projection' (interviews European Commission, June 2000). At the same time, the overall impact of this and subsequent public relations campaigns on popular attitudes towards European integration is difficult to ascertain, as is discussed below.

Cultural policy in the Maastricht Treaty

While these various cultural and PR initiatives were proposed, debated, implemented and had their impact assessed, the Community experienced the first legal development since the Single European Act. The negotiations that led to the Maastricht Treaty formally began with the launch of the two Intergovernmental Conferences on Political and Monetary Union in December 1990. The treaty was signed one year later. After a long and crisis-prone ratification process it came into force in November 1993.

In the period leading up to the Maastricht Treaty there was a relatively widespread anticipation that this time round the Community would receive some formal mandate in culture (and, as is shown in Chapter 5, also in educa-tion). In the first place, unlike the Single Act the Maastricht Treaty was not to be a purely economic document, which made it harder for member states to reject the Commission and the EP's lobbying for cultural powers on the habitual grounds that culture was not a primarily economic area (see Witte 1991). What is more, the cultural programmes that had been launched in the meantime were of dubious legality as was, by some accounts, the compromise formula of the 'Council and the ministers of culture meeting within the Council'. The German government in particular was keen to end this ambi-guity and place the Community's existing cultural actions on more solid legal foundations. Moreover, driven by Länder fears that the Community could encroach on their cultural prerogatives, it wanted a cultural clause to limit the kinds of cultural activities the Community could pursue in the future (inter-views European Commission, June 2000; Blanke 1994: 66[10]).

The other member states were, as always, divided on the issue. A first group, not surprisingly coalescing around Denmark and the UK, advocated the legal status quo. On the other end of the spectrum, a group of southern member states (Italy, Portugal, Spain and Greece) as well as Ireland signalled that they would be prepared to accept a more extensive cultural mandate for the Community but did not formally work out a common position on the issue (Blanke 1994: 66). In any event, as is shown next, it was the German position that broadly won out.

Three separate passages in the *Treaty on European Union* (1992) allude to culture and cultural policy. For a start, Part One of the treaty, titled 'Principles', features Article 3p (changed to Article 3q in the subsequent

Amsterdam Treaty), which stipulates that the activities of the Community shall include 'a contribution to education and training of quality and to the flowering of the cultures of the Member States'. Yet since Article 3p elaborates neither on what this 'contribution' should consist of, nor on what would make national cultures 'flower', its meaning remains very vague at best, pending potential future decisions by the European Court of Justice as to whether it should serve as an interpretative clause of sorts in determining the legality of particular policies.[11]

A second reference to culture resides in Article 92 of the Maastricht Treaty (Article 87 Amsterdam). Paragraph 3d therein reiterates and further elaborates on the exemption of some cultural 'goods and services' from the Community's free trade provisions already contained in the original EEC Treaty. It stipulates that among the measures that 'may be considered to be compatible with the common market' are 'aid to promote culture and heritage conservation where such aid does not affect trading conditions and competition in the Community to an extent that is contrary to the common interest'.[12]

The third, and for our purposes by far the most significant, allusion to culture is contained in Article 128 of the Maastricht Treaty. It gives the Community, for the first time, a limited cultural mandate:

> The Community shall contribute to the flowering of the cultures of the Member States, while respecting their national and regional diversity and at the same time bringing the common cultural heritage to the fore.

Article 128 further specifies that

> Action by the Community shall be aimed at encouraging cooperation between Member States and, if necessary, supporting and supplementing their action in the following areas: improvement of the knowledge and dissemination of the culture and history of the European peoples; conservation and safeguarding of cultural heritage of European significance; non commercial cultural exchanges; artistic and literary creation, including in the audiovisual sector.

In addition, Article 128 entitles the Community to foster cultural cooperation with third countries and international organisations. Lastly, it demands that 'the Community shall take cultural aspects into account in its action under other provisions of this Treaty'.

The cultural objectives spelled out in Article 128 are thus ambiguous. They oscillate between the themes of, on the one hand, putting the Community in charge of fostering cultural unity, and, on the other hand, entrusting it with the preservation of cultural diversity. Indeed, so pervasive is this ambiguity that at times either interpretation could be applied to the same sentence (for instance when the treaty refers to the 'culture and history of European peoples'). Overall, however, the rhetorical balance in Article 128 tilts towards the 'diversity' as opposed to the 'unity' side. In the first place, even when Article 128 does appear to allude to the 'unity' theme, it does not invoke a 'European culture'. Instead, while it starts out by referring to the 'common cultural heritage' which the Community should 'bring to the fore' it then quickly slides into the still weaker term 'cultural heritage of European significance'. Arguably, even national or local cultural heritage can be of 'European significance'. The notion that Article 128 favours 'diversity' over 'unity' becomes more plausible still if read in conjunction with Article 3p in the 'Principles' section of the Maastricht Treaty. As shown, it calls upon the Community to contribute to the 'flowering of the cultures of the *member states*' (emphasis added) while a 'common culture' or even only the 'common cultural heritage' is not mentioned.

Equally significant is the legal status of the measures that can be adopted under Article 128. Two types of measures are possible. First, the Community can 'adopt incentive measures, excluding any harmonisation of the laws and regulations of the Member States'; second, it may issue 'recommendations'. Neither is legally binding.[13] The terms 'incentive measure' and 'harmonisation' are both ambiguous. Overall, however, under any reasonably literal interpretation of the Maastricht Treaty the Community's cultural powers are essentially confined to encouraging cooperation between the member states. It may not issue legally enforceable standards, even if these were deemed to be of a 'non-harmonising' kind.

Worth noting, lastly, are the procedural requirements the Maastricht Treaty spells out for cultural policy decisions to be adopted. Such decisions are subject to the co-decision procedure as outlined under Article 189b of the treaty (Article 251 Amsterdam). This involves, notably, consultations with the Economic and Social Committee and the Committee of the Regions and requires approval by the European Parliament. Most importantly, Article 128 subjects all cultural decisions to the unanimity requirement in the Council and hence leaves them vulnerable to the veto of any single member state.[14]

In short, then, the Maastricht Treaty sought to square the circle between different cultural objectives that in many ways had seemed difficult to reconcile. First, it reflected a desire to enhance the Community's 'cultural dimension'. This went some way towards appeasing the EP and the Commission which had pressed for a legal mandate in culture throughout and it was in line with the Maastricht Treaty's mission of catapulting the Community beyond the status of a purely economic entity. Second, the Maastricht Treaty put the cultural policies already in place on a more solid legal basis, thereby addressing a (especially German) distaste for legal ambiguity. Third, it created potent safeguards to ensure that these measures could not be expanded or modified without the unanimous consent of all member states. Finally, by adding a harmonisation prohibition and ruling out legally binding measures, the member states ensured that such changes would, in any event, have to remain within very narrow parameters.

The Amsterdam Treaty of 1997 did not alter the Union's legal standing in culture, save for adding one further restriction. It converted the old Article 128 of the Maastricht Treaty into a new Article 151, and changed Paragraph 4 therein to read as follows: 'The Community shall take cultural aspects into account in its action under other provisions of this Treaty, *in particular in order to respect and to promote the diversity of its cultures*' (emphasis added). It is not entirely clear on whose behest the 'diversity of cultures' clause was inserted. At the time it attracted very little public attention, and given their own 'unity in diversity rhetoric' it would have been hard for the Commission and the EP to oppose it openly. Moreover, in strictly legal terms the new clause meant little, given that, as suggested, even the old Article 128 already privileged the 'diversity' over the 'unity' theme. In fact, strictly speaking the 'diversity of cultures' provision does not even apply to cultural policy, given that Article 4 refers to 'actions under other provisions'. Nonetheless, if nothing else the new clause served as a reminder to the Commission and the EP that the Community's cultural role was subject to very tight restrictions. As is shown next, this was reflected in the new batch of cultural initiatives that materialised from the mid-1990s.

From Raphael, Kaleidoscope and Ariane to Culture 2000

Within the Commission's cultural policy unit in DG X, different officials read the Maastricht Treaty in different ways. Some saw it as an imperfect but nonetheless promising basis for new Union initiatives and advocated that such initiatives be submitted to the member states without delay in order to sustain whatever cultural momentum the treaty had created. Others were much more sceptical. They, too, wanted to submit new policy initiatives, but took both the unanimity clause in Article 128 and the harmonisation prohibition as a bad omen for the Union's future cultural policy prospects (interview European Commission, June 2000). Nonetheless, after the Maastricht Treaty had come into force events moved relatively quickly. Following a cascade of Commission reports and communications the Council approved what became the Union's cultural flagship programmes in the post-Maastricht era.

The precise sequence of events that gave birth to these programmes need not concern us here in detail. For its part, the Commission (always staunchly supported by the EP) released several reports in which it professed its enthusiasm regarding the cultural clause in the Maastricht Treaty and attached cultural wish lists which often exceeded what, according to most standard interpretations, Article 128 in fact allowed for. For example, in its 1994 Communication on 'Community action in support of culture' (Commission 1994a; also 1992b), the Commission demanded, among other things, powers to organise 'large-scale emblematic activities' with a 'European dimension', including Europe Day festivities across the Union. Yet many member states opposed such requests just as they had done before the Maastricht Treaty. The traditional hard-core sceptics (Denmark and the UK) were increasingly joined by Germany and the Netherlands as well as by Sweden which was about to join the Union. These governments were driven by a mix of concerns. The German government pleaded mainly Länder fears while others claimed that the Commission's cultural proposals were unnecessary, too expensive or in violation of the subsidiarity principle and the anti-harmonisation provision in the Maastricht Treaty (interviews European Commission, June 2000; Council 1994).

Nonetheless, after much debate the national culture ministers (who, after the ratification of the Maastricht Treaty, could dispense with the 'mixed' formula and meet as a fully-fledged Council of Ministers) finalised three cultural programmes, after these had undergone the complicated co-decision procedure demanded by Paragraph 128.

The first was a programme in the field of heritage protection. Titled 'Raphael' it received thirty million ECU over a period of four years (Commission 1995a, 1995b, 1996a). The second programme, termed 'Kaleidoscope 2000', sponsored various transnational cultural events and exchanges – festivals, exhibitions, meetings and a host of 'partnership projects' involving participants from at least three different member states. Its total funding was 36.7 million ECU over a period of five years. After ferocious lobbying by the EP and the Commission and against initial resistance in the Council, Europe Day was declared a 'cultural event' eligible to receive Union funding (Commission 1995c). The third programme was named 'Ariane' and based on the Union's literature promotion programme in force since the early 1990s. Most of its combined funding of 11.1 million ECU over four years went into translation grants, with preference given to works in lesser-used languages, published after 1945 and/or 'representative of the culture of their country'.

In 1999, all three programmes were consolidated into a new programme called 'Culture 2000', with a total budget of 167 million euro for a period of five years, extended by a further two years in 2003 (EP and Council 2000a). As before, most funding went into transnational cultural cooperation, exchange, partnership and network programmes. The type of projects eligible for sponsorship and their objectives became defined more broadly, often to the point of becoming virtually meaningless ('facilitating access to culture', 'intercultural dialogue', 'spread of new forms of expression', release of 'synergies', etc.). Only ten per cent of Culture 2000 funding became eligible to go to 'special cultural events with a European or international dimension', such as 'European capital of culture' and 'European cultural month' festivities. This represented a clear defeat for the Commission and the EP which had consistently lobbied for giving such projects a larger share of funding.

Although the Commission kept a brave face in public, its culture officials were disappointed by the post-Maastricht cultural programmes. A series of consultation exercises, internal reviews and external evaluations all echoed this: while the Union supported hundreds of cultural projects, these suffered from high administrative overheads and low public visibility. In fact, one external evaluation found that even many *recipients* of Union sponsorship 'do not remember the results of the[ir] projects' once funding had run out (Commission 2004a: 10; see also Commission 2003a; EP 2001). Likewise, as is discussed below and further in Chapter 5, most 'emblematic events' supported by Kaleidoscope 2000 and later the 'special cultural events' provision in Culture 2000 (such as Europe Day) never managed to acquire much momentum in most member states.

This lack of visibility and popular resonance had several reasons: relatively low levels of overall funding (amounting to a few cents per Union citizen per year), the short duration of most projects (generally limited to one year), a focus on relatively uncontroversial but also unspectacular 'high culture' areas (such as literature and architecture) as well as the Commission's failure to use its (at any rate very small) budget allocated to 'emblematic public events' in a way that would have maximised publicity and media attention. In part this was due to fears of 'overexposure' and backlashes that had haunted the Commission's information strategists ever since the Olympics campaign in 1992. But most importantly, the low visibility of the Union's post-Maastricht cultural initiatives was an inevitable result of their preoccupation with 'networks'.

Cultural networks

Cultural networks were indeed the cornerstone of almost all the Union's post-Maastricht cultural programmes. By the Commission's own estimate, they received twenty per cent of the Union's cultural budget in the period between 1993 and 1998 (Commission 1999a) whereas eighty per cent of Culture 2000 funding goes to networks and other multinational cooperation programmes.

While spending more and more money on them the Commission has remained surprisingly vague on how, precisely, a 'cultural network' should be defined. Judging by the (itself often very vague) wording of the Culture 2000 programme and the projects the Commission has subsidised, the central idea seems to be that cultural networks represent some form of association between cultural groupings and organisations from different member states that collaborate in joint cultural projects. In line with stated priorities, most of these projects have fallen into the areas of performance art, visual and multimedia productions, literature, cultural heritage protection, conservation and museums, as well as cultural administration and management (see Commission 2001a).[15]

At the same time, many of the cultural networks supported by the Union have remained downright obscure ('European Network of Cultural Managers', 'EU NET ART', 'European Network of Art Organisations for Children and Young People' 'Women's Art Library-International Network' to name a few). Also, it is fair to suspect that many of the participating cultural bodies (sometimes quite 'virtual' entities in their own right) were driven to form transnational networks above all by the desire to become eligible for Union funding – something that many Commission officials privately accept while being more or less resigned to it.

From the Commission's perspective, however, the focus on cultural networks is in many ways attractive nonetheless. In the first place, funding them satisfies two key requirements of the Maastricht and Amsterdam Treaties: it respects the subsidiarity principle in that it offers a 'value added' to what national cultural policies typically seek to do, and it is not aimed at policy harmonisation. Second, the very term 'network' is evocative. Discursively it connects to notions of things modern, sophisticated, decentralised and flexible with a grass roots feel (not least of course the Internet) – a linkage the Commission does not tire of drawing time and again. Such notions, moreover, contrast favourably with criticisms of the Union's earlier cultural initiatives as rigid, dirigiste, bureaucratic, centralising and somewhat pompous. Add to this that the very ambiguity of what is (and is not) a cultural network, in conjunction with the relatively small amounts of money at stake for each individual sponsorship project, gives the Commission a fair amount of leeway in distributing its funds. It enables it to quickly adapt its sponsorship policy to changes in its own rhetoric (actual or perceived), changes in public or member state preferences, as well as to changing expectations as to where sponsorship would most enhance the Union's visibility and pinpoint particular target groups. The Commission clearly values this flexibility, even though it has provoked long-lasting complaints that it handles its cultural budget in an arbitrary, erratic and less-than-transparent manner (to which the Commission has responded by delegating more responsibility to formally independent selection panels).

Lastly, the Commission focused on transnational cultural groupings for yet another reason. Some officials hoped that strengthening transnational bodies with a direct stake in the continuation of existing cultural programmes would help the Union consolidate its cultural position. If not leading to outright interest group pressure for further integration as with political spillover, it might at least help entrench existing cultural programmes and prevent rollbacks. As one Commission official put it, if painters had as much a stake in European integration and as much political influence as farmers, the Commission would have been more successful in promoting its cultural agenda all along (interview European Commission, June 2000).

Nonetheless, by the turn of the century many Commission officials had come to a sobering assessment regarding the Union's cultural programmes in general and their network fixation in particular.[16] On the one hand, they accept that sponsoring cultural networks and similar 'horizontal' measures are among the few cultural activities the member states are willing to tolerate to any significant extent. But on the other hand, they have also come to accept the inherent limitations of such measures in fostering popular support for European integration. Too low is their visibility, and too ephemeral whatever 'European dimension'-flavoured output they are liable to generate. Even their ability to strengthen the Union's political position in culture has proved modest at best. As suggested, the transnational groupings that have emerged are often little more than ad hoc formations, created primarily for the purpose of attracting EU funding. To the extent that they developed a political agenda it typically serves to obtain still more EU subsidies for themselves. There is no evidence that transnational cultural networks have evolved into genuine interest groups championing a greater Union involvement in culture, much less European integration at large.

Public relations after Maastricht

As was shown earlier, 'information and communication' had already become a major area of Commission activity by the early 1990s, and after the Maastricht Treaty it became more important still. Of all the areas under investigation, 'information and communication' is the one in which the Commission made its greatest policy advances – to the point where by 1998 the annual budget allocated to it had risen to 107 million ECU[17] and has remained relatively stable since, with additional funding for some initiatives provided by member state governments.

As the Commission's 'information and communication' budget increased so did its attempts to establish a coherent framework for spending it. In early 1993, at the height of the Maastricht controversy in many member states and against the backdrop of a severe downturn in public support for the Union, the Commission received a report by an expert working group it had appointed to work out a blueprint for the Union's future information policy (see de Sélys 1996). The group's key suggestion was that the Commission should try harder to target particular 'messages' at particular sections of the population. The 'groups' it singled out for special consideration were young people and women (the latter because they 'are more liable than men to recognise quickly and intuitively the advantages of a better future'). The Commission itself, according to the report, 'must be presented with a human face: likeable, warm and conscious of the well-being of others', while the Union at large should be proffered 'like a good product'. A similar internal Commission document in 1994 advocated among other things that the Union should improve its media presence (Commission 1994b).

Advised by a plethora of advertising, polling and PR consultants and under strong pressure from the European Parliament, the Commission launched in 1995 what it called an 'integrated awareness campaign covering the fundamental basis of the European Union and the place of the citizen within it'. Its key ingredients were a 'targeted and decentralised information policy' and 'information and communication activities adapted to the culture and language of the different countries, or even regions, as well as to specific groups, in particular women' (Commission 2001b; Commission 1999b). At their heart was PRINCE (Programa de información para el ciudadano europeo), the successor of the 'priority information programmes' launched in the 1980s.

PRINCE
Established in its present form in 1995, PRINCE is to provide a 'global approach [to information] with clear and precise objectives and messages targeting specific audiences' (Commission 2001b: 21). To do so, it is divided into several 'priority information actions'. Initially, these were the 'Citizen's Europe' (defined largely in terms of practical EU-related issues such as consumer protection and freedom of movement rights), 'The euro, a currency for Europe' and 'Promoting the Union' (an umbrella heading for more general information campaigns about Union policies and institutions). Subsequent themes included the debate on a future EU constitution, enlargement, and the common 'area of freedom, security and justice' (the official euphemism for EU powers in policing, criminal justice and immigration).

Under each PRINCE heading the Commission publishes numerous brochures, leaflets, posters and fact sheets which it distributes through libraries, universities, citizens advice centres, European Documentation Centres, 'educational relay centres' (further discussed in Chapter 5), pro-Union organisations and other outlets. In addition, it maintains sites on the Internet, telephone advice services and sponsors or co-sponsors a vast range of events in the member states, often in cooperation with business organisations, trade unions and various pro-European associations. More recently, the Commission helped establish 'national-level information relay centres' in several member states, which it manages jointly with the respective host governments (such as the Jacques Delors Information Centre in Lisbon and Sources d'Europe in Paris).

Of all programmes under PRINCE, the campaign to promote the single currency has remained the most ambitious and expensive by far. It sponsored euro information tents, euro festivals, a euro newsletter ('Infeuro') euro advice meetings for business people, euro promotion packs for school children, euro advertising campaigns, euro exhibitions ('a time journey through monetary Europe'), the distribution of euro play money in order to familiarise citizens with the new currency, a euro calendar and 'Team Europe' speakers sent out by the Commission's regional representations to schools, youth groups, businesses, trade union gatherings and the like (see Gaserow 1997).

One notable aspect of the single currency promotion campaign was its implementation modus. Committees inside the different member states coordinated the campaign. These comprised one representative from the local Commission and EP representations each and one member appointed by the host government. While somewhat sceptical initially, Commission officials soon came to appreciate the decentralised and mixed implementation modus of the euro campaign. It fits in well with its targeted nature and ensures cooperation by national governments, which is especially important with regard to those measures that benefit from mixed funding. As a result, the Commission has sought to apply the decentralised information model to its other public relations campaigns under PRINCE and beyond, allocating greater responsibility to its representations inside the various member states (Commission 2001b).

Officials in the Commission's 'information and communication' department hail the single currency campaign a success. At the same time they stress its uniqueness. National governments and the Commission alike were eager to ensure the success of the currency, which created a convergence of interest between the various actors. The Commission found it comparatively easy to 'sell' its euro-promotion campaign to the member states and to obtain funding for it (interview European Commission, June 2000). A further factor was that Denmark and the UK remain outside the euro zone, were thus not targeted by the Union's euro campaign and thus did little to oppose it.

What stands out about the Commission's post-Maastricht information strategy in general and PRINCE in particular is the systematic targeting of information, i.e. the dissemination of different 'messages' to distinct audiences that are deemed to have particular 'information needs' and to be receptive to particular themes and approaches (Commission 2001b). In defining target groups, the Commission adheres to several concurrent and often crosscutting principles of differentiation. They include socio-economic status, presumed level of knowledge and cognitive ability, specific interests (e.g. employers, employees, small business owners), gender and age. However, the most frequent differentiation criterion is according to member state. A large proportion of the Commission's information output now seeks to appeal to specific national audiences by addressing issues deemed to be particularly relevant to the country in question. Following the pattern of the euro campaign, much of this material is produced and distributed by the Commission's representations inside the member states, which feed intelligence about their impact back to Commission headquarters where it is collated and used to plan future information campaigns.

In the UK, the best-known example of such a campaign, and one of the few that has attracted a fair amount of general media attention, has been the Commission's 'Euromyths and misunderstandings' brochure, first issued in 1992 and regularly updated since. It informed its British audience that, contrary to what it said were frequently levelled claims, the Union did not plan to outlaw mushy peas and double-decker busses and that it had not issued a directive to make fishing vessels carry condoms in order to prevent sexually transmitted diseases from spreading on board (Commission 2003b; Commission 1998a).

Age is the Commission's second most important criterion for targeting information, and the one age group that the Commission seeks to target more than any other is young people, defined as those aged 25 years and under. This concern with youth information goes back to the Adonnino Report, driving a 'Youth information action plan' by the Commission in the early 1990s (Commission 1992d; also *Bulletin* 1991 [No. 6], point 1.2.107). It saw the Commission using part of its discretionary budget to produce promotional videos and leaflets for schools and youth centres. Moreover, it sponsored the 'European Youth Olympics' and the 'Youth Forum of the European Communities', a confederation of national youth councils and non-govern- mental youth groups (Commission 1990a, Annex). It was only in the late 1990s, however, that such initiatives gained momentum, accompanied by ever direr warnings by the Commission that an 'information deficit' among the young could do irreparable harm to the Union's long-term development. In 1997, the Commission launched a programme to subsidise youth-targeted 'initiatives and projects in the field of information and communication with a European di- mension' (Commission 1997a). Public and private organisations alike can apply for funding, provided they 'develop young people's awareness of the creation of a People's Europe and European citizenship', further their knowledge of the European Union in general or of particular institutions and policies, or dissem- inate information about more specific themes such as the Maastricht Treaty or the single currency. As is shown in Chapter 5, this focus on youth information also shone through in the Commission's growing efforts at the time to produce information literature for children and in its creation of various Internet portals especially aimed at the young.

All the same, among officials in DG X the singling out of young people as a target group has remained controversial. In the first place, as Chapter 5 shows in greater detail, PR aimed at teenagers and children soon proved to have substantial backlash potential in the national media, forcing the Commission to downgrade or even withdraw some of its initiatives in this area. Moreover, some Commission officials object that the category 'young people' is too broad and call for a further fine-tuning of the Commission's 'information and communication' campaigns by taking into account more strongly criteria such as gender, education and social class (interview European Commission, June 2000). Nonetheless, even though other cate- gories have gained some ground in the meantime, 'young people' have remained one of the Commission's main 'information and communication' targets ever since.

Multiplier measures

While seeking to better target its 'information and communication' campaigns the Commission also has increasingly come to focus on measures with a presumed 'multiplier effect', i.e. measures that affect not only those whom they reach directly but, through them will, it is hoped, trickle down to broader sections of the public. Heading the Commission's list of 'opinion multipliers' are journalists through whom it hopes to gain more and more favourable coverage in the national media. For instance, in 1995, the Commission started its own satellite information service. It provides television stations across the Union and beyond with newsfeed about the EU and offers video footage with background information. To those radio and television journalists who visit its headquarters in Brussels the Commission offers a reception service, on-site editing facilities and a video library. Print journalists have access to a photo library (Commission 2003c). At the same time, in some respects the Commission's handling of the national media remains surprisingly amateurish. For instance, its ability to rebut EU-critical stories in the (especially British) weekend papers in a rapid fashion suffers from the fact that the Commission shuts down almost completely on weekends. Suggestions by some officials that the Commission should establish an all-weekend 'emergency rebuttal unit' have not so far yielded any results (interview European Commission, June 2000).

Also in the hope of attaining a multiplier effect the Commission has expanded its visitor service. Commission hosts and hostesses guide visiting groups through the Commission's Brussels headquarters. Those classified as 'high priority groups' ('made up of "opinion multipliers" likely to disseminate the information received within their social and professional circles') receive the most, 'general-public groups' the least attention. Visitors are invited to attend the Commission's 'Visit Point Europe' exhibition (Commission 2004b). It features the 'Panorama of Europe' which illustrates the history of European integration. Computer and video screens show clips about different EU policies, while a live satellite relay broadcasts debates in the European Parliament and press briefings by Commission officials.

Even though some of the Commission's PR measures seem tedious, 'information and communication' is the one area under investigation in which the Commission has continued to make the greatest inroads. This applies in a quantitative as well as in a qualitative sense. While the Union has spent more money on more 'information and communication' initiatives these have also become better targeted and more professionally designed and executed.

But just how effective are such PR measures in improving the Union's popular standing? At least in public the Commission itself is keen to claim that they work and seeks to expand them still further. At the same time, somewhat surprisingly it has abandoned many of its earlier attempts to evaluate their impact through surveys, focus group research and other means. What has taken their place are (far less illuminating) efforts to assess the *reach* of those programmes, for example by compiling statistics about visits to its Internet site. Different Commission officials give different explanations for this: some plead a lack of resources; others fear that overly zealous impact assessment exercises would make the Commission look too manipulative. Still others fear that if the impact of Commission PR were found to be low some member state governments might insist on cutbacks (interviews European Commission, June 2000).

With impact studies scarce the effectiveness of the Commission's various 'information and communication' campaigns is hard to gauge. One difficulty flows from trying to isolate their effect from that of a number of other variables that could have influenced public opinion towards the Union (and/or particular EU policies). For instance, while support for the Union stabilised somewhat after the Maastricht Treaty had been ratified (see the bi-annual *Eurobarometer* surveys), this might be due to a host of factors other than the 'information and communication' activities of DG X (e.g. changing economic conditions or a temporary decline in media coverage of the Union).

In any event, several factors are likely to mitigate the impact of the Commission's post-Maastricht public relations offensive. In the first place, while an average annual 'information and communication' budget of around 100 million euro seems impressive at first glance, it is below the annual advertising budgets of some larger multinational corporations. It becomes even less impressive if divided by the over 400 million Union citizens with whom the Commission seeks to 'communicate'. What is more, the Commission's information campaigns face an ever-present danger of triggering backlashes in popular opinion. For as these campaigns became more visible, aggressive and expensive, criticism that the Commission was wasting taxpayers' money for political propaganda also grew. Increasingly, such complaints emanated from beyond the traditionally most Eurosceptic parts of the national press and public opinion, and from beyond the traditionally most Eurosceptic member states. Indeed, it is now hard to find any recent press item on the Commission's 'information and communication' activities that does not adopt, at the very least, a decidedly cynical and derisory stance.

As a result, countering such criticisms has itself become an important objective for the Commission's public relations strategists. Paradoxically, some of their campaigns now seek to convince citizens that the Union is not in fact wasting taxpayers' money on costly public relations campaigns! For example, as part of its 'Euromyths and misunderstandings' and 'press watch' campaigns the Commission sought to assure the British public that contrary to what it claimed were frequent accusations to this effect it was not spending money on hot air balloons featuring the European logo, had no plans to sponsor a 'Euro-soap opera', did not insist that 'obscure European literature is being translated at a cost of £20m to Europe's taxpayers' and did not sponsor a 'Captain Euro' comic strip to 'brainwash children and students' (for recent examples see Commission 2003b).

Overall, while Commission officials are adamant that the euro-promotion campaign helped shore up support for the single currency, they are less upbeat about the other initiatives under PRINCE and related programmes. These have enjoyed much less support by the member states, have produced frequent backlashes in the national media, and are deemed even by the officials who run them to have 'gone stale' (interview European Commission, June 2000). Some fear that with the euro promotion campaign drawing to a close the 'information and communication' department in DG X will suffer cuts in staff and funding, despite the Commission's frequent attempts to depict enlargement and the proposed EU constitution as urgent 'communication areas' (e.g. Commission 2001b).

What is more, some other more emblematic measures at the interface of traditional cultural policy and public relations – such as Europe Day – are now widely perceived to have been a failure, due in part to a lack of cooperation from inside the member states and a dearth of funding (interview European Commission, June 2000; see also the discussion in Chapter 5). For its part, the European logo has become the most recognisable EU signifier by far, but its use is uneven. While the Commission has integrated it throughout its own campaigns and prescribes its display in certain contexts (e.g. to acknowledge EU funding on public works projects), its use often depends on national and local authorities. Generally, in countries where support for the EU is highest (such as Italy) it appears to be displayed most frequently and vice versa. Especially galling to Commission officials is the continued refusal by the British government to print the European logo on car licence plates. Over the years, successive UK governments have tried to justify this on various grounds, including the claim that the presence of the European logo would make licence plates hard for police officers to read and thereby encourage traffic offences.

The low turnout for the 1999 elections to the European Parliament was a further setback for the Commission's 'information and communication' strategists. It sparked accusations of incompetence and ineffectiveness from within other parts of the Commission and the European Parliament, no doubt further boosted by the still lower popular turnout for the EP elections in 2004. Yet here the Commission's underlying dilemma becomes once more apparent. Anxious to avoid accusations of interfering in domestic politics and fearful of potential backlashes, the Commission refrained from launching a special 'information' campaign related to the 1999 EP elections and even temporarily downscaled some of its other campaigns (interview European Commission, June 2000). Yet while this saved the Commission from accusations of being overly pushy and prone to 'overexposure', it also sparked complaints that officials had missed an opportunity to raise the Union's profile while allowing voter apathy to flourish. Caught between the need not to appear overly manipulative and constant pressure to 'sell' the Union and its policies to sceptical post-Maastricht national publics, the Commission's 'information and communication' officials face a dilemma from which they find it increasingly difficult to escape.

Conclusion

By the turn of the century the Union's accomplishments in culture and public relations had remained ambiguous. On the one hand, it had put in place a significant number of cultural and public relations measures. These ranged from Culture 2000 and a limited assortment of symbols (above all the European logo) to the many 'information and communication' measures launched in the post-Adonnino period. What is more, although the cultural clause in the Maastricht (and subsequent Amsterdam) Treaty was restrictive, it placed the Union's cultural involvement on a clear legal basis for the first time. If in the 1950s the Union was founded as an a-cultural entity, half a century later this was no longer completely so.

One factor that promoted the Union's cultural standing was the resilience and political skill of the Commission. After tactical mistakes in the 1970s when its proposals were overly sweeping and ambitious, the Commission switched to a more effective strategy, in some ways reminiscent of 'cultivated spillover' expectations discussed in the last chapter. First, it 'economised' much of its cultural agenda, calling for a borderless 'cultural space' in which 'cultural goods and services' could be exchanged freely. This fitted in well with the Union's economic mission and to some extent pre-empted legal objections. Second, often with respect to the same initiatives, the Commission (increasingly joined by the EP) relied on the Union's broader development to bolster its demands for a greater involvement in culture and public relations. When integration was stagnating, it argued that cultural policies could help reinvigorate it; when integration was making progress, it argued that cultural policies were needed to sustain it. Finally, on top of all this the Commission frequently relied on vague rhetorical commitments by the member states to foster a European identity, European values and so on. Though by the end of the 1990s these themes had faded into the background, they allowed the Commission to portray many of its earlier cultural proposals as merely giving substance to an objective to which the member states had already committed themselves in principle.

On the other hand, however, the nature, scope and funding of the Union's various cultural and PR initiatives remained very limited. Spending on all programmes combined amounted to no more than a few cents per EU citizen per year. Moreover, throughout the 1990s EU cultural policy became increasingly 'horizontalised' – to the point where Culture 2000 centres almost exclusively on subsidising cultural exchanges and networks of all kinds. Attempts to increase the Union's symbolic penetration into the everyday lives of its citizens – along the lines of what was suggested in the Tindemans and Adonnino Reports – yielded few tangible results. As for those measures that were not purely exchange-oriented, these became more and more punctual and PR-centred. They were aimed at generating support for narrowly defined Union policies (e.g. enlargement and the single currency), not at the more far-reaching objective of fostering a European identity or European values that so characterised official Community rhetoric in the 1970s and early 1980s.

The Maastricht experience further steered EU cultural policy in this direction. On the one hand, the sharp rise in public hostility towards the Union during the ratification debate seemed to lend a renewed sense of urgency to pleas by the Commission and the EP for measures to promote the Union's popular standing. On the other hand, however, the fact that this hostility often thrived on fears that the Union was braced to become more intrusive and erode national identities made an aggressive cultural offensive by the Union even less feasible than before. In fact, throughout the 1990s popular support for involving the Union in culture and the audiovisual sector (as well as education) was consistently much lower than for most other policy areas, including such contentious fields as foreign policy, monetary policy and defence (see the bi-annual *Eurobarometer* surveys; also Theiler 1999a for an analysis).

The Union's growing role in 'information and communication' reflected an attempt to overcome this dilemma. Many national governments found PR-type measures more acceptable than cultural policies of the traditional kind. They broke no new legal ground and violated no political taboos. Moreover, most PR measures were not geared towards the more grandilo-quent and increasingly divisive objective of European identity promotion. Instead, their aim was more narrow, i.e. to strengthen public support for particular EU projects and policies for which national governments them-selves wanted to secure public acceptance, above all the single currency. The logic at work here broadly seems to conform to that outlined in Chapter 2: European integration is among other things a policy of national governments which therefore, in principle, want to secure public support for it.

By the turn of the century the Commission and the member states had settled into a modus vivendi of sorts. National governments backed the Commission's public relations initiatives with relatively high levels of funding and gave the Commission a fair amount of leeway in designing and imple-menting them. At the same time, they denied the Union a more far-reaching cultural involvement along the lines of what had been suggested in the Tindemans and Adonnino Reports and many initiatives by the Commission and EP. For their part, the Commission and to a lesser extent also the EP appeared to have internalised these constraints, all but abandoning earlier attempts to broaden the Union's cultural role beyond cultural exchanges and narrowly targeted PR-type actions. As one culture official put it, these days such grander cultural policies are simply no longer on anyone's agenda (interview European Commission, June 2000).

Another way of conceptualising this shift is against the backdrop of the three levels of legitimisation discussed in the last two chapters. The Commission's early cultural ambitions had a strong 'third level' flavour; they sought to cultivate shared overarching communal identifications among Europeans, believing this to be the basis on which support for more specific EU institutions and policies could grow. By contrast, the PR-style measures which materialised instead had the much more modest aim of highlighting the Union's supposed economic utility to its citizens. What was to be legitimised were specific EU *policies* rather than the EU itself as corporate actor and identity category.

Yet what impact did all this have on public attitudes towards European integration? The concluding chapter explores this at greater length. Two preliminary observations, however, are in order. First, as was argued, 'top-down' political symbolism is most effective if it generates 'bottom-up' responses. The EU's own rhetoric has increasingly come to reflect this, depicting the encouragement of broad-based 'dialogue', 'debate' and 'deliberation' as central aims of its cultural and PR initiatives. Yet in reality very little of this has materialised. As suggested, most Union-sponsored cultural 'networks' have remained obscure to a wider public, much less actually involving it. For their part, most PR measures conceptualise EU citizens as little more than passive 'information targets', despite the loftier rhetoric that often accompanies them.

Likewise, the (at the time of writing still ongoing) debate on a future EU constitution has spurred little in the way of a genuinely broad-based popular involvement, even though the Commission has made this a 'priority objective' of PRINCE and devised a raft of public information and consultation initiatives to this end. Many factors may well have contributed to this, not least the lack of a shared language and pan-European media outlets and the barriers this poses to transnational communicative processes (see Chapter 4 below). But in part it also suggests that for most of its citizens the Union has not evolved into a salient identity category able to elicit much participatory effort. It reflects a 'third level' legitimacy deficit which most EU cultural and PR initiatives could not and, increasingly, were not designed to fill.

Yet contrary to what many Commission officials feared after the Maastricht ratification crisis, neither the introduction of the single currency nor the Union's impending enlargement triggered strong backlashes in public opinion. In fact, while public interest and participation in EU affairs has remained low (the lowest-ever turnout for the 2004 EP elections was yet another sign of this), the proportion of citizens who profess a diffuse sense of 'feeling European' has actually grown in recent years in most member states (see the biannual *Eurobarometer* surveys; also Risse in press). Overall (though with the UK being an important exception) public attitudes seem to have settled once more into the 'permissive consensus' of the pre-Maastricht era: marked by relative apathy, low mobilisation and few participatory ambitions but, at the same time, by a belief that on balance integration produces practical benefits. How much the Commission's many public relations campaigns contributed to this is, of course, hard to assess. As suggested, this is due to the dearth of reliable impact studies, their increasingly narrow focus on specific policies and the challenge of isolating their effect from that of other variables. Nonetheless, in so far as these campaigns had an impact at all, it was probably in promoting a belief that integration offers practical benefits. Increasingly this became their predominant aim, pushing aside the more far-reaching objectives that marked many earlier, ill-fated cultural initiatives.

The next chapter turns to audiovisual policy, the one part of the broadly defined cultural sector that has been left out of the discussion so far. It shows that even though the Commission and the EP's audiovisual ambitions enjoyed greater backing from the member states, their fate ultimately resembled that of the other cultural initiatives.

Notes

1 This was evident, for example, in the final declaration of the Congress of Europe in 1948. On the origins of the European Community between the end of the Second World War and the Rome Treaties see Loth (1991).

2 Most clearly the Janne Report of 1973, which is further discussed in Chapter 5. A further factor was the accession of the UK and Denmark in 1973. In both countries, public support for integration was much lower than in the original six, which moved the issue of public opinion further up on the Community's political agenda (also see Benzoni and Dumoulin 1999).

3 From the 1960s onwards, the French government had regularly proposed measures of this type (see Perriaux 1990; Bulletin 1987 [No. 3], point 3.4.1. *et seq.*). On the German situation (with reference to education but equally applicable to culture since the federal government–Länder division of powers is similar in both areas) see Rübsamen (1978).

4 Both the Genscher-Colombo Proposals (formally titled 'Draft European Act' [1981]) and the subsequent 'Solemn Declaration on European Union' issued at the Stuttgart Summit (1983) had called vaguely for greater 'cultural cooperation' between the member states, but not for new Community powers in the field (Perriaux 1990; Neville-Jones 1983).

5 Addressing the opening of the intergovernmental conference on constitutional reform in September 1985, Jacques Delors was quick to defend this decision on essentially pragmatic grounds. Culture and education, he contended, were more tricky areas in which to establish new Community powers than for example environmental policy (in which the Commission did demand, and obtain, new competences). There was, said Delors, 'no point in cluttering the Conference table with proposals on this, that and the other and plunging into ... interminable wrangling' (Delors 1985).

6 The original reads 'sind ohne weiteres als dysfunktional einzuschätzen'.

7 This was so in part because culture and education were emerging areas for the Community and as such still had relatively low staffing levels. Furthermore, many national and Community officials saw these policy areas as more suitable 'training grounds' for newly arrived officials than the Commission's established core departments (interviews European Commission, September 2000).

8 I am grateful to William Wallace for this information.

9 The account in this section draws on the extensive and detailed report by the

Commission (1992c) in which it reviews and seeks to evaluate its Olympic campaign. All quotes are from the same document. See also *Bulletin* 1992 (No. 1–2), point 1.3.263.

10 His account pertains in the first instance to the position of the member states on education policy as it is discussed in Chapter 5. For the most part, however, culture and (the non-vocational parts of) education were treated in tandem, and a given member state's stance with respect to one area tended to reflect its view on the other. See also Bekemans and Balodimos (1992).

11 The politics of translation make Article 3p harder to interpret still, given that some non-English versions of the Maastricht Treaty feature a rather different wording. In the German language version, for example, this article calls upon the Community to contribute 'zur Entfaltung des Kulturlebens in den Mitgliedsstaaten' [i.e. 'to the enhancement of cultural life in the member states'] while leaving it open whether this 'cultural life' might contain shared European elements.

12 This provision has been criticised for, among other things, its ambiguity (see Faroux 1993).

13 At the same time, there is some debate in the legal literature on whether 'incentive measures' and even 'recommendations' can evolve into 'soft law' and, if so, what precise legal implications this might entail (see Wellens and Borchardt 1989).

14 Furthermore, as are all areas of concurrent competences between the Union and the member states, cultural policy is in principle subjected to the subsidiarity clause as enshrined in the Maastricht Treaty under Article 3d. Yet, as has often been pointed out, the precise implications of the subsidiarity provision are unclear. Suffice to note that at least potentially it represents yet another obstacle that might be thrown in the way of concrete measures being adopted under Article 128. For a view that attributes a high significance to the subsidiarity clause in the context of Article 128 see Bekemans and Balodimos (1992).

15 For instance, in the field of performance art alone the 'networks' that benefited from Community aid have included: L' Union des Théâtres de l'Europe, la Convention Théâtrale Européenne, IETM, the European Network of Information Centres for Performing Arts, the Intercultural Production House for the Performing Artists, the European Music Office, the Europe Jazz Network, the Baltic Music Network, la Fête Européenne de la Musique, le Réseau Printemps, le Réseau européen des services éducatifs des maisons d'opéra, Dance Network Europe, Network Dance Web, P.A.R.T.S. – Performing Arts Research Training Studios, Euro Festival Junger Artisten.

16 By contrast, a faith in cultural policy as a motor of integration still reverberates through some EP reports (e.g. EP 2001).

17 See the Commission's annual General Report on the Activities of the European Union.

4

Audiovisual policy

From their very outset most of the Union's actual and attempted cultural policies as discussed in the last chapter were shrouded in relative obscurity; by and large they attracted little public and scholarly attention. An exception was audiovisual policy, the one part of the broadly defined 'cultural sector' that has been left out of the discussion so far. Once the Union had become active in this field this attracted a large amount of public scrutiny and sparked reactions that ranged from relentless hostility and ridicule to vigorous encouragement and praise. By the mid-1980s, audiovisual policy had become one of the EU's central cultural battlegrounds and has remained so ever since.

This attention has been due in part to the high economic stakes involved in the film and television sector. In part, it has also been spurred by the fact that its audiovisual ambitions often pitted the Union against the outside world, above all the United States. Yet perhaps the most important factor has been the role of television in the lives of most Europeans. Of all the 'cultural goods and services' available to them, television is by far the most widely 'consumed' (see *Eurobarometer* 2002) – a fact the Commission itself has not tired to stress time and again. This in turn has led many on either side of the audiovisual debate in the EU to credit television with an almost magical ability to mould popular attitudes – a view, incidentally, they were reluctant to shed even after most theorists of mass communication had abandoned or at least heavily qualified it (see Chapter 2 above).

Nonetheless, to date most studies of EU audiovisual policy have had a limited focus. They have concentrated on those audiovisual initiatives with the most direct bearing on the Union's core mandate of forging a single market at the inside and a unified commercial policy towards the rest of the world. The most prominent and most written-about of those is the Television Without Frontiers (TWF) Directive, first adopted in 1989 and slightly amended in 1997. The directive applied single market principles to the audio-

visual sector by abolishing most legal barriers to the transmission and reception of television signals between the member states. Moreover, it
imposed an (albeit non-binding and highly controversial) quota regime,
intended to aid European producers by curtailing the inflow of audiovisual
material from overseas, above all from the United States.[1]

In the context of this study the TWF Directive is relevant in as far as it
reflected not only economic but also identity-related considerations. This was
implicit in frequent claims by the Commission and the EP that making
Europeans watch television programmes from European countries other than
their own could make them discover shared cultural roots. Similarly, the
TWF debate often revolved around assertions that an 'overexposure' to US
audiovisual imports could inflict cultural damage on European audiences.
This in turn helped build up the United States as Europe's privileged 'cultural
other' and thereby established a discursive frame for many other audiovisual
initiatives as they are discussed below.

However, the present chapter leaves aside the TWF Directive and the
related quota row in order to concentrate on a second category of audiovisual
initiatives by the Union. Even though these have had a more proactive and
interventionist flavour they have attracted much less public and scholarly
attention. The first part of the chapter looks at Commission and EP-driven
attempts to promote a pan-European television channel, intended to
confront its audience with non-national (and thus presumably European and
'Europeanising') content. The second part turns to efforts by the EP and the
Commission to foster the Europeanisation of the audiovisual productions
sector by, in the first instance, subsidising multinational coproductions. Both
bodies hoped that a 'mixing and mingling' of national audiovisual formats
would over time lead to their partial cultural 'denationalisation', widening the
market for European audiovisual producers and nurturing a European identity in viewers.

Yet some two decades later the Union had achieved relatively little in
both fields. The pan-European television channel established with Commission support in 1985 faltered the following year over a widespread
audience aversion to its attempted non-national programming format and
the refusal by many national governments to adequately fund it and to secure
the Community-wide distribution of its signals. Similarly, many member
state governments blocked initial proposals for the Union to subsidise multinational coproductions. What audiovisual measures they did adopt in the end
amounted to little more than attempts to boost the production of domestic
output and its circulation throughout the Union. But these did little to overcome the cultural and linguistic obstacles that continue to tie many producers
to their national markets. As the 1990s drew to a close, the Commission
started to modify its audiovisual ambitions as well as the tactics it used to
promote them. It toned down its cultural anti-Americanisation rhetoric and
its audiovisual initiatives started to have a stronger economic and technolog-

ical focus, gradually abandoning hopes of using films and television programmes as vehicles to nurture a European identity in viewers.

The origins of Community audiovisual policy

Until the early 1980s, neither the European Commission nor the European Parliament attempted to involve the Community in audiovisual policy. This was for political as well as technical reasons. On the political side, until the 1980s most member states had maintained either strict public service television monopolies that excluded all commercial competition (as in West Germany), or regulatory frameworks that severely restricted the number and type of commercial broadcasters allowed to compete with their licence fee and/or taxpayer funded public service counterparts (as in the UK). As a consequence, television broadcasting was neither widely pursued nor widely conceived of as a commercial activity, which in turn denied the Commission an economic rationale under which it could have sought to enter the field under its existing legal mandate at the time (Noam 1991).

On the technical side, terrestrial television had little in the way of a self-evident transnational dimension to it. Broadcasting across national borders required expensive retransmitters and was not widely practised, apart from the inevitable 'spillover' of television signals in frontier regions. What is more, spectrum shortage restricted the number of television channels that could be carried terrestrially in any given area. The lack of a standardised European television norm further impeded broadcasting across frontiers, with some member states using the PAL standard and others the (without converter incompatible) SECAM system.

By the late 1970s, however, all this started to change. First, most member states weakened their public service monopolies by allowing commercial broadcasters to enter the market. In 1980, the European Court of Justice acknowledged the growing commercial dimension of broadcasting by declaring it to meet the EEC Treaty's definition of a 'service'. In principle, this obliged the member states to allow the unhindered distribution of television signals originating from anywhere within the Community on their territory (Wedell 1986: 288). Technical transformations were expected to push in the same direction. The evolution of low, medium and high powered broadcasting satellites facilitated the diffusion of television signals over large geographical areas, either for reception by private satellite dishes (whose size and price was steadily diminishing), or as feeders of local cable systems. Cable, too, was expanding rapidly in many member states (Negrine and Papathanassopoulous 1990). Taken together these political and technical developments appeared to usher in a growing transnationalisation of television in Western Europe. First, the ease with which television signals could now be transmitted via cable and satellite beyond their country of origin meant that Europeans could receive an increasing number of each other's domestic channels. Second, many observers also expected the emergence of truly pan-European television channels, as broadcasters would seek to target an international audience so as to maximise their viewing figures and thereby their advertising income.

It was against this broader political, economic and technological backdrop that the European Parliament and the Commission developed a sudden interest in the audiovisual sector. In part this was guided by economic objectives, but in part it was also motivated by a faith in television as a vehicle to affect loyalties and identifications in mass publics and strengthen support for European integration. And of all the initiatives to which this gave rise, the Community's attempts to set up a pan-European television channel stands out as the boldest by far. It led to what became the most fascinating – and ultimately also the most sobering – cultural experiment in the history of European integration to date, even though it has received surprisingly little scholarly attention.

The European television channel

The idea for a publicly funded pan-European television channel was first advanced by the European Parliament in 1980, in the form of a motion for a resolution on 'Radio and television broadcasting in the European Community' (EP 1980). Claiming that 'reporting of European Community problems by national radio and television companies and the press [... has] been inadequate, in particular as regards integration', it called for the 'establishment of a European radio and television company with its own channel'. It would cater to a general public and feature programmes in 'politics, education, cultural information, entertainment and also advertising'. It was to broadcast multilingually so as to appeal to the widest possible audience across Europe. The European Parliament adopted the motion in 1982, giving rise to an EP resolution similar in content and wording (1982b).

Earlier that same year, moreover, the EP Committee on Youth, Culture, Education and Sport had presented a unanimously adopted report 'on Radio and Television Broadcasting in the European Community' (EP 1982a). It argued that a 'new dimension must be added to European unification to enable Europeans to identify with European union' and that 'the instruments which serve to shape public opinion today are the media [... of which] television ... is the most important' and it, too, proposed the setting up of a pan-European, multilingual television channel. The latter would air programmes that would be 'European in origin, transmission range, target audience and subject matter', and thereby enhance popular understanding of and support for European integration. According to the report

European unification will only be achieved if Europeans want it. Europeans will only want it if there is such a thing as a European identity. A European identity will only develop if Europeans are adequately informed. At present, information via the mass media is controlled at national level. The vast majority of journalists do not 'think European' because their reporting role is defined in national or regional terms. Hence the predominance of negative reporting. Therefore, if European unification is to be encouraged, Europe must penetrate the media.

These repeated pleas by the European Parliament (which, as shown below, soon were seconded by the Commission) gave rise to two concrete projects in the 1980s. The first was the Eurikon experiment in 1982; the second was Europa TV some three years later.

Eurikon
The Eurikon experiment took place under the auspices of the European Broadcasting Union, a federation of national public service broadcasters which had hitherto been dedicated primarily to the exchange of news footage, sports transmissions and, most prominently, to staging the annual Eurovision song contest. Eurikon received financial support from fifteen European broadcasting organisations and the European Community. Five broadcasters (from Austria, Italy, the Netherlands, Germany and the UK) contributed programmes (Negrine and Papathanassopoulos 1990: 174; also Theiler 2001, 1999b; Collins 1993b: 162–175; Zimmer 1989).

Eurikon was never intended to be a permanent European television channel. Instead, it was designed as an experiment to provide its initiators with first-hand experience in pan-European broadcasting and help them evaluate the feasibility of a 'real' and permanent pan-European television channel in the future. To this end, Eurikon produced an experimental television programme for distribution in closed circuit format to 'invited guests of the participating broadcasters and to panels recruited for the purpose of audience research' over a period of five weeks (Collins 1993b: 165–166). It featured news, documentaries, sports, 'light' entertainment, 'serious' music, feature films and religious as well as children's programmes. About one third of all programmes were especially produced for Eurikon and each of the five contributing broadcasters assumed overall responsibility for one week of transmissions. They tried to fill programming slots in their respective week with their own productions in the first instance and the remaining slots with material solicited from the other four broadcasters (Collins 1993b: 167).

Yet the Eurikon experiment proved disappointing. National audiences found its programmes hard to comprehend and they were put off by its reliance on dubbing and subtitles. What is more, reactions of this type were registered throughout the duration of the Eurikon experiment, even though each of the five weeks featured different programming and scheduling formulas. Also, while viewers from different countries shared a dislike for Eurikon's output, the precise reasons for their misgivings varied from one national audience to the next (Collins 1993b). Overall, if the Eurikon experiment offered any clear lesson it was just how potent a set of cultural and linguistic obstacles any future pan-European broadcaster would have to grapple with.

Nonetheless, the Eurikon experience did not dampen the EP's enthusiasm for pan-European television broadcasting, in which it was soon joined by the Commission. In 1983, the Commission released an interim report to the European Parliament titled 'Realities and tendencies in European television: Perspectives and options' (Commission 1983). While the report also dealt with issues relating to the free 'flow' of television signals across the Community and support mechanisms for European audiovisual producers, it gave 'first consideration to the practical possibilities of getting a European television programme onto the screen …'. Echoing EP demands, the Commission called for a programming mix of 'news, politics, education, culture, entertainment and sport, in which the European viewpoint would be based on the ideals and realities of the cultural unity of Europe'. Moreover, like the European Parliament before it the Commission argued that the Community should help fund such a channel in recognition of what it saw as the vital contribution this could make to European integration.

Europa TV

After Eurikon it took another two years for the first publicly funded and truly pan-European television channel to take to the air. Europa TV started transmissions in October 1985, after protracted negotiations between the governments of the member states and their respective national broadcasting organisations. In the process, some major European public service broadcasters, such as the BBC and France's Antenne 2, decided (or were instructed by their respective national authorities) not to participate in the project, despite intense lobbying by the European Commission to ensure a large number of participants (interview European Commission, September 2000).

The intricacies of this preparatory phase need not further concern us here. In the end, Europa TV came into being as a consortium of five European public service broadcasters from Germany, Ireland, Italy, the Netherlands and Portugal (Maggiore 1990: 71). Its operational headquarters were in the Netherlands and its legal headquarters in Geneva, which also hosted the EBU. Initially, the channel was to be financed mainly through contributions from the Dutch government and the participating broadcast organisations, with advertising expected to generate substantial additional revenues over time. Its initial three-year budget was 35 million Swiss Francs (Dill 1989: 135–141; European Cultural Foundation et al. 1988: 98).[2]

In many respects Europa TV lived up to the Commission and the EP's expectations for a pan-European television channel. Most importantly, it aspired to be pan-European not only with respect to its geographical reach but also its programming content. The latter consisted of news, drama, sports, music and children's programming and 'was intended to meet the following criteria: it had to be European, complementary, independent, universal and original [... and it was to reflect] European culture and ... contribute] to it' (European Cultural Foundation *et al.* 1988: 99). Though Europa TV also featured domestic programmes produced by the participating national broadcasters as well as other national productions bought on the open market, its main mission was to produce and transmit programmes in a 'denationalised' format. For example, in order to cover news and current affairs from a 'European point of view' its news team 'was carefully structured to avoid the dominance of any single national group' and a 'non-national perspective was encouraged by all available means' (Maggiore 1990: 71). As a general rule, news events were covered by nationals of countries other than the one in which they took place (European Cultural Foundation *et al.* 1988: 99).

To overcome language barriers, Europa TV's visual image was transmitted alongside several sound channels. Facilities for simultaneous translation (in English, Dutch, German and Portuguese) enabled audiences to receive the channel in their native tongue. In addition, Europa TV provided subtitling in different languages through teletext.

After an initial phase during which Europa TV had only been available in the Netherlands, it expanded its reach to 4.5 million homes across Europe. This included access to 1.5 million households in Portugal where it was transmitted terrestrially (Negrine and Papathanassopoulus 1990: 176). Europa TV's initiators predicted that this expansion would continue at rapid pace and soon allow the channel to reach over thirty million homes and conquer a sizeable audience share in the process (European Cultural Foundation *et al.* 1988: 99). Moreover, the European Parliament and the Commission both hoped that by demonstrating the viability of pan-European broadcasting Europa TV would induce commercially operated broadcasters to follow into its pan-European footsteps and thereby become a catalyst for 'denationalised' broadcasting in Western Europe.

Yet things turned out very differently for Europa TV. Barely over one year after its founding it was forced to cease operations in November 1986. The causes of this failure merit some closer attention.

Why Europa TV failed

The most immediate reasons for Europa TV's demise were financial. After its first year of operations the channel had already exhausted its initial three-year budget (Zimmer 1989: 124). In the end, even the equivalent of a 720,000 pounds sterling emergency grant by the Commission could not save Europa TV, and at the time of its closure its debts had accumulated to 3.7 million pounds sterling (Negrine and Papathanassopoulus 1990: 176–177).

These financial difficulties stemmed in part from the failure of the participating broadcasters (and often indirectly of their respective national

governments) to ensure that Europa TV could operate on more than a frac-
tion of the annual budget available to most domestic public service
broadcasters. What is more, during its preparatory phase and throughout its
short life Europa TV's participants engaged in frequent rows and issued
demands that further reduced its economic viability. A good example was
Portugal's insistence that Europa TV broadcast not only in English, German
and Dutch but also in Portuguese. Given that the channel's signal was distributed widely in Portugal this seemed fair enough; but at the same time it so
increased the cost of translation facilities and multiple soundtracks that it ate
up half of Europa TV's budget (Negrine and Papathanassopoulus 1990: 176).
A further blow came when Belgium refused to carry Europa TV on its cable
system. This prevented it from reaching Belgium's sizeable Dutch-speaking
market and thereby reduced its potential to attract advertising revenues
(Lange and Renaud 1989: 236). Furthermore, even though Europa TV had its
operational headquarters in the Netherlands and received subsidies from the
Dutch government, the latter refused to exempt it from a rule prohibiting
foreign channels distributed in the Netherlands from carrying subtitles,
aimed at protecting Dutch broadcasters from foreign competition (Zimmer
1989: 130). This reduced Europa TV's appeal to those Dutch viewers who
would have preferred subtitles to dubbing and reduced its economic viability
even more.

On top of all this Europa TV was plagued by administrative problems and
by a general lack of direction and leadership. At the root of this were rivalries
between the participating national broadcasters and their refusal to allow the
EBU to effectively take charge of the channel. All the while their willingness
to do so themselves often remained wanting, as was borne out by their
frequent failure to fill the programming slots allocated to them. Even though
they themselves had brought Europa TV into being, it soon became clear that
the participating national broadcasters refused 'to regard Europa as their own
offspring' (European Cultural Foundation *et al.* 1988: 99; interview European
Commission, September 2000).

Yet what most sealed Europa TV's fate was its lack of audience appeal. It
was responsible for its failure to attract advertisers and thereby to become
economically viable. Indeed, so low was Europa TV's attractiveness to viewers that even after it had begun to offer commercial slots free of charge in an
effort to bring itself to the attention of potential advertisers these largely failed
to take up the offer (Negrine and Papathanassopoulus 1990: 177).

How to account for Europa TV's low popularity? As suggested, in part it
was due to its lack of resources and the Dutch refusal to let it carry subtitles,
while its 'high brow' cultural and educational aspirations clearly did not help
either. But more than any other factor it was Europa TV's attempt to appeal
to an audience as culturally and linguistically fragmented as the West
European one that posed a major stumbling block. A good way to illustrate
this is through the concept of 'cultural discount'. It denotes why 'a particular

programme rooted in one culture, and thus attractive in that environment, will have a diminished appeal elsewhere as viewers find it difficult to identify with the style, values, beliefs, institutions and behavioural patterns of the material in question' (Hoskins and Mirus 1988: 500). The concept of 'cultural discount' is applied most commonly to cross-national situations (e.g. Finnish films shown to Greek audiences). Yet it also captures viewers' resistance to programmes in a 'denationalised' format which Eurikon and Europa TV sought to develop. In proportion to how much this format clashes with the cultural habitus of viewers, its attractiveness to them diminishes.

A pan-European channel with an overwhelming financial and political backing, populist programming content and Europe-wide terrestrial distribution might have made up for some of these disadvantages. At the very least, a wider distribution would have helped compensate for a relatively low audience *share* by maximising audience *reach*.[3] In any case, Europa TV fell short on all these counts: it had weak financial and political backing, unrealistically strong 'high cultural' and didactic ambitions and only a very limited reach due to the refusal of all but one participating member state to distribute it terrestrially. By associating itself with Europa TV, the Commission thus bet on a project whose failure was almost a foregone conclusion.

With hindsight many Commission officials believe that the Commission should have distanced itself from Europa TV – or indeed even discouraged it – once it had become clear that a fully-fledged pan-European channel with adequate funding and operational autonomy was not attainable, and that some of the most important national broadcasters would not participate (interview European Commission, June 2000). Beyond this, the very notion of a publicly run pan-European television channel with a mission of fostering a European identity in viewers was by its nature destined to run into strong scepticism. Not least, it clashed with the prevailing ethos in all West European democracies that public service broadcasting should not be used for political purposes, at least not in such an explicit manner. Moreover, even within the Commission many officials simply could not imagine what a truly 'denationalised' television channel would look like, or indeed that such a thing could even be possible in the first place (interview European Commission, June 2000).

Interestingly, Europa TV was not the only channel to experience the difficulties linked to pan-European broadcasting. Its fate was shared by commercially operated pan-European satellite broadcasters in the 1980s. These channels, too, had started out with the aim of offering at least partially 'denationalised' programmes to a pan-European audience. Instead of adopting Europa TV's failed strategy of providing multiple sound tracks they broadcast in English exclusively, but sought to specialise in programmes for which linguistic elements are less significant. UK-based Super Channel, for example, promised in its press information package to '[take] into account that most viewers are not native English speakers. Presenters speak clearly, comedies and documentaries are selected for their visual content while music and sports programmes have a universal appeal' (quoted in Collins 1989: 365). However, echoing the fate of Europa TV these channels either perished or refocused on a predominantly mono-national audience. British-based Super Channel was one example. In 1989, it lost an average of one million pounds sterling per month (Collins 1989: 364). Its major pan-European competitor at the time fared little better: Sky Television had lost, by varying accounts, between 10.2 and 14.6 million pounds sterling in the year up to June 1987 (Collins 1989: 365). It, too, had little prospect of acquiring a sufficiently large audience share to survive as a pan-European channel in the long-run. Both broadcasters subsequently relinquished their pan-European aspirations and concentrated on the UK market, after which their financial lot improved. The Swiss-based European Business Channel encountered an even harsher fate. Founded in 1988 it beamed financial news across Europe, but in 1990 large financial losses forced it to close down permanently (Noam 1991: 193).

In 1988, after Europa TV's demise and the poor showing of commercially operated pan-European channels, the European Commission openly pondered whether it should support a renewed attempt at pan-European broadcasting. This 'provided it combines the following characteristics: a broadcasting organisation which is multinational within Europe, multilingual broadcasts; a multinational audience within a wide European area; European programme content' (Commission 1988b: 4). Until the launching of Euronews in January 1993, however, Europa TV's fiasco spelled an end to further projects of this kind. And in any event, Euronews was only a very diluted version of what Europa TV had once aspired to be, as is shown below.

Attempts to Europeanise the audiovisual productions sector

For the European Commission and the European Parliament, support for pan-European broadcasting was an important but not the only way in which they hoped to instrumentalise television to strengthen popular support for European integration. Especially once it had become clear that pan-European television channels were not viable, they turned their energies to the more modest project of encouraging a partial Europeanisation of the audiovisual productions sector. This would lead to what in Community jargon was often referred to as a 'European audiovisual space' or a 'Europe of viewers'.

Europeanisation versus Americanisation in EU audiovisual rhetoric

There was another, more subtle shift in emphasis. While the aim of promoting a European identity in mass audiences continued to resonate throughout the various audiovisual production initiatives by the Commission and the EP, it became complemented by increasingly vociferous calls to reduce the

Community's audiovisual trade deficit with the United States. With a growing sense of urgency, both bodies depicted Europe's reliance on US films and television programmes as costly not only in economic terms but also as a source of serious cultural damage to European audiences and as a threat to the survival of European culture – so much so that by the late 1980s the anti-Americanisation theme had become the predominant discursive frame for their various audiovisual initiatives.

Underpinning this focus on American audiovisual imports was hard statistical evidence. It showed that while enjoying a globally dominant position, the United States had also conquered a relatively large audiovisual market share in Western Europe, especially in fictional content. In fact, among European audiences US audiovisual imports carried a much lower 'cultural discount' than those from other European countries – signalling that, paradoxically, the United States had come closer to developing a 'pan-European' audiovisual format than any country in Europe (see Collins 1990). And by most accounts the US's audiovisual share in Europe was set to grow further, as new commercial television channels would turn to the United States as a source of relatively cheap, plentiful and popular programming input.

There are different ways to account for the popularity of US-made films and television programmes in Europe. One explanation focuses on the fact that Hollywood imports have had much longer exposure among most European audiences than those from other European countries. A further reason might well be the size and internal heterogeneity of the US domestic market. The former ensures sufficiently high economies of scale to allow for the production of more attractive output; the latter forces US producers to make films and television programmes which already carry some measure of cross-cultural mass appeal (Hoskins and Mirus 1988). Still other explanations emphasise the attractiveness of American cultural imports to European audiences as an alternative to the more 'elitist' and 'educational' fare traditionally offered by many European domestic producers, especially in the earlier days of rigid public service monopolies (see Morley and Robins 1989).

Whatever the explanation, it was against the backdrop of growing audiovisual imports from the United States that the Commission and the EP painted their 'cultural defence' scenario in ever starker colours. In their rendering, American and European audiovisual producers were pitted against each other in a relentless struggle for market share, audiences and cultural influence, with the former fighting for total hegemony and the latter for survival. And the success of US films and television programmes in Europe was portrayed not only as costly in economic terms but also as a threat to what was referred to more or less interchangeably, and with more regard for subtle ambiguity than conceptual consistency, as national cultures, European culture and European cultural diversity.

In 1986, for example, in defending the proposed MEDIA programme discussed below, the Commission warned that '[the] economic and cultural dimensions of communications cannot be separated. The gap between the proliferation of equipment and media and the stagnation of creative content production capacities is a major problem for the societies of Europe; it lays them open to domination by other powers with a better performance in the programming content industry' (Commission 1986: 4). Similarly, in 1988 it cautioned that 'while satellites are getting ready to overwhelm us with hundreds of new television channels, Europe runs the risk of seeing its own industry squeezed out and its market taken over by American and Japanese industrialists and producers [... A] European response is required ...'. (Commission 1988a: 5–6). But perhaps it was Jacques Delors himself who offered the most perfect synthesis of economic and cultural strands in his warnings against audiovisual domination by foreigners. In his first speech to the European Parliament after taking office as Commission President in 1985, he proclaimed that

> the culture industry will tomorrow be one of the biggest industries, a creator of wealth and jobs. Under the terms of the Treaty [of Rome] we do not have the resources to implement a cultural policy; but we are trying to tackle it along economic lines. It is not simply a question of television programmes. We have to build a powerful European culture industry that will enable us to be in control of both the medium and its content, maintaining our standards of civilisation, and encouraging the creative people amongst us. (Quoted in Collins 1994b: 90)

Whatever its factual merits, the Commission and the EP's use of the 'cultural defence' argument as a rhetorical pillar of their successive audiovisual policy proposals was tactically astute – and not just in the general sense that, as shown in Chapters 1 and 2, political identity-building benefits from accentuating perceived differences between in- and outsiders. First, as was argued, to some extent such anti-Americanisation warnings were rooted in hard economic facts which gave them a degree of underlying plausibility. There *was* an audiovisual trade deficit with the US, this deficit *was* likely to widen, and Europeans *did* spend a lot of time watching American films and television programmes. Certainly, claims that all this had a disastrous cultural impact were by their very nature impossible to arbitrate, appearing to some as far-fetched, hysterical or even absurd. Yet the Commission and the EP could not have made such claims in the first place had it not been for the underlying economic and statistical realities on which they were predicated. Warnings of an impending cultural takeover by the United States were discursive constructs, but they were not simply taken out of thin air.

Second, such warnings seemed all the more plausible since cultural resentments against the United States had a long history in many European countries. They reached back at least as far as the rise of Hollywood as a dominant cultural producer and exporter. In particular, they thrived on the appeal of American cultural imports to European working class audiences. Long before the Second World War, critics all over Europe bemoaned the alleged vulgarity, brashness and (bizarrely enough) effeminate and 'feminising' effects of American cultural imports, above all Hollywood-produced films. In Britain, for instance, cultural elites from all parts of the political spectrum

> were united by a fascinated loathing for modern architecture, holiday camps, advertising, fast food, plastics and, of course, chewing gum. ... These were the images of the soft and enervating 'easy life' which threatened to smother British cultural identity [and of] the process through which authentic working-class life was being destroyed by the 'hollow brightness', the 'shiny barbarism' and 'spiritual decay' of imported American culture. (Morley and Robins 1989: 19; also Delanty 1995)

It is hard to pin down the precise origins of these cultural resentments against the United States. More sociologically oriented accounts would focus on fears by national cultural elites of losing their own symbolic power to aesthetic influences beyond their control. Especially in Britain and France more general misgivings about a declining global influence in relation to the United States may also have fuelled cultural grudges after 1945.

In any event, frequently such elite concerns for the survival of 'authentic' national culture sparked policies that served as a precedent for what the Commission and the EP sought to implement at the EU level from the 1980s onwards. For instance, the early BBC had as one of its core missions the upholding of 'national standards' (Morley and Robins 1989: 19). Other public service broadcasters maintained official or unofficial restrictions on foreign content, directed mainly against imports from the US. Sometimes such quotas even applied to music played on the radio. In addition, almost all European countries instituted various schemes to subsidise their national film industries.

A further factor that encouraged the Commission and the EP's resort to the anti-Americanisation theme was the coming to power of the Socialist government in France in the early 1980s. For their warnings against 'cultural domination' by the United States coincided with that very theme evolving into a central plank of French cultural policy under the new government. Moreover, it started to resonate with some southern member states that had sided with French calls for protectionist quotas in the context of the Television Without Frontiers directive. Their commitment to the cause was epitomised by French culture minister Jack Lang's often-cited call for a crusade 'against financial and intellectual imperialism that no longer grabs territory, or rarely, but grabs consciousness, ways of thinking, ways of living' (quoted in Tracey 1988: 16–17). It was also evident in the denouncing by his ministerial colleague of American 'Coca Cola satellites' undermining 'our linguistic and cultural identity' (quoted in Noam 1991: 302). By making the anti-Americanisation cause a rhetorical pillar of its own audiovisual proposals, the Commission and the EP could, at the very least, hope to enhance their appeal to the French government. And as is shown below, it was indeed France which of all the member states became the staunchest and most consistent backer of an EU audiovisual involvement.

Lastly, the move of focusing on Europe's audiovisual standing in relation to 'other cultures' helped shift the terms of the audiovisual debate away from the question of European identity construction at the inside to that of Europe's position in relation to the outside world. As the Community's experience in other parts of the cultural sector had already shown, too outspoken a commitment to the former left it vulnerable to accusations of wanting to disseminate 'cultural propaganda', 'flatten national identities' and overstep legal constraints. The latter, by contrast, was less sensitive an area for the Community to be seen to concern itself with, giving its audiovisual initiatives seemingly greater normative validity and fewer manipulative connotations. Moreover, this external focus enabled the Commission and the EP to link the audiovisual sector to trade policy (where the Community enjoyed clear legal competences) as well as to issues of economic and technological competitiveness.

For all these reasons, the cultural anti-Americanisation theme had the makings of a potentially effective rhetorical pillar upon which the EP and the Commission could predicate their various proposals to Europeanise the audiovisual productions sector. Nonetheless, as is shown next, these proposals encountered significant resistance from the member states. And the policies that the Community eventually put into practice were a far cry from what the Commission and the EP had originally advocated.

The MEDIA programme

As far as its 'software' aspects were concerned, the audiovisual sector generally came within the competences of the national ministers of culture. As shown in the last chapter, these had started to meet more or less regularly in the early 1980s. Yet, when it came to audiovisual policy this initially produced little more than vague declarations of intent. Whenever the Commission managed to put more concrete proposals on the ministers' table agreement remained wanting, despite the 'metaphor of cultural war' (Schlesinger 1996: 10) against the United States which typically accompanied them and despite strong backing by France and the European Parliament (e.g. EP 1983, 1985).

For example, this became evident in April 1985 when the Commission proposed a Council regulation on a 'Community aid scheme for non-documentary cinema and television co-productions' (Commission 1985a). Its declared aim was to 'increase the number of mass-audience cinema and television co-productions involving nationals of more than one Member State'. To this end, it would have created a system to aid such coproductions through grants and loans, covering production as well as distribution costs.

But the Commission's proposal to aid coproductions ran into staunch opposition from several member states. Germany objected that it was too expensive, yet was also driven by the habitual Länder anxieties about protecting their constitutional powers, which include cultural policy in general and broadcasting in particular. Not surprisingly, the Danish government rejected it on the grounds that the Treaties of Rome did not allow the Community to pursue cultural policies even if these were adopted under a partly economic guise. Similarly, the Thatcher government in Britain rejected any Community intervention in the field and instead 'argued in favour of letting market forces have their way and of encouraging the television organisations [of the member states] to work together' (Wedell 1986: 284).

In late 1985, the Commission resubmitted its earlier proposal for an audiovisual support scheme (Commission 1985b; *Bulletin* 1985 [No. 12], point 2.1.125). In line with suggestions by the European Parliament it now listed support for coproductions involving partners from countries whose languages were not widely spoken as one of the 'objectives' that were to guide the distribution of aid. This, however, did little to appease those member states that had opposed the Commission's audiovisual plans from the outset (see Collins 1993b). As a result, the Commission's proposed Community-aid scheme for non-documentary cinema and television coproductions received its definitive burial.

This renewed setback prompted the Commission to revise its audiovisual wish list more thoroughly and to come up with proposals that would stand a greater chance of being accepted by the member states. This it did in 1986, when it presented a communication to the Council for an 'Action programme for the European audio-visual media products industry' (Commission 1986). It laid the foundation for the MEDIA programme which was passed later that same year.

The MEDIA (Mesures pour encourager le développement de l'industrie audiovisuelle) programme started at the end of 1986, initially comprising a range of pilot projects. Since then, MEDIA has been renewed several times, most recently in 2000 where its annual funding was increased to a total of 400 million euros for a period of five years (EP and Council 2001; Council 2000).

In contrast to the unsuccessful Commission and EP proposals that preceded it, MEDIA's main aim is to enhance the circulation of nationally produced audiovisual output inside the Community and beyond, not to promote transnational coproductions. From the very outset, MEDIA's 'top priority [...was] the creation of a European film distribution system, which will make it easier for national productions to move more freely throughout the Community' (Commission 1987b: 14).

The Commission distributes some MEDIA funding in the form of automatic subsidies to European film distributors. Beyond this, it supports selected projects on a competitive basis, similar to the Culture 2000 model discussed in the last chapter. An expert committee helps the Commission select projects and monitor their implementation, with projects generally receiving up to fifty per cent of their budget from the MEDIA fund.

In its two decades or so of existence MEDIA has supported a wide range of initiatives to encourage domestic audiovisual productions and their circulation throughout the Union and beyond. They have included a European Film Distribution Office to give loans to low-cost European feature films distributed in at least three different member states and a scheme called BABEL (Broadcasting Across the Barriers of European Languages) to refine dubbing and translation techniques. MEDIA has also supported various initiatives to help market independent productions as well as projects to promote cartoon films, audiovisual output in minority languages, the restoration and digitisation of the 'European audiovisual heritage', various training schemes for script writing, subtitling and the use of new technologies, and a European Film Academy which hands out the annual European film awards. Moreover, especially towards the end of the 1990s, MEDIA supported a myriad of 'networks' in charge of almost every imaginable part of the audiovisual sector.

The audiovisual output supported by MEDIA in recent years still gravitates towards the 'high brow' end of the spectrum, though there have been attempts to aid productions that stand a realistic chance of attaining some mass appeal. However, even those MEDIA-supported productions that do attract relatively large audiences have their appeal primarily confined to their country (or linguistic region) of origin. Very few enjoy the pan-European popularity enjoyed by Hollywood blockbusters.

Most importantly, despite substantial increases in funding over the years, MEDIA's main objective is still to increase the output of nationally produced material and its circulation throughout the Union and beyond, not the Europeanisation of audiovisual content by subsidising multinational coproductions. Demands by the European Parliament in a proposed amendment to the draft for a new version of the MEDIA programme in 1995 that MEDIA should incorporate measures to 'develop the ability of professionals to understand the European cultural dimension to audiovisual works in order to develop their ability to address a European, rather than simply a national audience' ('MEDIA II: Development and training' 1995: 198) failed to make their way into the programme.

In other words, with the advent of the MEDIA programme the Union's very Europeanisation objective had undergone a profound redefinition. According to the definition which had dominated the Commission and the EP's earlier audiovisual proposals that were rejected by the member states, Europeanisation was seen to entail, in the first instance, a measure of cultural harmonisation or 'denationalisation' – or at least a 'compatiblisation' of sorts – of different national audiovisual formats, and a corresponding harmonisation or 'compatibilisation' of viewing preferences (though the Commission and the EP were careful not to use such terms in public). To bring this about, these earlier proposals were aimed at fostering audiovisual coproductions involving as many member states as possible. Coproductions were expected to have a harmonising effect because they entail a 'mixing and mingling' of national audiovisual formats and because they must seek to minimise the 'cultural discount' attached to them since they are produced from the outset for consumption in several national markets and cultural regions. According to this logic, once a 'denationalised' audiovisual format has started to emerge and audiences grow amenable to it, producers will be able to market their output Community-wide, and pan-European channels will benefit from a suitably Europeanised supply of programming input. Moreover, even purely national television channels will acquire a greater 'European dimension' by airing more non-national programmes. And underlying all this was the hope that 'denationalised' audiovisual content would become a carrier of European values, fostering in audiences a European identity and, ultimately, greater support for European integration.

By contrast, in the second definition as it informed notably the MEDIA programme, Europeanisation constitutes above all a process of making audiovisual productions from one member state more attractive to audiences in other member states *without*, at the same time, inducing a partial cultural levelling of national audiovisual formats. To be Europeanised, in other words, is the market available to audiovisual producers rather than the style and content of their productions. To this end MEDIA subsidises dubbing and subtitling techniques, transnational distribution networks and the like. The hope is that by making productions from other member states more accessible to viewers they will spend more time watching and thereby become more 'acclimatised' to them, which in turn would lower the 'cultural discount' attached to these productions and promote their circulation still further. By way of such a virtuous cycle, then, European audiovisual producers would benefit from a larger market even without a cultural harmonisation or 'compatibilisation' of audiovisual formats. In this sense, even though MEDIA is still wedded to the Europeanisation cause, it in fact signifies a radical shift in EU audiovisual policy away from 'emphasising unity to emphasising diversity' (Collins 1994b: 96).

Conscious of this departure from its original audiovisual aspirations, the Commission's stance towards the MEDIA programme has remained ambiguous. On the one hand, many officials see it as a basic policy framework on which they hope to graft more ambitious and content-centred audiovisual measures at some later stage. On the other hand, echoing the general move away from interventionist and 'Europeanising' cultural initiatives discussed in the last chapter, the prospects of this happening anytime soon have worsened in recent years. On top of this, concurring with many other observers Commission officials doubt whether MEDIA in its present form will actually succeed in 'defragmenting' the European audiovisual market. Poor transnational marketing and distribution facilities are at least as much a symptom of a low demand for national audiovisual productions beyond their country of origin as they are its cause. In this sense, many officials suspect that MEDIA simply has its priorities the wrong way round (interview European Commission, June 2000).

Audiovisual Eureka and Eurimages

If MEDIA thus focuses mainly on mono-national audiovisual productions, this does not apply to the same extent to two other audiovisual support programmes that came into operation in the late 1980s. These were launched outside the Community framework yet provided for its participation in one form or another. The first was the Audiovisual Eureka programme, founded in 1989 on the initiative of the French government. Twenty-six countries signed its original charter, including some from Central and Eastern Europe (Sandell 1996: 274). By the end of the 1980s its membership had grown to thirty-five countries, with the Council of Europe and the European Commission as associate members. During its lifetime Audiovisual Eureka received some Community funding and the Commission supported its small secretariat ('Audiovisual Eureka' 1999; Collins 1994a: 136; Commission 1994c; 'Joint declaration' 1990).

Audiovisual Eureka's clout remained severely limited by the fact that it had no significant funds of its own to hand out. Instead, its role was that of a 'marriage bureau' of sorts. It brought together companies in the audiovisual sector to collaborate on specific projects, including coproductions and distribution arrangements. One of its priorities was to involve the new democracies from Central and Eastern Europe in such projects. Audiovisual Eureka also promoted the use and development of new production techniques, and in 1992 it gave birth to the European Audiovisual Observatory which compiles statistics about the audiovisual sector. In 2003 the participating governments decided to dissolve Audiovisual Eureka (though not the European Audiovisual Observatory). This was due in part to policy disagreements, and in part to the fact that some of its activities had been incorporated into the new MEDIA programme which had also been extended to the Central and East European accession countries in the meantime (Communication on Audiovisual Eureka 2003).

Equally launched on the behest of the French government and also outside a formal Community context was the Eurimages programme. It was initiated in 1988 based on the Council of Europe's Cultural Convention. Most Community member states (with the notable exception of the UK) participate, joined by a range of Council of Europe members that do not (or at the time did not) belong to the Community. Eurimages' declared aim is to support 'the co-production, distribution, broadcasting and exploitation of creative cinematographic and audiovisual works' through a range of financial incentives (Council of Europe 1988). Thus far, Eurimages has come to the aid of around 900 full-length feature films and documentaries, ranging from *Astérix et Obélix contre César* to a documentary about the conflict in Northern Ireland (Council of Europe 2004).

In so far as Eurimages fosters transnational coproductions it clearly goes farther than most aspects of the MEDIA programme and indeed resembles the Commission's unsuccessful coproduction proposals in the 1980s. At the same time its funding has remained tiny and its overall impact on the European audiovisual sector negligible. At present, it expends around nineteen million euro per year on average, far below the production costs of many single Hollywood films.

Officially, the Commission has been an enthusiastic supporter of both Audiovisual Eureka and Eurimages. In private, Commission officials are more ambivalent. On the one hand, they fear that programmes of this kind could herald a gradual 'de-Communitarisation' of audiovisual policy altogether. On the other hand, so far these programmes have proven the only way 'to "end-run" the veto over cultural initiatives enjoyed by single Member States within the Community and to establish outside the Community programmes and policies impossible to achieve within it' (Collins 1994b: 97). What is more, there is at least a theoretical possibility that over time Eurimages could be incorporated into the EU proper, or at least inspire future additions to the MEDIA programme. However, as is shown next, as the 1990s drew to a close the prospects for this became ever more remote.

Maastricht and beyond

As discussed in the last chapter, the Maastricht Treaty gave the Union a formal mandate in cultural policy for the first time. Article 128 (changed to Article 151 in the subsequent Amsterdam Treaty) mentions the audiovisual sector as an area of potential Union intervention. Yet as in other parts of culture it may only take 'incentive measures' and issue 'recommendations'. These must be legally non-binding, 'non-harmonising', respect the subsidiarity principle and must be adopted unanimously. Many of these terms are unclear, and after the Maastricht Treaty had come into force in late 1993 Commission officials in charge of audiovisual policy disagreed on how best to proceed. Some wanted to submit at least one major new audiovisual initiative to the member states with a minimum of delay – mostly advocating a new coproduction-oriented initiative modelled after Eurimages and its own defeated proposals from the first half of the 1980s (interview European Commission, June 2000). This, they hoped, would sustain the momentum created by the Maastricht Treaty and push for a liberal interpretation of Article 128. Yet other Commission officials were more cautious, wanting to focus at least initially on the gradual expansion of the MEDIA programme. As did their colleagues responsible for other areas of cultural policy, they feared that too ambitious and pushy an offensive by the Commission might create a backlash in some member states and cause them to retreat into a restrictive interpretation of Article 128 from the outset.

As is shown below, the Commission did indeed start to work on a new coproduction initiative which it formally submitted to the member states in 1995. Parallel to this, it invested a large portion of its post-Maastricht audiovisual energies in a stream of reports, memorandums, position, strategy and green papers as well as impact and feasibility studies, hoping to turn the Union's limited audiovisual mandate in the Maastricht Treaty into tangible policies that would eventually take it beyond the confines of the MEDIA programme. Many of these pronouncements came to centre on the objective of creating a 'European information area' – a term that, by the mid-1990s, had replaced the earlier concept of the 'European audiovisual space'. Moreover, they contained very similar findings, all suggesting that the measures hitherto taken (mainly under the MEDIA umbrella) had done little to 'defragment' the European audiovisual sector. Cultural and linguistic barriers between the member states had remained strong and most audiovisual producers continued to be tied to their national markets, depriving them of sufficient economies of scale to successfully compete against their US counterparts.

Figures on television consumption were one indication of this. By the mid-1990s, viewers watching their respective domestic channels still accounted for ninety-four per cent of television consumption in Europe (Stewart and Laird 1994: 5). The remaining six per cent consisted mainly of viewers watching domestic channels from neighbouring countries in their own language (e.g. Austrians watching German channels), or diaspora communities tuned to television stations from their home countries (e.g. Italian immigrants in France watching channels from Italy). Furthermore, in as far as domestic channels featured non-domestic programmes, these mostly came from the United States rather than from elsewhere in Europe.

Cinema statistics pointed in the same direction. A Commission study in 1997 found that the year before some sixteen per cent of cinema tickets sold in the EU were for national films in their respective home markets. A mere six per cent of cinema admissions were for films produced elsewhere in the EU (Commission 1997b). The remaining seventy-eight per cent of cinema admissions were for films originating from overseas, overwhelmingly of course from the United Sates. A study by the European Audiovisual Observatory in 1996 showed very similar results (Commission 1997b). Of the forty commercially most successful films in the EU, only ten were European. In fact, apart from *Trainspotting* (which ranked thirteenth) the first twenty were all from the US. The comparatively most successful European films were 'on a par with comedies like *Werner – Das Muß Kesseln!*, *Il Ciclone* and *Les Trois Frères*, having only a limited geographical distribution, which demonstrates the limited market potential for this genre outside national frontiers' (Commission 1997b). Six years later the situation had barely improved, despite significant increases in MEDIA funding. The EU-wide market share of European films shown beyond their home markets in 2002 was a mere 7.9

per cent. The US scored 71.2 per cent, whereas 19.2 per cent of cinema admissions were for domestic productions shown in their home markets (European Audiovisual Observatory 2003). Likewise, a mere eight per cent of European-made films were seen by more than one million EU-Europeans while sixty-one per cent of US films shown in Europe attracted an EU audience of one million or more (Commission 2003d: 40). The Union's combined audiovisual trade deficit with the US in 2002 was estimated at around 8.2 billion dollars (European Audiovisual Observatory 2002).

Yet despite the starkness of these figures and the intensity of its pleas, the Commission's audiovisual policy achievements after the Maastricht Treaty have remained modest. On the audiovisual productions front there were no qualitative leaps but merely a continuation and expansion of existing initiatives. This is borne out by the new MEDIA programme which, as was shown, is still aimed largely at boosting the circulation of domestic audiovisual output throughout the Union.[4]

Throughout the second part of the 1990s, repeated attempts by the European Parliament and the Commission to overcome these constraints ran into opposition from some member states, which had remained as strong as throughout the decade before. For example, in 1995 the Commission issued a proposal for a 'European guarantee fund' (Commission 1995d). It was to run parallel to the MEDIA programme and foster the development of fictional works – mainly coproductions – 'with considerable European and international market potential' by providing credit guarantees. The proposal was approved unanimously by the European Parliament and (not surprisingly) welcomed by the audiovisual industry yet the Council refused to adopt it. The most vociferous objections came from the usual suspects, above all the UK, Denmark, Germany, the Netherlands (and, after it had joined the Union, also Sweden), but even many other governments were lukewarm at best. Then as now, a role for the EU in shaping audiovisual content – however indirectly – has remained unacceptable to many national governments.

Similarly, the Union has not attempted to set up another multilingual pan-European television broadcaster along the lines of Europa TV. One partial exception is Euronews. It was established in January 1993 as a consortium of (mostly public) broadcasters from several European countries and Egypt. Subsequently, the British ITN acquired a forty-nine per cent stake in its operating society, which was bought back in 2003 by the public consortium that runs Euronews (see European Broadcasting Union 2003). Yet other than being multilingual with a pan-European reach, Euronews bears little resemblance to the failed pan-European broadcasters of the 1980s. In the first place, its programmes are limited to news and current affairs. Second, it does not, for the most part, attempt to repeat Europa TV's failed strategy of seeking to cover national events from an elusive 'European point of view'. Instead, the bulk of its news footage comes from the participating national broadcasters and Euronews then produces multilingual soundtracks to accompany it. In this sense, Euronews is a plurinational rather than a non-national broad-caster. The European Commission subsidises Euronews by running frequent 'infomercial' type programmes that straddle the boundary between 'citizen's advice' and blatant pro-Union PR, but otherwise does not use the channel to promote a 'denationalised' programming format. As have other parts of cultural policy, pan-European broadcasting, too, has become 'PR-ised' to an extent.

With initiatives to promote 'denationalised' pan-European television channels and audiovisual coproductions seemingly ruled out for the foresee-able future, the latest innovations in EU audiovisual policy have largely been confined to a discursive level. There the Commission has come to treat audio-visual policy – in its technical as well as content-related aspects – as a sub-sector of what it refers to as the 'multimedia' field, depicted to involve everything from the Internet to mobile phones and digital broadcasting. What is more, in the Commission's rendering 'multimedia' in turn is but one dimension of the broader group of issues it bunches together under the heading of 'information society', which is defined so vaguely as to apply to almost every imaginable sphere of social, cultural and economic activity. By the late 1990s, 'multimedia', 'information society', 'digitisation' and 'techno-logical convergence', along with ubiquitously invoked 'networks' and 'information gateways' had all become buzzwords in official Commission rhetoric, liberally strewn across numerous reports, position, discussion and strategy papers.

Still on the level of Commission rhetoric, moreover, audiovisual policy has become largely 'deculturalised'. On occasion the Commission still claims that the Union should devise audiovisual policies to foster 'enhanced social solidarity', promote the 'dissemination of European cultural values' and the like. But as these themes failed to make its audiovisual Europeanisation agenda more palatable to many member states, the Commission (and to a lesser degree also the European Parliament) gradually abandoned them. Instead, the Commission has come to treat audiovisual policy primarily under economic and technological rather than cultural guises. Time and again, it stresses the economic stakes involved in the audiovisual sector and the supposed link between its 'software' and 'hardware' aspects, the latter encompassing areas such as new distribution techniques (mainly the Internet), digital broadcasting and high definition television (Commission 1997c, 1994d; more recently Reading 2004; Commission 2001c, 1999c).

As for the cultural anti-Americanisation theme it, too, has lost its former place in Commission rhetoric. The Commission still makes frequent refer-ence to the United States. However, rather than depicting the US as a cultural menace it now portrays it mainly as a technological competitor, together with Japan and other countries in Asia. For the Commission, the audiovisual 'struggle' is now mainly about money rather than identity.

Yet just as the embrace of the 'European culture' and cultural anti-

Americanisation themes in the early 1980s did not spawn effective measures to Europeanise the audiovisual sector, so the gradual abandonment of these themes a decade later had little impact either. In fact, the Commission may well have started to bow to the limits of the politically possible: it has not, as of late, tried to submit a new and farther-reaching audiovisual initiative to the member states, along the lines of its ill-fated proposals to support transnational coproductions in the 1980s.

In sum, judged by the Union's policy record to date, the Europeanisation and 'defragmentation' of the audiovisual productions sector is not a project that is in the process of building up momentum. On the contrary: efforts to implement such policies may well turn out to have been no more than a sustained but largely inconsequential episode that began in the early 1980s but started to run out of steam some two decades later. So, too, did pleas for the protection of 'European culture' against the United States.

Conclusion

The Union's audiovisual record thus broadly mirrors that in other parts of culture. The Commission and the EP started out with ambitious proposals aimed at 'denationalising' audiovisual content and viewing habits through pan-European television channels and transnational coproductions. In part they were driven by the hope that this would foster a European identity in viewers and foster support for European integration. Yet these proposals either failed to materialise or, as with the European television channel, proved unsustainable. What followed in their wake were much more modest measures aimed at enhancing national audiovisual output and its circulation throughout the Union, mainly through the MEDIA programme. Measures of this type were relatively easy to swallow for even the most culturally protective member state governments: they did not interfere with national audiovisual content or with national audiovisual policies, and in fact complemented what the latter had already been trying to achieve for many decades. By the end of 1990s the Commission (and to some extent also the EP) seemed to have bowed to the limits of the politically possible and abandoned their earlier aspirations to use audiovisual policy as tool to Europeanise mass audiences.

How to explain the Union's meagre audiovisual record? As in other parts of culture, national governments were clearly the main obstacles, and frequently their opposition extended beyond the usual suspects such as Denmark, Germany, Sweden and the UK. As was discussed in the last chapter, the Union's weak legal mandate in culture (which did only marginally improve in the Maastricht Treaty) made it easy for national governments to block the Commission and the EP's audiovisual proposals, allowing them to simply invoke the Union's lack of legal competences rather than having to make their case on more substantive grounds.

All the while, the Commission and the EP once more employed a great deal of ingenuity and tactical skill in promoting their audiovisual agenda, above all by using an eclectic variety of discursive frames. Some sought to highlight the economic significance of the audiovisual sector and its link to issues such as technological competitiveness and the development of the 'information society'. Others stressed the fragile nature of public support for the EU and the potential of audiovisual measures to improve it. A third type centred on the cultural anti-Americanisation theme. The latter in particular seemed promising, and not just in the broader sense that, as argued in Chapters 1 and 2, the construction of political communities benefits from emphasising boundaries. In fact, it was uniquely suited to the audiovisual sector, given that Europe's audiovisual trade deficit with the US was real and that cultural resentments against the United States were firmly entrenched among elites in many member states.

Yet while warnings against a 'cultural colonialisation' by the United States found some resonance in France and some southern member states, many others remained thoroughly unconvinced. In countries ranging from Denmark and Ireland to the Netherlands and the UK, such fears appeared grossly exaggerated if not downright weird. And for wider publics across the Union the anti-Americanisation argument was bound to be even less convincing, given that these very publics were avid *consumers* of American films and television programmes. In the end, even in France this theme could only get the EP and the Commission so far. While broad sections of the French elite (far beyond Jack Lang and the various Socialist governments during the period) were receptive to the 'resistance to American cultural imperialism' theme, their primary concern was for *French* culture and the *French* language, not for a concept of European culture, however defined. French cultural and language policy at the time clearly bore this out. In sum, the anti-Americanisation theme enjoyed some plausibility in some member states, but to serve as a viable rhetorical underpinning for ambitious and culturally intrusive audiovisual policy initiatives by the EU it was simply not plausible enough.

Much the same applied to the 'European culture' theme. It was the discursive flipside of the anti-Americanisation coin, and its use by the Commission and the EP represented in many ways a throwback to their early cultural initiatives of the 1970s and to the Tindemans and Adonnino reports. But this theme, too, enjoyed only limited appeal. In many member states, 'Brussels" insistence on defending 'European culture' could only be grist on the rhetorical mill of EU opponents who depicted the Union as an intrusive and manipulative entity determined to erode national identities and homogenise national cultures. Against this backdrop, the Commission was well advised to gradually drop the 'European culture' theme in the 1990s, especially after the Maastricht debate had revealed widespread anxieties regarding the effects of European integration on national cultures. In fact, along with other parts of culture and education, audiovisual policy is among the areas in which national publics are least willing to accept a Union involvement (see the bi-annual *Eurobarometer* surveys; Theiler 1999a).

This chapter raises many more questions which go to the heart of the issues discussed in Chapters 1 and 2. Most importantly, even if the Union *had* launched major initiatives to support transnational coproductions their likely impact is far from clear. Claims by the Commission and the EP that multinational coproductions would cultivate 'denationalised' audiovisual formats are problematic, not least because they risk glossing over prevailing linguistic differences which are not liable to be easily 'denationalised'. Perhaps, even a large-scale, sustained and aggressive sponsorship of multinational coproductions would not have caused a significant 'denationalisation' of audiovisual formats and viewing habits. But even if this had occurred, it would not necessarily have led to a Europeanisation of political allegiances. As was suggested in Chapter 1, simply watching the same films and television programmes does not inevitably create overarching identifications or communal sentiments, just as using similar airports and shopping malls does not necessarily have such an effect either. The Commission and the EP's confidence in the ability of television to shape political allegiances often smacked of the 'hypodermic needle' and 'remote control' conceptions of media impact to which few contemporary students of mass communication subscribe (see Chapter 2). More broadly, it reflected too uncritical a faith in the ability of technology to act as a European identity forger.

As for the pan-European television channel, had it survived it might conceivably have provided a state-transcending communicative forum for Europeans, facilitating the kind of 'bottom-up' deliberative and interactional processes without which third-level legitimisation cannot materialise. But here, too, the mere ability to communicate does not ensure that communication actually takes place, much less its actual content and effect on those involved. At this point, then, one of the basic dilemmas that looms over the entire political symbolism project in the EU once more comes into view: as suggested in Chapters 1 and 2, effective political symbolism requires a conscious 'top-down' shaping of cultural content, at least during its initial stages. But the early twenty-first century liberal pluralist context within which the Union operates and which informs its own ethos makes interventionist policies of this kind very difficult to implement in the first place. The backlashes against the Commission's 'information and communication' campaigns discussed in the last chapter (which, though arguably both manipulative and 'interventionist' were hardly culturally homogenising) are a good example. Aggressive attempts to instrumentalise a pan-European television channel for political ends might well have elicited similar responses and thereby become self-defeating.

The concluding chapter explores these issues at greater length. In any case, because most audiovisual 'denationalisation' proposals were never implemented we cannot be sure what their impact would have been. If this chapter supports one clear conclusion, it is thus above all how strongly many member states and national publics alike continue to resist an EU involvement in audiovisual policy, and how difficult it is for the Commission and the EP to overcome this resistance. As is shown in the next chapter, the Union's experience in educational policy leads to very similar conclusions.

Notes

1 The most recent version of the TWF Directive is EP and Council (1997). Also see Collins (2002, 1995, 1994a, 1993a). On the world trade issue see Schlesinger (1997, 1996).

2 The Swiss franc was used as Europa TV's accounting unit because of its legal base in Geneva.

3 Audience reach refers to the number of viewers who can receive a given television channel; audience share pertains to the proportion of viewers that actually choose to watch it. Therefore, even if a channel's audience share remains stable, its actual net audience grows as its reach increases.

4 Also, in 1997 the Union adopted a slightly amended version of the Television Without Frontiers Directive (Collins 2002; EP and Council 1997). It contained additional provisions on issues such as teleshopping, the protection of children and the right of reply. The famous 'where practicable' provision attached to TWF's European content provision, however, was left intact. While the French government had lobbied hard to erase the escape clause from the directive, this stumbled over resistance led by the UK.

5

The 'European dimension' in schools

Unlike cultural policy where the Community had no powers under its founding treaties, the situation in education was less clear-cut. Potentially, the Community could become implicated in those aspects of educational policy that touched on its broadly defined economic mandate. These included vocational training (Article 128 EEC), the Community-wide recognition of educational and professional qualifications (Article 57 EEC) and, on a more limited scale, the promotion of some types of scientific research (Articles 7 and 9 EURATOM). In addition, according to some interpretations there was again the potential for involving the Community in educational domains beyond those mentioned in the founding treaties by resorting to Article 235 of the EEC Treaty. As discussed in Chapter 3, however, the extent to which Article 235 lent itself as an alternative legal foundation was disputed.

During the Community's first decade and a half of existence, neither the European Commission, the European Parliament nor any of the member states challenged its legal limitations in education. The few educational initiatives launched in this period were strictly confined to vocational training and the mutual recognition of educational qualifications and they were justified with economic arguments rather than with the desire to use education as a tool to strengthen popular support for European integration (e.g. Council 1963; also Hölzle 1994; Müller-Solger, Czysz, Leonhard and Pfaff 1993; Peege 1973).

It was not until the early 1970s that the Commission made its first cautious forays into 'general' (as opposed to vocational) education. Like parallel attempts to implicate the Community in culture as discussed in Chapter 3, this occurred against the backdrop of what many inside the Commission and beyond held to be a growing public alienation from the integrative process. And driving it was a belief that mass education in general and school curricula in particular could be instrumentalised to cultivate a

European identity in national publics and shore up support for integration.

However, reflecting the expected sensitivity of the issue and the Community's lack of legal competences in 'general' education, the Commission proceeded very cautiously. In July 1972, it appointed an advisory panel chaired by the former Belgian educational minister Henri Janne and composed of eminent academics including Carl Friedrich von Weizsäcker, Hendrik Brugmans, Jan Tinbergen and Alfred Grosser. The panel received the task of defining a set of fundamental objectives that were to guide the Community's educational activities in the future. It released its report in February 1973 (Field 1998: 29–31; Commission 1973).

From the Janne Report to the action programme

The official title of what is commonly referred to as the Janne Report is *For a Community Policy on Education*, and the report's title encapsulates its content: much of it centres on the attempt to devise potential rationales for why the Community's educational involvement should be extended beyond vocational education and diploma recognition. The report put forward two main arguments. First, it claimed that 'the economic (and therefore "professional" [i.e. vocational]) needs for training are not separable from the education system in general'. As the Community was tackling the former already, the latter allegedly could (and thus, according to the somewhat eccentric logic that marked the Janne Report's chain of reasoning, *should*) no longer be kept completely beyond its reach. Second, however, for the Janne committee a Community involvement in 'general' education was not just logical-cum-inevitable but it was also necessary. It was required to, among other things, add a 'European dimension' to the educational experience of young Europeans and thereby help them develop 'positive attitudes with regard to Europe':

> The Europeans' feeling of political, social and cultural belonging can no longer be exclusively national if a part of the attributes of the nation-state has been tested in the Community: the territory in as far as the frontiers disappear, the transfers of powers of decision to supranational bodies, the supranational jurisdictions, the right of establishment of foreigners, etc. This being so, is it possible to escape from the idea that education should comprise a European dimension wherever this is possible?

The Janne Report then identified a range of elements that should constitute this 'European dimension'. They included:

> (i) insertion into teaching practices of a suitable proportion of examples and illustrations as well as reading texts ... tending to increase knowledge of Europe and the other peoples which are members of the Community; (ii) Continuation of the 'correction' of history textbooks with a view to expurging or amending na-

tionalistic, biased passages or those of a kind which would create hostile or erroneous judgements; ... (iv) Use of geography to transcend national frontiers and to mark the relative nature of the differences and similarities of human groups; positive influences of the frontier regions; (v) Creation of linguistics teaching, throwing light in particular on the common structures of the European languages; (vi) Prudent and gradual teaching of European 'civics' to be based mainly on Community practices and institutions, on pluralism and on democracy; (vii) Examination of the opportuneness of creating an 'agency' at [the] Community level to produce (or to promote the production of) didactic equipment ... with a view to supplying teaching establishments ... with instruments of study of high pedagogic quality and creating or strengthening positive and well-informed attitudes with regard to Europe.

The Janne Report further recommended the promotion of foreign language learning and measures to enhance student and teacher mobility. Finally, it advocated the creation of a Community 'cultural and educational committee', and the drafting of a European charter of education as a 'framework for the whole of educational thought in our region of the world ...'.

Although the Janne Report was advisory only it represented an important initial step in what became the Commission's protracted fight on behalf of the 'European dimension' in schools. The most important factor was its timing, as its release virtually coincided with the 'Declaration on European identity' at the Copenhagen Summit as discussed in Chapter 3. This meant that those who championed a greater educational role for the Community – above all the Commission itself – could construe the Janne Report as merely one step towards translating existing verbal commitments by the member states into concrete policies. For much the same reason, even those national governments that had gone along with the Copenhagen Declaration in the expectation that no concrete actions would ensue were now in a poor position to reject the Janne Report out of hand.

Furthermore, the release of the Janne Report roughly coincided with a redistribution of responsibility for the educational portfolio within the Commission, which boosted its determination and – on the face of it – its ability to advance the educational agenda outlined in the report. In 1973, the Commission created a new Directorate for Education and Training integrated within the equally new Directorate-General for Research, Science and Education (DG XII) (*General Report 1973*: 320–321). The new Directorate-General became headed by the (then) German Commissioner Ralf Dahrendorf, who is widely noted for his enthusiasm in translating the Janne Report's educational wishlist into concrete policy initiatives with which to confront the Council and the individual member states. According to one former high-ranking Commission official, had it not been for Dahrendorf's arrival the Janne Report might well have faded into obscurity, and the Commission might well have failed to develop an agenda in 'general' education until well into the 1980s (interview, February 2001).

A few months after Dahrendorf's taking charge of the education portfolio, the Commission issued an initial draft for a Community action programme in education, titled 'Education in the European Community' (Commission 1974a) which largely repeated the 'European dimension'-related recommendations in the Janne Report. These were affirmed once more in a draft resolution for 'Cooperation in the field of education' which the Commission submitted to the Council shortly thereafter (Commission 1974b). Yet despite the Commission's cautious way of proceeding it soon ran up against strong resistance from some member states. In fact, when the national educational ministers met under their habitual 'mixed' formula of the 'Council and the ministers of education meeting within the Council' (the same formula later used in culture)[1] to debate the draft resolution, they failed to adopt it. Instead, they referred the issue to a newly created 'education committee'. It was composed of representatives from the Commission and national education ministries and was to draw up a blueprint for a comprehensive Community action programme in education (Neave 1984: 13–15). The committee reported to the education ministers in 1975, and an 'action programme' in education was passed in February 1976 (Council 1976; also Field 1998: 31–33; Maaß 1978).

The action programme contained a wide range of provisions, touching on areas such as the schooling of immigrant and 'guest worker' children, equal opportunities in higher education, language teaching, exchange visits for educational administrators, networking between educational institutions and, once more, the mutual recognition of educational qualifications. Yet as far as the 'European dimension' in school curricula was concerned it was a major disappointment for the Commission. Almost all of its initial proposals on the subject (and by extension those in the Janne Report) had vanished from the action programme – so much so that the 'European dimension' in school curricula did not even receive its own heading. Instead, it was subsumed under the title 'promotion of closer relations between educational systems in Europe'. There the action programme stipulated that 'in order to give a European dimension to the experience of teachers and pupils in primary and secondary schools in the Community', the member states (and not the Community itself) should

> promote and organise short study visits and exchanges for teachers, with special emphasis on student language teachers; development of the national information and advisory services necessary to promote the mobility and interchange of pupils and teachers within the Community; contacts between the authorities of establishments concerned with teacher training; educational activities with a European content.

There were no further guidelines on what these 'educational activities with a European content' (or, for that matter, the 'European content' itself) should consist of.

For the Commission this was all the more painful as the overall importance of the action programme was considerable. Never before had the education ministers been able to agree on a similarly comprehensive and far-reaching declaration of intent regarding the Community's educational role, and its approval by the ministers 'brought to a close the protracted and often difficult quest to find a basis for cooperation in education. It set ... down the areas in which such cooperation should concentrate and develop' (Neave 1984: 11; also Field 1998: 32–33; Winter 1980). For many years to come, almost every educational initiative by the Community relied heavily on the action programme, both in rhetoric and substance. Yet it was precisely the role of the action programme in defining those areas of educational policy in which some Community involvement *would* be broadly acceptable to the member states which renders the almost complete absence of the 'European dimension' in school curricula among these areas so significant. It turned the action programme into a clear setback for the Commission in its efforts to make the introduction of 'European content' into national school curricula a pillar of its educational involvement.

After the action programme had been passed, the Commission and the EP both continued to lobby on behalf of the 'European dimension' in school curricula but the earlier momentum had been lost. A Commission initiative in 1978 entitled 'Educational Activities with a European Content: The Study of the European Community in Schools' (Commission 1978) largely reiterated the recommendations in the Janne Report. It was accompanied by a country-by-country survey which highlighted the large-scale absence of 'European content' from national school curricula and the alleged danger this posed to the Community's long-term development. But this initiative, too, elicited strong resistance from some member states, which became so strong that the 'Council and the ministers of education meeting within the Council' did not meet for the next three years. The most vociferous opponents were Denmark and France. As in cultural policy, they invoked the Community's lack of legal powers in 'general' education and now even argued that the 'mixed' formula 'Council and the ministers of education meeting within the Council' carried too strong an allusion to Community competences where none in fact existed. At the same time, such objections enjoyed the more or less tacit support of other member states. These included the UK (especially after the Thatcher government had come to power) and Germany which was driven by the habitual Länder fears of a Community encroachment into their constitutional prerogatives which include education (Janssen 1981: 213; Schmitz-Wenzel 1980; Rübsamen 1978).

If anything the cause of the 'European dimension' in schools lost further momentum by a partial reversal of the administrative reforms of 1973 inside the Commission. Effective from January 1981, the education portfolio moved from the Directorate-General XII into DG V (Employment and Social Affairs). This represented a setback to attempts spearheaded by Commissioner

Dahrendorf in the 1970s to develop education into a field of Community activity in its own right instead of treating it as a mere auxiliary instrument to help the Community achieve its economic objectives (Janssen 1982: 267). The broader implications of this were clear: while a Community involvement in education for economic ends was now broadly acceptable, attempts to in-strumentalise education for symbolic and identity-related purposes were not. It was only with the Adonnino Report in the mid-1980s that the 'European dimension' in school curricula received a new impetus.

From the Adonnino Report to the Maastricht Treaty

As was shown in Chapter 3, the Adonnino Committee (formally named 'Committee on a People's Europe') was appointed at the Fontainebleau Summit and instructed to work out a strategy by which the Community could enhance its symbolic presence in the lives of its citizens and attract greater popular support (*Bulletin* 1984 [No. 6]: point 1.1.9 [subheading 6]). To some extent the Adonnino Report was a consolation prize for the European Parliament, the Commission and the more culture and education-ambitious member states, compensating them for the likely absence of those two policy areas from the upcoming Single European Act. To some extent it also reflected a desire on the part of many member state governments to ensure popular acceptance of the Single Market programme, not least under the impression of a disappointingly low turnout for the European Parliament elections in June 1984.

The first of the two Adonnino reports did not touch on education other than to demand the better mutual recognition of educational and profes-sional qualifications under the rubric entitled 'Community citizen's rights'. The second report, by contrast, dealt much more extensively with education, under the title 'Youth, education, exchanges and sport' (both reports in 'A People's Europe' 1985). As in culture, Adonnino's educational proposals fell into two broad categories. The majority covered the already familiar terrain ranging from the promotion of language learning to school and youth exchanges and pan-European youth camps. A second category of proposals, by contrast, fell under the heading of the 'European image in education'. It included

> (i) the creation by each Member State, wherever this has not yet been done, of centres whose task ... it would be to facilitate the work of schools and teachers and inform and help them from an educational viewpoint; (ii) the preparation and availability of appropriate school books and teaching materials; (iii) confirming 9 May of each year *Europe Day* with a view to creating awareness and giving information in schools in particular as well as on television and in the other media. ...; (iv) the setting-up of a Centre displaying European achieve-ments, and the common heritage, backed up by a collection of documents and works relating thereto.

It is difficult to establish a direct link between the Adonnino Report and the launch of concrete educational initiatives shortly thereafter. After all, Adonnino's recommendations were not binding and, as shown in Chapter 3, their wider reception was far from unanimously enthusiastic. Even so, just as in cultural policy several factors strengthened the Commission and the EP's educational clout in the immediate post-Adonnino period. This included the accession in the early- to-mid-1980s of Greece, Spain and Portugal whose governments were generally more open to involving the Community in cultural and educational policy, and whose nationals helped boost staffing levels in the Commission's culture and education departments. Moreover, Adonnino's central claim that cultural and educational measures could help the upcoming Single Market programme succeed was bound to resonate favourably in some national capitals. In the 1970s, the Commission's argument that European identity-enhancing measures were needed to lift the Community out of its stagnation could do little to convince national governments which were ultimately responsible for this stagnation; in the 1980s, by contrast, such measures could be depicted as part of an effort to ensure the success of a wider economic and political agenda to which the member states had already committed themselves in principle. At the very least, by formally accepting the educational recommendations in the Adonnino Report national governments increased the accumulated weight of their commitments for a 'European dimension' in education. This in turn could only encourage the Commission and the EP to step up their push for tangible policies in this field and made it more difficult for sceptical member states to reject them out of hand.

And it was indeed in the immediate post-Adonnino era that the Community made its most significant forays into 'general' education to date, launching three initiatives which – albeit under changing titles and formats – have formed the backbone of its educational agenda until the present day: Erasmus, Lingua, and Youth for Europe.

The chronologically first and most expensive of these was the Erasmus programme (Council 1987c). First adopted in 1987, Erasmus' core objective is to enable university students to pursue part of their studies in another member state through mobility grants and exchange agreements between universities. As is shown below, in 1995 Erasmus became part of the new Socrates programme and experienced significant increases in funding.

The Lingua programme was initiated in 1989 and sought to promote the learning and teaching of Community languages (Council 1989). It supported students and pupils wishing to learn the language of another member state on location, as well as language teaching in the context of vocational and technical education. Lingua, too, was later subsumed into the Socrates programme and its funding rose significantly.

Youth for Europe (Council 1988a), finally, also had as its core objective to foster the movement of people across borders through youth exchanges of various kinds and periods of duration. Exchanges deemed to 'make young people aware of the European dimension' (for example by being multi- rather than merely bilateral), and those involving participants from underprivileged backgrounds received priority. In subsequent years, Youth for Europe, too, was renewed and its funding increased significantly.

All three initiatives were controversial and their drafting was mired in numerous quarrels and legal challenges pertaining to their funding, legal foundations and implementation rules. In particular, given the Community's continued lack of legal powers in 'general' education at the time they had to be based in part on Article 235 of the EEC Treaty, subjecting them to the unanimity requirement in the Council (Blanke 1994: 57). In addition, apart from accepting much lower funding levels than it had originally demanded for all three programmes, the Commission made several substantive concessions. First, national authorities received a key role in implementing the three programmes. Second, with the very limited exception of Lingua they did not seek to affect curricular content, much less infuse European symbolism into school curricula. Instead, their key objective echoed that of the various cultural programmes passed almost simultaneously: to promote transnational mobility and communication and therefore to make Europeans from different member states more visible to and more knowledgeable of each other. Though the Community had managed to involve itself in 'general' education at last, this involvement, too, had become thoroughly 'horizontalised'. Finally none of the three initiatives had a direct bearing on elementary schooling. In devising Lingua, the Commission had originally planned a comprehensive Community language programme that would have covered elementary and secondary schools, vocational training and adult education. Yet upon the insistence of notably Germany and the UK, all references to elementary schooling were dropped. And it was left to each member state to decide whether it wanted to extend Lingua into secondary education (Janssen 1989: 195).

Erasmus and Lingua both benefited from a measure of interest group pressure on their behalf. One Commission official singles out the role of the Confederation of British Industry, which had good links to some high-ranking members of the Commission as well as to ministers in the Thatcher government and which championed the two programmes as a cost-effective way of addressing a dearth of foreign language skills among the British workforce. The official insists that the CBI's stance was decisive in preventing a British veto (interview European Commission, September 2000).

In addition, at a European level Erasmus was supported notably by the European Round Table of Industrialists as well as by the European Council of Rectors, although they supported it for different reasons. Employers were after a net increase in student mobility in order to improve language skills and 'cross cultural competences', whereas higher education institutions saw in Erasmus a way of *managing* intra-Community student flows. This became a more pressing issue after some of the traditional obstacles to transnational student mobility (such as differential student fees, difficulties in obtaining residence permits and the imperfect transnational recognition of educational qualifications) had been reduced through a mixture of ECJ rulings and Single Market-related decisions in the 1980s. The desire to curtail student inflows from other parts of the Community was especially strong among British universities. Largely due to the language factor these were attractive to Continental students but generally preferred fee-paying students from countries outside the Community (Hackl 2001; Shaw 1999; Field 1998: 36).[2]

Youth for Europe, for its part, also benefited from the Commission's skill in political framing. When drawing up the programme the Commission shrewdly avoided any allusions to formal education. Instead, it advanced it as a 'youth measure', thereby locating it in a policy domain that was less contested than education (Janssen 1987: 218–219). Most importantly, the policy area which in some Continental member states is referred to as 'youth policy' (sometimes looked after by 'youth ministries') has no real formal equivalent in the UK. This made it harder for the Thatcher government to argue that Youth for Europe encroached upon a national policy domain and thereby preempted a great deal of potential resistance to the programme (interview European Commission, September 2000).

Yet when it came to the Adonnino Report's push for a 'European dimension' in school curricula these factors did not apply and, accordingly, progress was much slower. After ferocious lobbying by the Commission and the EP and various drafting stages, (e.g. *Social Europe* 1988 [Supplement No. 5]: 23–24; Council 1987b [1985]), the education ministers adopted a new resolution on the issue in 1988 (Council 1988b) whose content largely reflected the Adonnino Report. Its declared objective was to 'strengthen in young people a sense of European identity and make clear to them the value of European civilisation and of the foundations on which the European peoples intend to base their development today ...' through a series of 'concerted measures'. The member states pledged, 'within the limits of their own specific educational policies and structures' to, among other things, 'include the European dimension explicitly in their school curricula in all appropriate disciplines, for example literature, languages, history, geography, social sciences, economics and the arts'. They also promised to organise seminars on the subject and encourage 'school twinnings', the formation of 'European clubs' in schools, educational activities as part of Europe Day (9 May) and transnational cooperation in school sports. For its part, the Commission was to 'examine the possibilities' of using 'European dimension'-related audiovisual material in schools, promote the exchange of information between educational authorities and carry out 'comparative analysis'.

Overall the 1988 resolution had little impact (see the survey below). What tangible measures it produced at the time revolved around the odd pilot programme in teacher training and curricular development, as well as numerous conferences, colloquia and seminars that attracted little public attention beyond the narrow ranks of educationalists, academics, and education ministry officials who frequented the Community-sponsored conference circuit.[3] Moreover, by the early 1990s even the Commission itself had become more muted on the 'European dimension' in school curricula, with most of its educational reports, memoranda and discussion papers released in anticipation of the Single Market deadline at the end of 1992 preoccupied with social and economic rather than political and identity-related issues (e.g. Commission 1991a, 1991b). All the same, there was one notable exception to the Commission's general restraint at the time, which was its attempt to sponsor a pan-European history textbook. Together with Europa TV, the history textbook was one of its boldest political symbolism initiatives to date, but in the end turned out to be one of its most spectacular failures.

The European history textbook

The European history textbook originated with an umbrella project launched by the Franco-British-Norwegian industrialist Frédéric Delouche, which the Commission began to support in the late 1980s. The first stage of the project was to entail the production of a 500-page survey of European history written for a general audience; the second the book's adoption into a television series; and the third the production of a European history survey for use as a prescribed text in schools throughout the Community (see Davies 1996: 43–44).

The European history book for a general audience had as its chief author the historian Jean Baptiste Duroselle who was assisted by a multinational panel of advisors. It was published in 1990 under the title *Europe: A History of its Peoples* (Duroselle 1990). The volume's objective as spelled out in its introduction was to compile 'for the general reader a one-volume history of Europe, set in overall European as opposed to national perspective'. Such an account would overcome the lingering national biases which according to the authors overshadowed traditional national historiography. By extension, it would bring home to its readers Europe's presumed underlying social and cultural unity and the necessity to speed up political unification. And indeed, in every regard the narrative that unfolded on the subsequent 500 pages or so sought to live up to these aims:

> Chapter One opens with the rape of the Greek Goddess 'Europa', and proceeds to discuss the geographical complexity and uniqueness of the continent ... Chapter Three describes the Celts and Teutons as the first Indo-Europeans. Chapter Four proceeds under the heading 'Classical Antiquity: Greek Wisdom, Roman Grandeur'. Chapter Five ('the First Four Centuries AD in the West') is devoted exclusively to the expansion of Christianity. Chapter Seven is a lengthy discussion of whether Charlemagne's empire marks the 'beginnings of Europe'. Chapter Eight ('Europe under Siege') opens with a vivid image of banner-waving Saracens on horseback – 'European civilisation' thus being equated unequivo-

cally as Christendom defending itself against the resurgent forces of Islam. The book continues in a similar vein until Chapter Seventeen ('The Road to European Disaster') which deals with nationalism, Chapter Eighteen ('Europe Destroys itself') …, and finally Chapter Nineteen, 'Europe's Recovery and Resurgent Hopes', which focuses on the 'makers of Europe' and the 'building of Europe in the face of Gaullism'. [Overall] European history is presented as a gradual coming together: a moral success story of reason and unity triumphing over disunity and nationalism. (Shore 1996: 485–486)

Most reviews of the European history book were scathing. One critic de-nounced it as 'history in the service of an idea' and likened it to Soviet-bloc historiography (Zamoyski 1988: 13). Another, alluding to the book's defini-tion of Europe as limited to the then-EC-Twelve plus Scandinavia, Austria and Switzerland, accused it of peddling 'half-truths about half of Europe' (Nicholas 1991: 22). The strongest protests, however, came from Greece. Many critics there took exception to Duroselle's alleged lack of regard for the contributions of ancient Greece and Byzantium to European history, and for Greek and Slavic cultures in his discussion of 'the ancient peoples of Europe'. Several Greek MEPs lodged stern protests with the Commission, as did the Archbishop of Athens. Some Greek commentators likened the Euro-history book to the *Satanic Verses* (Davies 1996: 43).

Taken aback by such criticism and by a barrage of media ridicule, the Commission distanced itself from the European history enterprise and stopped funding it.[4] Nonetheless, the schoolbook project survived, thanks to the continued support by Delouche, the French Hachette publishing house as well as translation grants from a private German foundation and the French ministry of culture.

The didactic volume, co-produced by twelve authors from eleven member states plus Czechoslovakia (Delouche 1993), was completed in 1992 and eventually published in sixteen languages, after it had struggled to find a publisher in Britain (Nundy 1992: 15). Prior to this, various drafts had provoked extended quarrelling between the different co-authors and under-gone various 'corrections'. For example, a 'French account of "the Barbarian Invasions" was changed to "the Germanic Invasions". A Spanish description of Sir Francis Drake as a "pirate" was overruled. A picture of General de Gaulle among the portraits on the cover was replaced by one of Queen Victoria' (Davies 1996: 44; also Nundy 1992).

In any event, in the end the book's initiators had to compromise on their two most central objectives. First, they did not achieve a completely homogenised European format: the different language versions of the text display substantial differences in content and interpretation (Hörner 1996: 28). Second, in light of the looming refusal by most national education authorities to approve the European history book for school use (which seemed almost a foregone conclusion, especially after the adverse publicity it had generated), its authors were forced to compromise even on that issue.

In the introduction to the German language edition they concede that their work does not satisfy 'the narrow criteria for authorisation' as a school text-book and should thus be seen as a 'prototype' of sorts which would hopefully appeal to a more general public.[5] The foreword to the English language edition does not even mention the authors' initial intention of producing a textbook. Thus re-targeted at a general audience, the would-be textbook could at the most hope to duplicate the Duroselle volume published two years earlier to which at any rate it bears strong resemblance.

Not surprisingly, the European history textbook saga has not left Commission officials with fond memories. Comparing it to Europa TV, they view it as an embarrassment they are determined not to repeat. All the while, it remains unclear who exactly decided to associate the Commission with the project in the first place. The sponsorship decision was made without formal involvement by national education ministries. Some suggest that a link between Delouche and an extremely high-ranking Commission official at the time might have played a role, while others speculate that the Commission might have given in to informal pressure by the French government whose own culture ministry helped sponsor the project (interviews European Commission, September 2000).

Whatever the case, there are strong parallels between the attempted European history textbook and Europa TV – parallels that go beyond the fact that both projects ultimately floundered and earned the Commission wide-spread criticism and embarrassment. In the first place, both Europa TV and the textbook saga bear out the risks to which the Commission exposes itself by leaping ahead with a 'European dimension'-related project that many consider overly ambitious at best and blatantly propagandist and manipula-tive at worst. Whatever the intrinsic merits of these projects, the adverse coverage they attracted sealed their fate. Moreover, both projects highlight the dangers the Commission faces by associating itself with cultural and educational projects over whose implementation it has only limited control. The lack of formal Council involvement in the Commission's decision to support the European history project proved a mixed blessing. While it prob-ably enabled the Commission to go ahead with it in the first place it also meant that its officials had to weather the ensuing barrage of criticism all by themselves. Its hasty withdrawal from the project was justified on pragmatic grounds but it was also a sign of its vulnerability and lack of support over the issue.

Beyond this, the failures of Europa TV and the would-be European history textbook both point to a deeper problem that lingers over the entire gamut of European identity and 'European dimension' projects in culture, audiovisual policy and education. As was suggested, even if projects with a consciously designed 'European dimension' manage to be *produced* in defi-ance of the many legal and political obstacles that usually stand in their way, it is far from self-evident what this 'European dimension' should consist of, let alone that it will actually be 'absorbed' by its intended recipients. Ultimately, covering European history from a 'non-national' point of view proved as elusive as Europa TV's 'non-national' programming format. As the concluding chapter argues, constructing the 'European dimension' in a way that – inevitably – *national* publics can relate to might well pose the greatest challenge to the EU's political symbolism project in culture, education and beyond.

Education in the Maastricht Treaty

As was the case with cultural policy and for similar reasons, the period leading up to the Maastricht Treaty saw a relatively widespread expectation that 'general' education would be included in the range of new Community competences (e.g. Witte 1991: 196). Yet the member states were again divided on the issue. Some, not surprisingly coalescing around Denmark and the UK, opposed giving the Community even a very limited mandate in the field. Other (mainly southern) member states were willing to accept a relatively broad Community mandate in 'general' education, akin to what it already enjoyed in vocational education. The German government, finally, again had two main objectives. On the one hand, it wanted to place those educational programmes that were already in force on a more solid legal foundation. On the other hand, driven in part by the habitual Länder fears, it wanted to limit the kinds of programmes which the Union could launch in 'general' education, and especially those that would extend beyond mere educational exchanges (Blanke 1994). As in cultural policy it was again the German position which broadly won out.

Three separate passages in the Maastricht Treaty (which were left unchanged in the subsequent Amsterdam Treaty) allude to education. Part One of the treaty, titled 'Principles', features the aforementioned Article 3p (3q Amsterdam). It stipulates that the Community should make 'a contribution to education and training of quality and to the flowering of the cultures of the Member States'. As was argued, the legal standing of Article 3p is ambiguous, but it has potential significance as an 'interpretative clause' for the more specific cultural and educational articles in the treaty.

Article 127 of the Maastricht Treaty (Article 150 Amsterdam) pertains to vocational education. As was shown, in this field the Community had already enjoyed some powers under the Rome Treaties and the Maastricht Treaty further expanded them. It authorises the Community to 'implement a vocational training policy which shall support and supplement the action of the Member States' in areas such as vocational training and the reintegration of unemployed people into the labour market. Decisions under Article 127 are subjected to the co-decision procedure as spelled out in Article 189b of the Maastricht Treaty (Article 251 Amsterdam), and again exclude 'any harmonisation of the laws and regulations of the Member States'. At the same time, Article 127 is relatively far-reaching. It authorises the Community to 'implement a policy' rather than merely to enact 'incentive measures' and issue recommendations. Moreover, once adopted policies in vocational education are legally binding (Blanke 1994: 66–67).

Yet it is the Maastricht Treaty's implications for non-vocational – i.e. 'general' – education that are of primary interest in the present context. Here the treaty contains a new Article 126 (Article 149 Amsterdam) which gives the Union a limited legal standing in 'general' education (as well as in the adjacent area of 'youth policy') for the first time.

> The Community shall contribute to the development of quality education by encouraging cooperation between Member States and, if necessary, by supporting and supplementing their action, while fully respecting the responsibility of the Member States for the content of teaching and the organisation of education systems and their cultural and linguistic diversity.

Such Community action, according to the treaty, should be aimed at

> developing the European dimension in education, particularly through the teaching and dissemination of the languages of the Member States; encouraging mobility of students and teachers, *inter alia* by encouraging the academic recognition of diplomas and periods of study; promoting cooperation between educational establishments; developing exchanges of information and experience on issues common to the education systems of the Member States; encouraging the development of youth exchanges and of exchanges of socio-educational instructors; encouraging the development of distance education.

In addition, the Community may foster educational cooperation with third countries and international organisations, especially the Council of Europe. As in culture, decisions under Article 126 are subject to the co-decision procedure as outlined under Article 189b as well as to the subsidiarity principle.

As far as the 'European dimension' in school curricula is concerned Article 126 has only modest implications at best. First, the possible areas of Community action it enumerates are almost exclusively concerned with fostering the mobility of students and teachers but do not include educational content of any kind. In this sense, Article 126 stays well behind even the educational action programme of 1976 (Janssen 1992: 202). As with cultural policy, legal experts disagree on whether the list of educational measures contained in Article 126 is exemplary or exhaustive (Blanke 1994: 69–70). But even if it were deemed to be merely exemplary, any curriculum-related initiative in the Community could at the most be of a 'soft' and non-binding type, rather like the many resolutions and declarations drafted in the past. And this is not only due to the 'while fully respecting the responsibility of the Member States for the content of teaching' clause, but above all because the same article does not give the Union *any* competences in 'general' education of a kind that would enable it to define and enforce binding standards. Instead, it stipulates that the Council 'shall adopt *incentive measures*, excluding any harmonisation of the laws and regulations of the Member States' (emphasis added). In addition, the Council may issue recommendations. As was argued, these terms are ambiguous. Nonetheless, just as in culture the setting of legally enforceable standards is not permitted under Article 126 of the Maastricht Treaty, even if they were deemed to be of a 'non-harmonising' kind.

In sum, under the Maastricht Treaty the Community's role in 'general' education is one of encouraging educational cooperation between the member states. Depending on which legal interpretation one follows, this could potentially include the promotion of legally non-binding agreements on curriculum design. But these areas remain under the exclusive control of the member states and, as in culture, the Community lacks legal powers of enforcement (Blanke 1994; Bekemans and Balodimos 1992).

By designing the educational provisions of the Maastricht Treaty in the way they did the member states managed once more to reconcile a host of different and at first glance contradictory objectives. On the one hand, they gave the Community a legal mandate in 'general' education for the first time. This went some ways towards accommodating demands by the EP and the Commission and conformed to the Maastricht Treaty's declared purpose of taking the Community beyond the status of a purely economic entity. It also helped place those educational policies already in force on a more solid legal basis. Yet on the other hand, the Maastricht Treaty contains powerful safeguards to ensure that any amendment to or extension of these existing initiatives must stay within very narrow parameters. In particular, it excludes any supranational challenge to the member states' monopoly over educational content.

One of the earliest repercussions of the Maastricht Treaty for educational policy was at an administrative level. In 1995, education once again received a fully-fledged Directorate-General for 'Education, Training and Youth'[6] (DG XXII) placed under the auspices of Commissioner Edith Cresson, the former French Socialist prime minister. This administrative upgrading reflected the Union's expanded competences in vocational and first-time formal mandate in 'general' education. It also anticipated an increase in funding and organisational complexity of some educational programmes in preparation at the time.

Cresson's arrival provoked mixed feelings among her new subordinates. Some saw her as poorly briefed, heavily dependent on her advisers and lacking the necessary skills to compile and push through new policy initiatives. Yet at the same time Cresson was energetic and well connected and seemed more strongly committed to expanding the Community's educational role than her immediate predecessor, the Irish Social Affairs Commissioner Pradaig Flynn. In fact, not since Dahrendorf's reign in the 1970s did an Education Commissioner appear to harbour such a strong commitment to education as a political and cultural rather than merely an economic tool (interviews European Commission, September 2000; Field 1998: 63–64).

Even before Cresson took charge, and even before the Maastricht Treaty had entered into force, the Commission's education officials had started to work on a strategy for the immediate post-Maastricht period. The Union's three existing flagship programmes in 'general' education and youth policy – Erasmus, Lingua and Youth for Europe – were scheduled to run out by the middle of the decade, and the Commission was set on trying to renew and if possible expand them into compulsory education. Yet as in cultural policy it had to proceed with caution. The Union's new mandate in 'general' education was legally ambiguous, and some Commission officials feared that too aggressive a move by the Commission could provoke the member states into a restrictive interpretation of Article 126, just as the overly enthusiastic approach by the Dahrendorf Commission in the 1970s had provoked some member states into complete intransigence that lasted for several years (interview European Commission, September 2000).

Such fears were aggravated by the behaviour of the UK government. Soon after winning the 1992 election, the Major administration started to show itself no less hostile to many of the Community's educational activities than its predecessors under Margaret Thatcher. This was borne out by the British reaction to a Commission Green Paper on the 'European dimension' in education (Commission 1993a). The contents of the Green Paper were modest and vague, essentially reiterating what the education ministers themselves had already agreed to in the 1988 'European dimension' resolution. But the British reaction was furious all the same. One British minister denounced what he claimed were the Commission's schemes for a 'statutory curriculum, modules or themes which would be commonly used throughout Europe' and pledged to ensure that 'common-sense not common education' would prevail (quoted in Field 1998: 65). Faced with such hostility the Commission refrained from submitting further proposals of the kind until the latter part of the decade.

In addition, Commission officials were at odds over how the upcoming educational initiatives should be 'packaged'. Some wanted to combine all 'general' and most vocational education programmes into a single overarching initiative for 'lifelong learning'. They hoped that this would eliminate the 'Berlin Wall' which according to one official had been erected between vocational and 'general' education and stifled Community progress in the latter. This position also had some support in the European Parliament. By contrast, a second group of Commission officials insisted that the basic division between 'general' and vocational education needed to be maintained, fearing that the Union's vocational initiatives could be dragged down by becoming too closely associated with 'general' education where its legal basis was much more fragile and the member states more reluctant to grant the Union a significant role (interviews European Commission, September 2000).

Socrates

Emerging out of this were two new umbrella programmes in education which both had a long and arduous journey through the co-decision procedure demanded by the Maastricht Treaty. The first is called 'Leonardo da Vinci' and combines expanded versions of most of the Union's vocational programmes from the preceding decade. The second programme is in 'general' education. Named 'Socrates', it was passed in March 1995 with a funding of 850 million ECU for a five-year period and based on both Articles 127 and 126 of the Maastricht Treaty. In 2000 it was renewed for a seven-year period with its contents amended and its funding raised to 1,850 million euro (EP and Council 2000d; Fritsch 1998).

Socrates incorporates expanded and amended versions of the old Erasmus and Lingua programmes as well as a range of measures in areas such as adult education, distance learning and educational technologies – areas in which by the mid-1990s a coalition of interest groups and some national governments were pushing for a Union involvement.[7] But most importantly in the present context, Socrates includes the Union's first-ever programme in primary and secondary education, called Comenius, which must receive at least 27 per cent of its overall budget.

Comenius offers financial and logistical support for transnational school partnerships. Each partnership revolves around a particular project (loosely defined as having to be 'of common interest to the participating schools') and leads to school-based activities ranging from exchange visits to the production of videos, exhibitions and Internet websites (see below). In addition, Comenius sponsors a variety of teacher mobility programmes, transnational 'networks' pertaining to almost every conceivable aspect of school education as well as multilateral cooperation projects in areas such as didactic methods and curriculum development.

In its initial Socrates proposals, the Commission had sought to give itself the bulk of responsibility for implementing the programme. Yet during the subsequent negotiation process it was forced to surrender important powers to national Socrates agencies (interview European Commission, September 2000). These are designated by national governments and are interposed between the Commission on the one hand and individuals, groups and educational institutions on the other. Depending on the member state in question, they are more or less tightly subjected to national educational ministries. As regards those Socrates programme items that are officially designated as 'decentralised' (which, crucially, includes the entire school partnership section of Comenius), applicants for funding have their application evaluated directly by their respective national agencies. The Commission is shut out from the decision-making process altogether and has no possibility of recourse. Many member states depicted this as a decentralising measure justified by the subsidiary principle. However, seen from a different angle it subjects Socrates to a curious form of 'multiple centralism', in many ways resembling a conventional international cooperation programme (Janssen 1994: 211).

How, then, has Socrates been implemented thus far? Its Erasmus part, for a start, has helped stimulate a growing transnational mobility of students and university teachers. For instance, in the 2003/2004 academic year Erasmus funded transnational mobility arrangements involving almost two thousand higher education institutions and around 120,000 students (Commission 2002b).[8] Moreover, it has supported a variety of projects to facilitate the mutual recognition of university courses (and thereby indirectly encouraged the mobility of students still further). Increasingly, moreover, Erasmus has been brought into overlap with other Union activities in higher education. This includes the Jean Monnet programme. Financed up to now from the Commission's information budget, it promotes the teaching of European integration at universities by subsidising Jean Monnet chairs (over 600 since 1990), as well as teaching projects, centres and course modules (Commission 2004c).[9] Finally, some key Erasmus objectives also tie in with the intergovernmental 'Bologna Declaration' and the subsequent 'Bologna process', which seeks to compatibilise national higher education systems through a unified European degree structure, degree recognition provisions and the full-scale implementation of the European Credit Transfer System (Hackl 2001).

Yet of primary interest in the present context is of course Comenius, given that it pertains to 'general' education at the primary and secondary levels. In 2003, more than 10,000 schools were involved in Comenius-sponsored partnerships, with some 25,000 pupils and 35,000 teachers visiting partner schools in other member states (*General Report on the Activities of the European Union 2003*). These numbers look impressive at first glance but they call for two important qualifications.

First, they seem significantly less impressive if one considers that Comenius covers an area (the EU and some adjacent candidate countries) that comprises around 300,000 schools, four million teachers and seventy million primary and secondary school pupils. Second, merely focusing on quantitative indicators does little to illuminate what the various school partnerships sponsored by Comenius actually consist of, or their impact on pupils' educational experience. For example, how much teaching time is typically devoted to partnership-related activities? What other parts of the curriculum do these activities replace? Does a typical Comenius partnership lead to the transmission of knowledge and symbolic representations of the European Union or merely of other countries and cultures?

Surprisingly little comparative work has been carried out on these questions. The Commission's own Comenius database pertains mainly to formal criteria (such as project titles, age of the participating children and location of the partner institutions) and gives few indications as to how Comenius activities are actually carried out in practice and perceived by the participants (see 'PartBase' 2004). Similarly, the Commission's regular assessment exercises (usually conducted by external auditors) deal mainly with financial and managerial rather than content-related issues (e.g. Commission 2004d; Commission 1997d).

In the absence of more systematic, fieldwork-centred studies, the following two examples give a fairly good flavour of typical Comenius school partnerships. The first partnership linked a village primary school in Kinloch Rannoch in the UK to two schools in Sweden and Italy (Haigh 1998). By 1998, it had led to teacher visits and pupils' involvement in two projects. The first project was labelled 'playground games'. Each school contributed a few games typical of its respective country or region. From this sprang the production of a 'game pack' and of a video illustrating the different games. As their second project the schools produced a calendar. Pupils from each school contributed illustrations and sold copies of the calendar to their parents. They also exchanged regular newsletters, and many children found pen friends in partner schools. A second example of a typical Comenius school partnership links three junior secondary schools in Germany, Sweden and Finland (Karolina-Burger-Realschule 2004). In preparatory meetings, teachers agreed to start a project labelled 'Life and work by the river or by the sea – geographical, historical and economical aspects'. Pupils prepared posters in German and English, a joint exhibition and an Internet site and some pupils visited each other's schools.

By and large, Comenius-sponsored school partnerships resonate well with the (in relation to the Union's population size extremely few) pupils and teachers that have participated in them. Moreover, in contrast to some other EU-sponsored educational and cultural initiatives – Europa TV and the would-be European history textbook being prime examples – what media coverage it has attracted has been largely favourable. At the same time, except for the new member states from Central and Eastern Europe and some candidate countries, applications for Comenius funding have started to level off somewhat in recent years. In part this may be due to an increase in teacher workloads in many member states and, linked to this, to increasingly crowded, 'three-Rs'-dominated and centrally steered national curricula. This leaves less room for optional add-ons such as Comenius (Commission 2004d). In any event, there is little evidence that Comenius has led to a significant increase in the transmission of positive representations of the European Union or of particular EU-related policies or institutions. Indeed, themes relating to the EU or even only to European integration broadly defined are largely absent from the list of the most popular projects around which Comenius school partnerships revolve (see 'PartBase' 2004). And given that the selection of partnerships (and, by extension, of projects) is in the hands of the national Socrates agencies rather than the Commission, the latter has no means of changing this.

Commission officials view this with mixed feelings. On the one hand, they would welcome an increase in EU-related Comenius projects. On the other hand, still smarting from the debacle of the would-be European history textbook and the widespread hostility to its 'information and communication' material for school children (further discussed below), they want to avoid Comenius being seen as an outlet for 'EU propaganda'. The Commission's ability to include Comenius into the Socrates programme was due in part to it revolving around exchanges, language learning and the promotion of transnational 'cultural literacy' rather than the Europeanisation of school curricula. Any move away from this might well place the entire programme at risk (interview European Commission, September 2000).

Finally, more or less closely tied in with Comenius are a range of educational initiatives that emerged from within the member states themselves from the mid-1990s, often devised and initiated by semi or non-governmental bodies such as teacher associations, local school boards and even individual schools or teachers. Some benefit from material or logistical support from non-EU organisations such as the Council of Europe and the European Cultural Foundation (Council of Europe 2003; Bell 1995; Brock and Tulasiewicz 1994; Hopkins, Howarth and Le Métais 1994) while others are spin-offs from various Comenius-sponsored 'networks' and collaboration programmes involving teachers and educational administrators. Examples include the formation of 'European clubs' in some schools, their participation in the annual 'European schools day competition' as well as Council of Europe-sponsored brochures and events on subjects such as racism, multiculturalism, general democratic values and the environment. Yet the presence and visibility of such initiatives varies greatly from one member state to the next, with some smaller ones (such as Ireland and Portugal) but also to some extent Germany and some new member states from Central Europe in the lead. Moreover, like Comenius-sponsored school partnerships many of these initiatives do not centre on the European Union, but instead on language learning or on broader social issues that are worthy but largely 'European dimension'-free.

Other post-Maastricht initiatives

Negotiated parallel to Socrates was the new version of the Youth for Europe programme, aimed at what in Union jargon are now referred to as 'young people in non-formal learning contexts'. It was originally passed in 1995 with Article 126 of the Maastricht Treaty as its legal basis, a funding of 126 million ECU and implementation provisions similar to those of Socrates (EP and Council 1995). In 2000 it received the less 'propagandist' title 'Youth' and was renewed for a period of seven years with a total funding of 520 million euro (EP and Council 2000b).

Youth's centrepiece has remained the funding of different kinds of transnational youth exchanges, similar to those supported by the original Youth for Europe programme. In addition, it now includes a 'European voluntary service programme for young people' (EVS), which supports volunteers working in other member states or in selected third countries for up to one year.[10] A further part of the Youth programme is 'Eurodesk', officially defined as a 'European network' that disseminates information about the EU notably through a telephone answering service and an extensive Internet presence. Eurodesk's principal task is to provide information 'relevant to the education, training and youth fields, and the involvement of young people in European activities'. In addition, the Commission has sought to put Eurodesk at the service of its broader 'youth information' and PR campaigns. Sometimes in collaboration with pro-EU youth organisations inside the member states, it disseminates more general information and PR material on Union policies and institutions.

Closer to school teaching is the Union's involvement with educational software and, more generally, with information technology in schools. The 'Delors White Paper' on 'Competitiveness, growth and employment' (Commission 1993b) already featured stark warnings that Europe had fallen behind the United States and Japan in this area, and a specially appointed 'task force on educational multi-media software' reiterated them (Commission 1996b). Reminiscent of the Commission's take on the audiovisual sector, the taskforce blamed US dominance in this field on Europe's linguistic and cultural fragmentation, which results in low economies of scale for European producers. To remedy this, it called for EU initiatives to support the development and distribution of European educational software, the training of teachers and pupils in its use and the universal connection of schools to the Internet. Echoing the 'multiple-use' character of its audiovisual rhetoric, the Commission suggested that involving the EU in educational technology would yield economic benefits and defend Europe against technological domination by outsiders, as well as 'bring different cultures together, strengthen European identity and reinforce European integration'. The same theme reverberates throughout the Commission's various follow-up reports on the implementation of the 'Education & Training 2010' strategy. It features a range of (non-binding) educational targets based on the pledge by the Lisbon European Council in 2000 to turn Europe into the world's leading 'knowledge economy' – a term, incidentally, that has become as ubiquitous in Union rhetoric as it has remained ill-defined (e.g. Commission 2002a).

From the second part of the 1990s, the Commission and the EP managed to push through a range of concrete initiatives to support information technology in schools. Some of these were incorporated into the Socrates and Leonardo da Vinci programmes, while others formed part of broader technology initiatives such as ESPRIT and its successors. The most visible programme in this domain is the annual 'Netdays Europe'. Apart from general awareness-raising, it seeks to encourage the design of educational projects using the Internet. By 2002, 471 projects were awarded the Netdays Europe label of which 45 per cent were submitted by schools (see Commission 2004e; Netdays 2002: Summary of Results). Related to this, the Commission has set up the 'European schoolnet', which it uses among other things as a vehicle for its school-centred public relations campaigns further discussed below. Lastly, it sponsors a growing number of other websites such as 'Myeurope' and the 'European youth portal'.

Commission officials depict the Netdays and related initiatives as a success. Given the obvious technological, economic, and transnational dimension of the Internet, the Union's involvement in this area was comparatively easy to justify and offered a plausible 'value added'. By the mid-1990s, many member state governments – especially in southern Europe – had come to see information technology as an area in which they were seriously lagging behind, and the Commission's various educational technology initiatives skilfully played to such anxieties (interview European Commission, September 2000).

At the same time, these various educational technology initiatives, too, are not likely to have increased pupils' exposure to EU-related themes and symbols in any significant way. The Internet itself is hardly a specifically European medium, and the Commission's numerous reports and policy statements do surprisingly little to clarify what, precisely, the 'high-quality digital educational content' (Commission 2002a) it wants to foster might consist of. Accordingly, Netdays' aims have remained vaguely defined, revolving around 'dialogue', 'cultural knowledge', 'quality educational content', 'appreciation of cultural diversity' 'technological competence' and so on, and many Netdays projects focus on themes such as language learning, poetry and the performing arts. Such coyness is no accident. As with Comenius, Commission officials fear that too aggressive an attempt to graft 'European content' onto its educational technology initiatives could trigger backlashes inside the member states and thereby place these initiatives at risk.

On balance, the EU's educational technology initiatives are mainly about helping to build an educational communications infrastructure as opposed to Europeanising educational content. As regards their value as an outlet for political symbolism as defined in Chapters 1 and 2 this is obviously a major limitation. Moreover, at least as far as the Internet is concerned it might also limit their potential for further growth. Some member states have connected almost all their schools to the Internet and the latter has become so popular that initiatives to train teachers – let alone students – in how to use it are increasingly redundant.

Commission PR in schools

Most EU educational initiatives have thus left little room for the 'European dimension' in school curricula. Moreover, as is shown below, if only for pragmatic reasons the Commission itself became increasingly reluctant to press for it overtly. Even so, as in cultural policy this does not mean that the Commission has shed all ambitions to use schools as instruments to strengthen popular support for European integration. Instead, in some measure educational policy, too, has become 'PR-ised', with the Commission producing a barrage of promotional material aimed at children and trying to convince schools and teachers to integrate such material into the curriculum. Many of these initiatives have benefited from close collaboration between the Commission's education officials and its 'information and communication' department as discussed in Chapter 3.

Like its PR campaigns aimed at a general public, the Commission's promotional drive in schools received a critical boost with the introduction of the single currency. In May 1997, the Commission appointed a group of external advisors from the education and PR fields to 'ponder the relevance of conducting a campaign [for the euro] via the school system, the organisational aspects of this, its timing and, lastly, the possible role of the Commission in supporting and supplementing action taken by the Member States' (Commission 1998b; also Commission 1998c; Commission 1998d). The expert group released its report in January 1998 (Commission 1998b). It called for a publicity drive on behalf of the euro among young people, not only because they 'have substantial potential for assimilation' but also due to their 'obvious capability for conveying information to their parents and grand-parents'. Moreover, according to the report 'school information programmes on the euro can provide an excellent opportunity to familiarise pupils with the other peoples of Europe and their history. A platform of knowledge of this kind is a step in the direction of European citizenship, a step school pupils could take in conjunction with the introduction of the single currency'. In this sense, the euro should not be handled 'as simply yet another piece of information, but as the core of an important message'.

When it came to concrete policy recommendations the expert group report was surprisingly modest, however. It cautioned that too aggressive a euro promotion campaign could trigger backlashes inside the member states and create an impression that '"Brussels" [is] looking out for propagandists at school'. To avoid this, a school-centred euro information campaign would have to be implemented by national educational authorities in the first instance with the Commission limiting itself to some 'added value' measures such as the exchange of experience and the production information literature.

Accordingly, most of the Commission's attempts to promote the euro in schools have centred on the production of promotional material, often in close cooperation with the PRINCE programme discussed in Chapter 3.

'Information and communication' output produced for school children included numerous brochures, posters, sketches of euro notes and coins, 'umbrella-type display stands', and a selection of videos. These bore titles such as 'A single currency for Europe', 'The European ABC: the single currency', 'From the electrum to the euro', The euro – it's child's play', and 'The euro isn't witchcraft; this way to the currency' (Commission 1998b). In addition, the Commission produced material, both in print and on the Internet, to inform teachers whose alleged ignorance on the subject it did not cease to bemoan, about the euro.

Parallel to distributing material on the single currency the Commission sought to take advantage of the momentum created by the euro promotion campaign by intensifying its more general drive to promote the EU in schools. This led to numerous 'overview of the EU and European integration'-type booklets such as a 'passport-sized mini-brochure' aimed at children between five and ten, and, most famously, several hundred thousand copies of a comic booklet titled *The Raspberry Ice Cream War: A Comic for Young People on a Peaceful Europe without Frontiers* (Commission 1998e). It

> tells the story of Christine (who has 'already made friends all over Europe'), Max (who wears a baseball cap with the EU flag) and Paul (who wants to study languages and travel to as many countries as possible – first of all, of course, right across Europe). Our three young heroes are busy surfing the Internet one day when they get sucked into the computer and dumped in a land of borders, passports and levies. ... Europe in the dark ages. Frontiers and barriers everywhere and people fighting wars for the stupidest reasons ... The kids are arrested for refusing to pay a border levy and are hauled before the king – who suspects them of trying to steal the recipe for raspberry ice cream. Our enlightened trio explain what life is like in the EU paradise they hail from. 'There are no borders anymore and the governments put their heads together to decide what's best for everyone ... you can go anywhere you want, work, study, buy things, go on holiday', Christine helpfully explains. (Harding 2003: 2)

The Commission also put material of this kind on its 'European schoolnet' as well as on sister sites such as 'Myeurope', a self-styled 'unique community of teachers who work for the development and the enhancement of our common European identity'. In addition, the Commission distributes its information output through its representations in the member states, through 'European resource centres for schools and colleges' (which have steadily proliferated in recent years), and sometimes through the local Socrates implementation agencies. In line with the general tendency discussed in Chapter 3, the Commission has increasingly sought to target such promotional output according to age, educational level and, above all, member state.

All this raises the question of whether schools and teachers actually use such Union-produced material in their daily teaching, whether this has led to an increase in teaching time devoted to the EU, and ultimately of course whether it has shaped pupils' attitudes towards European integration. These questions are hard to answer. As discussed, the Commission itself has become reluctant to conduct systematic impact studies of its PR initiatives. All the same, several factors are bound to mitigate the use and effectiveness of Union PR in schools. First, while the Commission's promotional campaigns aimed at a general public as discussed in Chapter 3 allow it to appeal directly to national audiences by bypassing national governments, media, political parties and other opinion formers, the use of Union-produced material in schools inevitably requires the *cooperation* of the relevant authorities inside the member states: national or regional education ministries, local educational authorities, school boards, head teachers and not least individual classroom teachers. Yet especially where school curricula are under relatively tight central control, even those schools and teachers that would otherwise be willing to do so have little leeway to deviate from the officially prescribed curriculum so as to provide their pupils with a greater dose of European content.

Add to this that the Commission's promotional material for children faces strong hostility in some member states. Not surprisingly, the UK again took the lead in this, causing the Commission to withdraw 75,000 English-language copies of its *Raspberry Ice Cream War* comic (Bamber 1998), reputedly moving most of them into the basement of the Commission Representation in Dublin.[11] This came after a barrage of criticism from the conservative press and (mainly) Conservative politicians, some of whom had been inspired by the Commission comic to veritable tirades. Conservative MP Teresa Gorman, for instance, likened the comic to 'extreme propaganda aimed at children ... reminiscent of the one-sided stuff put out by the Third Reich' (quoted in Bamber 1998). Parts of the national press in the UK soon joined in such criticism, and the *Raspberry Ice Cream War* provoked angry questions in the House of Commons (*UK Parliament Hansard* 11 Nov. 1999, pt. 6; *UK Parliament Hansard* 28 Oct. 1998, pt. 4). In the end, even the Labour government felt compelled to denounce the comic as 'undoubtedly an ill-judged and, in part, factually inaccurate publication' (quoted in Harding 2003: 2).

In other member states such opposition is generally less animated. But along with criticism of the Commission's general PR activities discussed in Chapter 3 it has grown in recent years and made the Commission tread more carefully: much of its more recent material for schools deals with worthy but largely 'European dimension'-less issues, ranging from drugs and racism to environmental protection and gender equality.

In fact, just as in culture and the audiovisual sector the Commission has increasingly come to respect the limits imposed on its attempts to use education as a European consciousness-raising tool. On the one hand, its education officials have continued to release a steady stream of ambitiously titled position papers and Green Papers, reports, feasibility studies, working group documents, draft 'action initiatives' and the like: a communication on

'Learning in the information society' (Commission 1996c); a White Paper entitled 'Teaching and learning, towards the learning society' (Commission 1995e); a Green Paper on 'Education – training – research: The obstacles to transnational mobility' (Commission 1996d); a report titled 'Towards a Europe of knowledge' (Commission 1997e); and numerous documents on the implementation of the 'Education & Training 2010' strategy, which revolves around a range of (aspirational) educational targets intended to turn the EU into the 'most competitive and dynamic knowledge-based economy in the world' (Commission 2003e, 2002a).

Yet, on the other hand, most of these reports and initiatives led to little tangible action, other than of a kind which itself was largely symbolic and centred on awareness raising and the production of still more studies, reports and expert meetings. An example was the Union-sponsored 'European year of lifelong learning' held in 1996. According to one official, it was designed not only to popularise the issue of lifelong learning itself but also to create 'positive momentum' for the EU's educational involvement more generally (interview European Commission, September 2000). Apart from sparking a further cascade of reports and expert meetings, the 'year of lifelong learning' included some eye-catching initiatives, such as 'pub-based learning' in West Yorkshire. Some of these managed to attract a fair amount of media attention but had little lasting impact overall. Much the same applied to the Union-sponsored 'European year of languages' in 2001 (EP and Council 2000c) which led to a host of conferences and awareness-raising measures but in the end did little to enhance the Union's clout in 'general' education.

In fact, save for a few exceptions (e.g. Commission 1997e) the Commission's educational rhetoric has increasingly abandoned the European identity theme altogether. In its place have come frequent allusions to what the Commission refers to more or less interchangeably as 'active citizenship', 'modern citizenship', or 'active (or modern) citizenship in the Union'. 'Learning for active citizenship', in the Commission's rendering, 'can be described as a process of critical accompaniment in which individuals are offered structured opportunities – at cognitive, affective and pragmatic levels – to gain and renew the skills of self-directed participation and to experience the negotiation of social purpose and meaning' (Commission 1998f; also Commission 2003e, 2002a). Yet once the Commission's 'active citizenship' rhetoric is stripped of its accompanying jargon one is left with a rather more prosaic concept. Teaching 'active citizenship' then reveals itself as little more than a strategy to encourage labour mobility; to, as the Commission puts it in the same working document, give pupils 'access to the skills and competencies that young people will need for effective economic participation under conditions of technological modernisation, economic globalisation, and, very concretely, transnational European labour markets'. The engendering of popular identifications with the EU and its policies is not part of the Commission's 'learning for active citizenship' definition.

Different Commission officials account for this shift in different ways. Some highlight the need for pragmatism and rhetorical caution – all the more pressing once the Blair government in Britain had turned out to be almost as hostile to much of the EU's involvement in 'general' education as its Conservative predecessors, and once the member states had implicitly agreed not to use qualified majority voting in 'general' education even though the Maastricht Treaty provides for it. The Commission's more docile approach in recent years was further boosted once Edith Cresson had resigned over corruption allegations in 1999 and was replaced by the more consensus-oriented Viviane Reding. On a different note, one Commission official points to the 'rationalist wave' that has swept through the Commission, causing it to redirect its policy agenda towards ever more narrowly defined economic ends. Yet another colleague points to generational turnover within the Commission's education department. Most officials associated with the Janne and Dahrendorf agenda have retired from the Commission and with them went out much of the energy and idealism they had brought to the task. Much – though not all – of the more recent intake of education officials are sceptical of what one of them dismisses as the 'flag and anthem approach' to European identity promotion in schools (interviews European Commission, September 2000).

This group of Commission officials can be subdivided into two camps. Some see the Commission above all as a champion of various progressive educational causes and their implantation in national educational practice – ranging from multiculturalism to non-traditional gender conceptions, gay rights and the 'mainstreaming' of children with learning difficulties and physical disabilities. Others, by contrast, argue that attempts to instrumentalise education for *any kind* of broader social, cultural, or identity-related objective should best be left to the member states. They believe that the Union should limit its educational ambitions to the economic and technology-related areas that remain closest to its core mandate and where EU involvement has consistently proven much more acceptable to the member states. In this rendering, education may still be instrumentalised to strengthen support for European integration, but the responsibility for this should lie with national governments rather than with the Union itself.

The 'European dimension' in educational practice

So far this chapter has focused more on policy formation and formulation than on policy implementation; it has traced the fate of the 'European dimension' in schools by, in the first instance, exploring the content of the Union's various educational initiatives. In so far as it has focused on how these initiatives relate to actual educational practice, this was mainly with regard to the use of Union-produced material in schools and the impact of Comenius school partnerships. Yet initiatives of this latter type could of course never hope to do more than to provide relatively marginal European 'add-ons' to regular, nationally defined curricular content. The following question thus remains: to what extent have regular national school curricula and teaching practices come to include EU-related elements and what do these elements consist of? This final section of the chapter seeks to shed some light on this and, in particular, on whether the 1988 'Resolution of the Council and the ministers of education meeting within the Council on the European dimension in education' (which has thus far remained the last initiative of its kind) has had a tangible impact on educational practice inside the member states.

Clear data is hard to come by. Stimulated by the 1988 resolution (and a stream of research funding that followed in its wake) the few existing studies on the subject are relatively dated, mostly going back to the early- to mid-1990s. Reflecting the fact that the 1988 resolution has thus far remained the last of its kind and that in the period since the 'European dimension' in school curricula has slipped on the Commission's list of educational priorities, most of these studies have not been updated since. Likewise, the Union's own educational statistics are only of limited use in this regard. 'Eurydice', the EU's main educational database, contains audited figures on almost every conceivable aspect of educational policy but not on 'European content' in school curricula. Also, the bibliography it compiled on the subject has not been updated since 1996 (Eurydice 1996).[12]

Against this backdrop, two country-by-country surveys are especially useful for our purposes because of their comparative and fieldwork-based approach and their adherence to a set of relatively coherent and consistent criteria of evaluation. The first study was commissioned by the Association for Teacher Education in Europe (ATEE) (Ryba 1992) and the second is published in a volume edited by Cremer and Schmuck (1991). Even though these studies are relatively dated (both were directly stimulated by the 1988 resolution), they nevertheless give an approximate insight into the status of the 'European dimension' in the Union's schools – a status which, for the reasons suggested below, is not likely to have changed significantly in the years since. For some countries, moreover, these surveys can be usefully complemented with more recent material with conveys a similar overall impression.

Turning to the situation in individual countries, the best range of quantitative and qualitative data on the 'European dimension' has been compiled in the Netherlands. A 1990 study of Dutch textbooks and teaching syllabuses (which focused on geography, history, economics, social studies and 'civics') is a good example. It found that in geography 48 per cent of all textbooks and 83 per cent of syllabuses dealt with questions pertaining in one way or another to the European Community. Yet the proportion of time and space devoted to the Community was a mere 3.9 per cent in textbooks and 3.3 per cent in syllabuses. In social studies, 45 per cent of Dutch textbooks dealt with the EC as did 50 per cent of syllabuses, but the proportion of time and space devoted to the Community was a tiny 1.9 per cent in both textbooks and syllabuses. The picture was similar in the subject of history. While 59 per cent of all textbooks and 80 per cent of syllabuses dealt with EC-related issues, the space and time devoted to them was only 2.6 per cent in textbooks and 2.5 per cent in syllabuses (Plas 1991: 284). The ATEE study came to similar conclusions regarding the presence of EU-related material in Dutch textbooks and further criticised its poor presentation and substandard didactic quality (p. 21).

The situation was similar in the Irish Republic. The contribution on Ireland in the Cremer and Schmuck survey found little evidence of there being 'in the curriculum at the primary or secondary levels a particular interest in EC-related themes' (Doran 1991: 227, my translation[13]). Overall, it concluded that Ireland's membership of the European Community did not significantly enhance its treatment in Irish school curricula. The ATEE study came to similar findings: It detected elements pertaining to the EC and Europe throughout Irish textbooks and syllabuses, yet found that the emphasis was typically on '"foreign" languages and on "other" countries [...i.e. on] "them and us rather than us"' (p. 17). Similarly, 'the history of Europe is not painted or portrayed as "our history" but rather as the history of "other countries"' (p. 17).

This 'us and them' matrix prevailed in Spanish schools as well. Ninety per cent of Spanish history and social science syllabuses mention 'Europe'. 'However, many of the themes that deal with Europe do not really have a European orientation. Most are influenced by the involvement of Spain in European history, especially from the sixteenth to the eighteenth century, and often amount to pure descriptions of historical facts. Though these themes provide a wealth of information about Europe, much remains to be done to get from this nationalistic approach to a European one' (Palacio-Villa 1991: 313, my translation[14]).

In France, too, the status of the 'European dimension' in schools is generally precarious. The contribution in the Cremer and Schmuck survey notes the continued strength of specifically national elements in the French '*éducation civique*' which is explicitly aimed at engendering 'republican loyalties' (Hickel 1991). When it comes to 'European content' in French curricula, however, no comparable ambition exists. What traces there are of it are confined to history and geography lessons. The ATEE report confirms this impression. It senses in France a 'brick wall of fundamental scepticism' towards the inclusion of a 'European dimension' in school curricula and notes that 'the study of foreign languages, mother tongue and art hardly take account of the European dimension' (p. 18). The same applied to teachers training (p. 19).

The picture worsens when one turns to the UK. In the 1970s, an attempt to increase the presence of 'Europe' in British education led to the introduction of 'European studies' as a distinct subject in some schools

(Blackledge 1991). But 'European studies' generally enjoyed a low academic status and quickly became seen as an easy alternative to 'serious' language learning (Goodson 1995, Chapter 4). The ATEE report confirms this as it cites 'evidence for the very low status of European studies [... which are] generally pursued only by the less able students' (p. 20). When the first National Curriculum came into force in England in 1988 under the Thatcher government, the 'European dimension' was largely excluded. And the revised National Curriculum of 1995 'had virtually eliminated the European dimension' (Morrell 1996: 12) even in its most prosaic and factual aspects, with the term 'European Union' excluded from all curricular subjects other than geography. Consequently, in history 'the study unit entitled "The Twentieth Century World" does not include the establishment of the European Community or Union' (Morrell 1996: 9). But even in geography 'the Union is not identified in any of the three maps provided – of the UK, Europe and the World' (Morrell 1996: 13). The ATEE study concurs, noting that in Britain 'most students ... receive no specific teaching about Europe' (p. 20).

In Danish schools the 'European dimension' has remained equally scarce. The ATEE study concludes that on the available evidence 'it will take considerable time before the European dimension and European awareness ... become part of the Danish education system' (p. 18). The contribution on Denmark in the Cremer and Schmuck survey found that what little mentioning there is of the Community in Danish schools is often embedded in a 'discussion of contemporary problems' framework. There, the Community tends to surface in relation to unflattering topics such as unemployment and the fisheries crisis. Meanwhile, 'civics' lessons in Denmark deal overwhelmingly with Danish society, institutions and political processes while 'only a very small proportion of teachers is of the opinion that school teaching should be used to instill in pupils positive attitudes towards European integration' (Kledal and Lauridsen 1991: 100, my translation[15]). Overall, the study concludes that in Denmark it is 'politically still unthinkable to introduce the fostering of a European consciousness as an educational objective' (Kledal and Lauridsen 1991: 98, my translation[16]).

In Germany, the responsibility for curricular content rests largely with the Länder. Even though on average they have gone further than the educational authorities in most other member states, the presence of the 'European Dimension' in German school curricula is still very limited. A content analysis of German 'political studies' (*Politikunterricht*) curricula found that while all but one Land included in it some elements pertaining to European integration, the Community received a low priority compared to other topics. 'The survey shows clearly that European themes are emphasised in only a few school curricula. In most curricula, European themes are "taken care of" under broader subject headings (e.g. "international relations"). Compared to other topics dealt with in political studies Europe is clearly given less weight' (Renner and Sander 1991: 129, my translation[17]). Similarly, 'Europe' takes up an average of only three percent of German political studies textbooks and many treat European integration from a purely economic angle (Renner and Sander 1991: 133).

As in many other member states, the Greek education system is heavily and explicitly instrumentalised as a national consciousness-raising tool. According to the 1985 education law, pupils are to be turned into 'free, responsible democratic citizens, [willing] to defend national independence, the country's territorial integrity and democracy, imbued with love towards human beings, life and nature, and faithfully committed to the fatherland and to the true Christian Orthodox tradition' (quoted in Gikopoulos and Kakavoulis 1991: 179–180, my translation[18]). When it comes to the EU, no comparable ambition exists. Accordingly, 'the examination of the Greek curriculum and [teaching] materials showed that only two subjects in the sixth grade of the primary school in Greece have devoted some time for [sic] teaching about the European Community. These subjects are history and social and political education. All other textbooks present the concept of Europe via war events, conflicts, aggression, as well as by geophysical and geopolitical aspects' (Flouris 1995: 117). Further, '[a] more in-depth content analysis of both subjects revealed that in history, approximately 12 minutes of instructional time has been allocated for teaching about the EEC. The situation is worse in social and political education, since only four lines constitute the total amount of instructional time that has been allocated. No other learning activities could be found in the written curriculum and materials that focus on the European Community' (Flouris 1995: 117–118). In sum, 'the Greek elementary school curriculum and materials during all six years of attendance do not reflect any of the aspects of the European Dimension as stated in the Resolution of the Council and the Ministers of Education of the EU countries [of 1988]. The concepts of European identity and citizenship as proposed by the Resolution do not exist in Greece's curriculum and textbooks' (Flouris 1995: 118).

These findings echo those for most other member states and they broadly converge on three basic observations. First, in all cases the share of curricular content devoted in one way or another to 'Europe', the European Union or even only to other member states is small, if one leaves aside foreign language teaching. Second, to the extent that 'European content' is detectable in national school curricula, it tends to be (a) not primarily concerned with the European Union or European integration and, (b), about 'our country in relation to other countries in Europe' rather than about 'we together with other countries/peoples as part of Europe/as Europeans'. This, finally, places the 'European dimension' in stark contrast to the continued strong presence of specifically national content in the school curricula of most member states, which are often explicitly instrumentalised as vehicles for the transmission of national myths and symbols.

To such findings one could object that most of the research on which they

are based is by now somewhat dated, and that in the meantime the 1988 resolution on the 'European dimension' together with new programmes such as
Comenius and the Commission's various school-centred PR initiatives might
have had more impact. Nonetheless, to the extent that such gains occurred
they are bound to have been relatively marginal. In the first place, the few
somewhat more recent studies that *are* available for some countries suggest
no significant progress.[19] Second, as far as Comenius is concerned the number
of pupils affected by it is tiny in relation to the Union's size. Third, Comenius
(as well as the Commission's PR campaigns) seeks to complement rather than
replace regular national curricula and thus can hope to account for no more
than a small share of overall teaching time and curricular content. Finally, as
shown, most Comenius partnerships do not revolve around EU-related
themes in the first place, and even Commission-produced literature for
schools increasingly deals with issues other than EU structures and institutions. Especially if compared to the fervour with which most member states
continue to design their 'civics', history, and geography curricula to advance
their specifically national socialisation agendas, the 'European dimension' is
still a negligible entity in school curricula throughout the Union.

All this does not exclude the possibility that events could take a sudden turn
and make the 'European dimension' in schools a reality at last. But judged by the
Union's educational record in recent years this seems unlikely. The
Commission's actions since Maastricht suggest that it has understood the 'while
fully respecting the responsibility of the Member States for the content of teaching' clause in the Maastricht Treaty as a signal by the member states that
curricular content is not a part of educational policy in which they want the
Union to be involved, however indirectly. Increasingly, moreover, the
Commission appears willing to abide by this wish, not least so as not to risk the
development of its other educational programmes. In light of this, the
'European dimension' in schools is not a project that is in the process of building up momentum. On the contrary, like parallel attempts to 'denationalise' the
audiovisual sector, efforts to involve the European Union in the design of
national school curricula – or even only to include elements pertaining to the
EU therein – may well prove to have been a largely inconsequential episode that
started in the mid-1970s and came to an end some two decades later.

Notes

1 They had met under this formula since 1971. For a discussion of the extremely
  complex (and never entirely clarified) legal implications of the 'mixed' formula in
  education see Rübsamen (1978).
2 Erasmus further benefited from the fact that universities have always had a much
  stronger international outlook than elementary and secondary education and, at any
  rate, more autonomy from direct state control in most member states. This made a
  Community involvement in higher education generally less sensitive (Hackl 2001).

3 Sometimes other bodies such as private foundations or German regional govern-ments also supported such conferences. For conference reports see Janssen (1993). See also Janssen (1990). One more tangible 'European-dimension' related measure at the time was the European Parliament's decision to unilaterally fund the distribution of Community maps to schools (*Social Europe* 1989 [Supplement No. 8]: 46; *Social Europe* 1987 [Supplement No. 3]: 16).

4 I was unable to find out at precisely what stage the Commission pulled out of the European history project. According to one report, it still subsidised 'first meetings' of the panel of twelve historians that compiled the subsequent textbook version of the history project (Nundy 1992: 15).

5 Though the German edition is still labelled as a 'historical work for schools to be used in the first and second years of secondary school'.

6 Subsequently, culture was added to DG XXII's brief.

7 An example was an influential report by the University-Industry Forum, a partner-ship between the European Round Table of Industrialists and the European Council of Rectors. Released in 1992, it warned that the underdevelopment of the adult educa-tion sector in many member states carried serious economic risks and called for a Europe-wide programme for 'lifelong learning' to remedy the situation (Otala 1992; also Field 1998: 54). In preparing Socrates the Commission went to great lengths to consult various NGOs interested in education and it encouraged them to form Europe-wide umbrella organisations or 'networks'. Many have done so in recent years, with the larger ones establishing representations in Brussels. One Commission official estimates that by the end of the 1990s the Commission's education depart-ment was in regular contact with over 300 such groups (interview European Commission, September 2000).

8 This second figure pertains to the preceding year.

9 In 2003, the Commission proposed to subsume the Jean Monnet programme into a new 'Community action programme to promote bodies active at European level and support specific activities in the field of education and training', together with exist-ing subsidies for other higher education bodies such as the European University Institute in Florence and the College of Europe in Bruges (Commission 2003f).

10 EVS started in 1998 with a budget of 47.5 million ECU for the first two years. It reached back to an EP resolution (EP 1995). A Commission-initiated pilot pro-gramme began in 1996 with an action programme approved in 1998.

11 Many thanks to Daniel Dunne for this information.

12 What little information it contains on that subject is limited to policy statements or declarations of intent provided by the national ministries of education. Yet for the most part these lack specificity. For instance, while most national educational author-ities now indicate that the founding of the EU forms part of the history curriculum, they rarely specify the actual share of teaching time and reading material devoted to the EU in relation to other items such as national or world history. What is more, as the Commission's own surveys ascertained as far back as the 1970s, such declarations are often aspirational in nature and at odds with actual educational practice (Commission 1978).

13 'Es gibt wenig augenscheinliche Beweise dafür, daß es im Lehrplan sowohl der Primar- als auch der Sekundarebene ein besonderes Interesse an EG-Themen gibt ...'

14 'Allerdings sind viele dieser Themen, die Europa behandeln, nicht wirklich europäisch ausgerichtet. Die meisten von ihnen werden berührt von der Verwicklung Spaniens in die europäische Geschichte, insbesondere vom 16. bis zum 18. Jahrhundert, und sind oft reine Beschreibungen historischer Tatsachen. Diese

Themen vermitteln zwar eine Fülle von Informationen über Europa, aber es bleibt noch viel zu tun, um von diesem nationalistischen Ansatz zu einem europäischen zu gelangen.'

15 'Nur ein sehr geringer Teil der Lehrer ist der Meinung, daß den Schülern eine positive Einstellung zur europäischen Integration im Rahmen des Unterrichts vermittelt werden sollte.'

16 'politisch noch undenkbar, ein europäisches Bewußtsein als Erziehungsziel einzuführen'.

17 'Die Übersicht macht deutlich, daß europäischen Themen nur in einzelnen Lehrplänen eine herausgehobene Bedeutung beigemessen wird. In der Mehrzahl der Pläne werden europäische Themen im Rahmen eines übergeordneten Themas (z. B. "Internationale Beziehungen") "mitbehandelt". Im Vergleich zu anderen Themen des Politikunterrichts hat Europa ein deutlich geringeres Gewicht.'

18 'freie, verantwortliche, demokratische Bürger zu werden, die nationale Unabhänigkeit, die territoriale Integrität des Landes und die Demokratie zu verteidigen, beseelt zu sein von der Liebe zum Menschen, zum Leben und zur Natur und in Treue zum Vaterland und zur wahren orthodoxen Christlichen Tradition zu stehen'.

19 For instance the updated study by Morrell (1996) on the UK and the one by Flouris (1995) on Greece.

6
Political symbolism and the future of European integration

Some fifty years after its founding the Union's record in culture, the audiovisual sector and education remained mixed. It had become involved in some economically oriented areas such as the free movement of cultural 'goods and services' and vocational training. Moreover, it had initiated some more proactive exchange and circulation-enhancing programmes, above all Youth, Socrates, MEDIA and Culture 2000. Finally, from the 1990s onwards it pursued a myriad of PR-style measures, mostly aimed at shoring up public support for particular EU policies such as enlargement and the single currency. Yet when it came to instrumentalising culture and education to increase the Union's symbolic presence in the everyday lives of its citizens, far less had been achieved. From EU-sponsored Europe Day celebrations to the 'European dimension' in schools, most proposals in this area stumbled over resistance mounted by shifting configurations of national governments. Others were accepted by the member states in the form of vague declarations of intent but never implemented. Indeed, resistance to these proposals became so strong that the Commission itself abandoned many of them.

Two major questions arise from this. First, why were the European Commission and Parliament so unsuccessful in involving the Union in the more symbolically charged parts of culture, audiovisual policy and education – a failure that on the face of it seems all the more paradoxical as it coincided with important advances in economic and to some extent also political integration? Second, what are the potential consequences of this for legitimacy, identity, and public consent in the European Union?

Addressing the first question it is useful to return briefly to the 'spillover versus countervailing pressures' framework outlined in Chapter 2. As was suggested, in this rendering three types of policy spillover have the potential to further the Union's position in a given policy area: functional, political and cultivated.

Functional spillover, to begin with, did play some role in advancing the Union's clout in some more economically charged parts of culture, audiovisual policy and education. For instance, many initiatives for language learning, mutual diploma recognition and educational mobility were launched on the coattails of the Single Market programme in the late 1980s and early 1990s. Though such policies were hardly indispensable for the successful implementation of the Single Market, they nonetheless represented a logical complement to and extension of economic integration and could be justified in these terms. By contrast, proposals ranging from Union-sponsored Europe Day celebrations to the 'correction' of history textbooks had little direct bearing on economic and Single Market-related issues, and except for some initiatives in the audiovisual sector the Commission did not even try to justify them on economic grounds.

All the same, as discussed in Chapter 2 'functional pressures' may also result from public opinion-related as opposed to just economic developments. Other things being equal, as the Union's perceived salience and visibility increases so does the need for corresponding 'legitimacy transfers' to maintain popular support, with cultural, audiovisual and educational policy representing a potential tool to help achieve this. The Commission and the EP, the Tindemans Report and the Janne and Adonnino committees predicated their proposals on precisely this logic. When integration was stagnating, they portrayed cultural and educational measures as necessary to reinvigorate it; when integration was progressing, they claimed that such measures would help sustain it. Yet in the end these arguments, too, carried little weight. Throughout much of the 1970s and 1980s the Union's popular standing was in fact relatively solid, thus depriving the Commission's 'crisis talk' of credibility. Similarly, in the 1970s claims that the Community could be helped out of its stagnation by shoring up popular enthusiasm for it did little to sway national governments which were chiefly responsible for this stagnation in the first place.

In the 1990s all this changed, as the Maastricht ratification crisis brought the long-lasting permissive consensus for integration to an (at least temporary) end. But at this stage the Union faced a new dilemma. For as popular scepticism of the Union grew so did fears that it was braced to become culturally more intrusive and erode national identities. In conjunction with opinion surveys which suggested that an EU involvement in culture, audiovisual policy and education was extremely unpopular, this meant that the Commission found it difficult to justify its ambitions in these areas on the grounds that they would improve the EU's popular standing. At the most, the perceived need to shore up popular support for the EU and particular EU policies (above all the single currency) fuelled the growth of the Commission's PR budget at the time.

Turning to political spillover, it, too, played only a limited role overall. To the extent that interest group pressure did enter the equation it was again chiefly in the more economically charged parts of culture and education, such as language learning, vocational training and some audiovisual support and liberalisation initiatives. This is not surprising, given that the most influential interest groups at the national and European levels alike pursue broadly defined economic agendas. By contrast, using culture and education as European identity forgers had few outspoken advocates, save for the relatively weak pro-European movements and some related organisations. In the 1990s, the Commission attempted to change this by encouraging the formation of various 'cultural networks' and educational NGOs at the European level. Yet the transnational groupings that emerged were often little more than ad hoc formations, created primarily for the purpose of obtaining EU funds and without a broader policy agenda. Similarly, the Commission's attempts to liaise with governmental and semi-governmental agencies in culture and education (such as curriculum development units within national education ministries) and/or to help them form ties with educational NGOs had little lasting impact.

Cultivated spillover, finally, seems to have played the greatest role by comparison. Commission officials at all levels remained staunchly determined to strengthen popular support for European integration through cultural, audiovisual and educational policies. Only in the late 1990s did this commitment fizzle out somewhat as a younger and more pragmatic batch of cultural and educational officials rose through the ranks and as resistance from some member states had proven impossible to overcome. Also, in trying to advance their cultural, audiovisual and educational agenda Commission officials often displayed impressive tenacity and tactical skill. They resorted to formally independent expert panels to elaborate or reinforce particular policy agendas, encouraged a generous interpretation of existing legal constraints, interpreted previous Council commitments as constituting more than the Council itself had intended and grafted proposals for symbolically charged cultural, audiovisual and educational proposals onto more economically oriented ones. The Commission also experimented with various rhetorical 'frames', ranging from the 'rediscovery of European culture' and 'public apathy threatens the Community's future' themes in the 1970s to the anti-Americanisation and 'cultural performance conditions economic performance' headings in subsequent decades. Finally, as noted the Commission liaised with and encouraged the formation of pan-European interest groups in culture, the audiovisual sector and education from which it hoped to obtain rhetorical and political support, above all through its various 'network' initiatives.

However, these cultivation attempts, too, faced important obstacles. They ranged from the seeming elusiveness of discursive 'frames' that would appeal to all member state governments to the difficulty of ensuring that the would-be lobbying groups which the Commission sought to create would develop into effective champions of its broader cultural, audiovisual and educational policy agenda. Yet the central obstacle throughout was resistance to this agenda from within the ranks of the member states and, linked to this, the very unequal distribution of powers in culture, audiovisual policy and education between the Commission and the EP on the one hand and the Union's intergovernmental elements on the other. Due to this resistance many of the Commission's efforts to 'cultivate' particular cultural and educational agendas were choked off from the outset. In other cases the Commission's 'cultivation' effect was limited to pruning initial proposals to the point where they satisfied the lowest common denominator among the member states and where they were only a pale shadow of what the Commission itself had originally sought to accomplish.

Certainly, to assert that spillover failed to operate in culture, audiovisual policy and education is another way of saying that countervailing pressures prevented it from succeeding. As suggested in Chapter 2, such pressures can emanate from 'above' (i.e. from governments and other elites) as well as from 'below' (i.e. from national mass publics), and this study suggests that both were frequently present.

Resistance from national governments, to begin with, remained strong throughout. Usually it was spearheaded by Denmark, the UK, Germany and Sweden while enjoying more or less explicit support of many other governments as well. The precise causes of this resistance varied between different countries, governments, periods and issue areas and the position of individual member state governments was often neither clear nor consistent. Even so, seen at the broadest level the tenacity and seemingly insurmountable nature of this resistance bears out a central claim of consociational and many other broadly intergovernmentalist approaches to European integration as discussed in Chapter 2: national elites refused to share their monopoly over the symbolic tools of political legitimisation and community-building because they do not see European integration as a socially, culturally and psychologically state-transcending undertaking in the first place. Then as now, such a conception is not widely shared beyond the confines of the European Parliament and the Commission. Most importantly, it is not shared by political elites in many member states which continue to bear the main responsibility for policy outcomes in the EU and which have continued to refuse the EP and the Commission's quest for a greater symbolic role.

At the same time, national governments were not the only source of opposition. Resistance also came from 'below', from within broader sections of the various national publics. The low popular appeal of Europa TV, the widespread apathy towards Union-invented rituals such as Europe Day, and the popular aversion to extending the Union's legal mandate in culture and education all were signs of this. What is more, the Union's cultural and educational initiatives found a poor reception among many national opinion formers – journalists, academics, columnists and so forth. The scorn widely heaved on the Commission-sponsored European history textbook, television channel and many of its 'information and communication' campaigns bears this out. Their critics were quick to portray such initiatives as a waste of taxpayers' money, or even as sinister and manipulative attempts to brainwash national publics in the name of 'Euro nation-building'. Some of this criticism came from the usual suspects such as the conservative press and Conservative politicians in the UK. However, some of it also came from those who were relatively benevolent towards the EU in other respects.

This resistance 'from below' could only strengthen the determination of many national governments to deny the Union a greater cultural, audiovisual and educational role. It also meant that those policies which were enacted were less likely to accomplish their objective of improving the Union's popular standing. Partially as a result of this, the dynamic familiar from domestic state- and nation-building contexts whereby 'top-down' political symbolism triggers 'bottom-up' responses which in turn makes further 'top-down' policies more viable could never take root in the EU. Generally weak spillover pressures in conjunction with strong resistance from national governments and mass publics alike account for the Union's meagre cultural, audiovisual and educational record.

None of this is likely to change significantly any time soon. In the first place, *Eurobarometer* still suggests strong public opposition to involving the Union in areas such as culture, education and the audiovisual sector. Likewise, the media in many member states are as keen as ever to denounce anything that remotely reeks of attempted 'Euro-nation-building' or 'Commission propaganda'. Most importantly, many national governments have remained staunchly opposed. Even if enlargement should eventually lead to a deepening of the Union's powers in some areas, cultural, audiovisual and educational policy will probably not be among them. Still in the early stages of consolidating their own democratic institutions and polities, the new members from Central and Eastern Europe have so far seemed no less keen on defending their symbolic prerogatives than many of their West European counterparts (see Auer 2004).

But even if the Union did manage to initiate more symbolically charged policies in culture, audiovisual policy and education these would still face formidable challenges. Above all, they would continue to have to grapple with the wider social and cultural realities in the EU as well as with the practical limits of an analogy between historical cases of state- and nation-building on the one hand and contemporary European integration on the other. For unlike the former, the EU must legitimise itself in the eyes of populations that inhabit industrialised democracies, boast high average levels of education and advertising literacy, are politically enfranchised and, for the most part, remain firmly socialised into their existing national contexts. These continue to be reproduced through by and large stable and well-functioning mechanisms inside the member states, involving not least national policies in culture and education. To further complicate matters, apart perhaps from the vaguest notions of 'Western heritage' and the like, Europeans share few meanings and reference points on which EU political symbolism could draw. The widely perceived artificiality of the 'non-national' programming formats attempted by Eurikon, Europa TV and their commercial counterparts and the low popularity of domestic audiovisual productions beyond their country of origin (both of which were not merely due to linguistic barriers) all are signs of this. The inability of the authors of the would-be European history textbook to agree on a shared version of European history illustrates much the same point.

Following the example of some culturally divided domestic systems, the Union could seek to mitigate these problems through symbolic 'targeting' – something the Commission's 'information and communication' strategists have increasingly sought to do. But to be effective even such a strategy probably must draw on some kind of underlying common psychological denominator – a shared denominator which has remained elusive among Europeans, as the fate of many cultural and educational projects suggests. It might well turn out to be still more elusive in an enlarged EU which encompasses populations long disconnected from the West European mainstream.

Again, the point here is not to argue that political legitimacy requires fully-fledged cultural homogenisation. Post-national theorists as well as empirical examples such as Switzerland convincingly show this not to be the case. What is required, by contrast, is at the very least a shared cultural baseline which allows 'thinner' (e.g. 'civic') myths and symbols to be transmitted to and 'processed' by the different national publics at which they are aimed. So far, the few more symbolically oriented cultural, audiovisual and educational measures which the Union managed to put in place failed to appeal to national publics not because their largely 'thin' and 'civic' content would have been intrinsically meaningless to them (after all, they all inhabit broadly defined liberal democracies), but because their 'denationalised' cultural packaging proved impenetrable. The European story has potential appeal, but there is no shared language in which to communicate it, both literally and metaphorically.

Cultural denominators are, of course, socially constructed and as such they are malleable. As was shown in Chapter 2, there are many examples of political elites moulding cultural patterns among their subjects and using this as a basis for their political symbolism campaigns. This ranged from a cautious 'cognitive compatibilisation' in Switzerland to full-blown cultural and linguistic homogenisation in many other countries. But here, too, the domestic analogy may be of little relevance for the Union, as its margin of manoeuvre is much narrower. The early twenty-first century liberal and culturally pluralist ethos within which the Union operates and which underpins its 'thin' and 'civic' self-understandings is incompatible with overt attempts to 'denationalise' cultural patterns and such attempts have remained unacceptable to national governments and mass publics alike. The strong resistance to plans by the Commission and the EP to influence cultural content (e.g. through their various ill-fated audiovisual coproduction and 'European content' in school curricula proposals) illustrates this well. In some ways, the very ethos on which the Union seeks to predicate itself rules out some of the means it would need to further propagate that ethos in the first place.

The road to effective political symbolism in the EU faces many additional obstacles. Of those, the EU's frequently noted lack of definitive geographical boundaries might well be among the most important. Since, as was shown, an overarching 'entity process' thrives in part on the drawing and accentuation of boundaries with outgroups, this further reduces the feasibility of such a process in the EU for the time being (Risse in press; Delanty 1995). More broadly, demarcating 'Europe' is complicated by the absence of commonly recognised cultural, geographical or historical others against which this demarcation could take place, even assuming for the moment that it would not be frustrated from the outset by the inclusivist and culturally pluralist self-understandings on which the Union seeks to predicate itself. In fact, many EU member states were *each other*'s primary 'others' during much of their history and in some instances it was not until quite recently that this legacy of fervently pursued national self-differentiation faded. Even the United States, perhaps the EU's most 'obvious' cultural and increasingly also political competitor has not amounted to a suitable 'EU-other'. The Commission's unsuccessful attempts to link its audiovisual initiatives to the cultural anti-Americanisation theme throughout the 1980s and 1990s demonstrate this.

In light of this, the most plausible and most widely recognised 'EU other' is Europe's violent past – something the Union stresses with almost ritualistic regularity, not least in its educational material for schools. Time and again, the Commission and the EP – along with many governing elites in the member states – contrast Europe's 'bloody nationalist past' with a 'peaceful European future' while depicting further integration as a safeguard against slipping back into the horrors of the past (Shore 2000; Wæver 1996). For the Union to make the past its other is probably more practicable and by most accounts also more palatable than focusing on cultural or geographical outsiders – be they Islam, Asia, third-world would-be immigrants, the United States or whatever. All the same, its long-term viability, too, is far from clear. Paradoxically, the very fact that in most readings another war in Western Europe has become almost unimaginable *regardless* of what happens to the EU makes the 'integration or war'-theme an increasingly implausible rationale for present-day European integration – even for those who afford the Union a causal role in building the West European security community over the past half century in the first place. In this regard the Union may well have become a victim of its own success.

For all these reasons, the social, political, cultural, and psychological obstacles in the way of effective EU political symbolism are substantial. For the time being they may well remain insurmountable, even in the unlikely event that the member states decided to give the Union greater cultural and educational powers at last.

Such an insight leads to the second broad question growing out of the account in this study, which pertains to its possible consequences. More precisely, one must ask whether in the long term the Union could sustain a sufficiently high level of public commitment even without being able to resort, or at least resort effectively, to the kinds of symbolic strategies that once helped foster domestic political legitimacy and popular consent.

By so asking one moves into largely uncharted waters, much in line with the *sui generis* character of the European Union itself. Going by the earlier discussion, one factor to consider is the impact of cultural and educational exchanges (along with other contact- and circulation-enhancing measures) on popular perceptions of the EU. This was one area of cultural and educational policy where the Union made significant progress and where the potential for further expansion seems greatest, augmenting the at any rate growing volume and density of economic and social interaction between European societies.

Yet as was suggested, while such interaction may well induce some levelling of lifestyles and consumption patterns, this would not necessarily translate into greater legitimacy and support for the policies and institutions of the European Union. Underpinning this is a core postulate of social constructivism, namely that material transformations do not have inexorable (i.e. pre-determined) social and ideational consequences. Empirically, the state- and nation-building literature bears this out: no successful project of domestic political identity formation has ever relied on exchanges and other forms of interaction alone.

Nonetheless, a continuously high volume of interaction between its member societies may benefit the Union in two ways. First, following Deutschian thinking it could steadily improve mutual perceptions between these societies and thereby help solidify and further entrench the security community they have built over the past half-century. Possible reservations notwithstanding,[1] it is reasonable to assume that a growing interaction and mutual interpenetration in Western Europe has had, on balance, a tolerance-building and pacifying effect. Attitude surveys have long pointed in this direction. While popular perceptions of the EU are often fragile, perceptions among its constituent populations *towards each other* have improved dramatically since the end of the Second World War, just as many transactionalist scholars predicted. For instance, for French respondents Germany became the second most 'trusted' country on earth (Inglehart 1991). Of course benevolent mutual perceptions between different societies do not equate to an overarching sense of community (some transactionalists were too quick to draw this link), nor do they necessarily help legitimise overarching institutions. Yet overall they are more likely to benefit rather than to impede European integration. Above all, they could constitute a kind of horizontal social 'glue' between the EU's member populations, which in turn is a necessary (though not sufficient) psychological condition both for the emergence of an overarching sense of community and 'entitativity' and, by extension, quite possibly for European integration in its more vertical (i.e. institutional) dimensions (see Chapter 1).

Second, at a more tangible level a partial homogenisation of cultural patterns among the EU's member populations could help bring about a 'denationalised' cultural baseline which, as suggested, is a prerequisite for successful political symbolism (no matter how 'thin' and 'acultural') yet which the Union has been prevented from trying to generate through more proactive and interventionist policies. To return to the earlier metaphor, it could help develop a shared 'language' in the form of common cultural experiences and reference points through which the Union's symbolic project could be communicated more effectively to its member societies. Moreover, in principle this could happen regardless of whether these shared cultural patterns were specifically European or linked to broader globalising tendencies. Speaking the same symbolic language is more important than where that language comes from.

Granted, on this score the evidence is not particularly strong so far. While there are signs of some cultural levelling in Western Europe (whatever its origins), policies which could have 'activated' the resulting common cultural patterns and thereby turned them into symbolic building material or symbolic transmission channels have largely remained elusive, as was shown throughout this study. It would be fascinating to analyse Europa TV's popular appeal had it been allowed to survive into the present or, still more interestingly, twenty or thirty years hence. Perhaps a growing cultural levelling in the meantime would have made its 'denationalised' programmes more palatable to viewers; perhaps the EU might even have succeeded in subtly instrumentalising it as an outlet for its symbolic agenda, akin to many national public service broadcasters. Yet neither of this would of course be certain. European integration is still a relatively young project, it lacks close historical precedents, and many of the cultural tendencies in evidence today are still weak and contradictory.

What about the Union's public relations measures – one area in which it made relatively strong inroads by comparison? As was argued, the effect of Union PR on public attitudes is hard to gauge. This is due to a lack of reliable impact studies and to their increasingly narrow focus on specific policies such as enlargement and the single currency. Moreover, it is difficult to isolate the impact of Union PR from that of other factors that might affect public attitudes towards the EU such as changes in economic conditions and in the popularity of domestic governments. Nonetheless, given that the Union's PR initiatives have predominantly sought to convince citizens of the practical benefits of European integration, it was in this area that whatever impact they have had is likely to have been greatest.

Another way of capturing this is with reference to the three levels of legitimisation outlined in Chapter 1. Many of the earlier political symbolism proposals put forward by the EP and the Commission were aimed at creating third-level legitimacy; they sought to symbolically represent and transmit notions of the EU as a corporate actor and of Europeans as an overarching communal category, both with values, needs and aspirations and a self-referential claim to survival. Later, more PR-oriented initiatives, by contrast, have sought to contribute primarily to first-level legitimisation by highlighting the utilitarian benefits of integration. Their aim is less to promote the EU qua communal category and corporate entity than to shore up support for particular EU policies. To a lesser extent they also involve second-level moves by seeking to 'reshape' the member states' interests as perceived by their citizens so as to make them more amenable to European integration. For instance, this is reflected in the Union's constant assurances to its member populations (seconded by many national governments) that 'pooling' sovereignty in certain areas comes naturally to advanced European democracies and strengthens rather than weakens their ability to shape their destiny in an interconnected world.

Of course these different levels overlap in practice. Even the most narrowly targeted PR initiative typically features the European 'logo' as an overarching corporate symbol, and the very talk of 'Europe doing' and 'Europe benefiting' contributes to its reification and to some overarching 'entity process' (more below). Nonetheless, conceptually the distinction between these different legitimacy mechanisms is quite sharp, and attitude surveys reflect this. On the one hand, public interest and participation in EU affairs has remained chronically low – the poor turnouts for the 1999 and 2004 EP elections are potent signs of this. But on the other hand, with the UK being the most important exception public attitudes towards the EU seem to have settled once more into something resembling the 'permissive consensus' of the pre-Maastricht era: marked by relative apathy, low mobilisation and few participatory ambitions but also by a conviction that on balance integration produces practical benefits and should therefore be tolerated.[2] Interestingly, prompted by *Eurobarometer*'s questioning a growing proportion of EU citizens in most member states profess feeling 'European' in addition to harbouring their national affiliations. But this sense of Europeanness has remained so weak as to have few behavioural consequences and it does not seem to have translated into stronger identifications with the EU. For example, this is evident in the lack of 'European' issues debated during EP election campaigns in many member states.

Returning to the earlier question, could the EU secure a requisite level of popular support in the long term without at the same time generating a strong sense of overarching community, 'entitativity' and corporate actorhood, and the kind of self-referential quality and 'end in itself'-status that flows from third-level legitimacy? Going by the discussion in Chapters 1 and 2 the prospects for this are far from certain, despite the Union's relatively secure standing in recent public attitude surveys. After all, from Rousseau to Habermas, almost all political theory on offer sees the development of shared political loyalties as contingent on an overarching sense of community – or, more cautiously, sees communal sentiments as giving rise to a shared discursive realm within which such political loyalties may develop over time. Empirical observations seem to bear this out: even the most politically decentralised and culturally plural domestic systems have acquired a measure of third-level legitimacy, though it is typically weaker than in their more centralised and culturally homogenised counterparts.

Whether the European Union can remain an exception to this depends on several factors. Most obviously, it would require that national mass publics continue to believe that integration yields economic (and/or other tangible) benefits while not gravely threatening their respective national identifications. If first- and second-level legitimacy remain strong, moving to the third level becomes less urgent.

Furthermore, taking the earlier concept of the authority-legitimacy balance as a guide much hinges on the Union's broader political development. In particular, in the absence of strong third-level legitimisation processes the Union would do well to emulate the central authorities in culturally plural and political decentralised states and minimise its impact on its citizens: by acting as discreetly and as inconspicuously as possible, by curbing its intrusiveness and visibility in relation to national and sub-national levels of government, and by generally under rather than overstating its significance and clout. In part this would be a matter of the EU adjusting its appearance. But most importantly, it would require a curb on the formal and de facto transfer of power from national and sub-national levels of government to European-level institutions. While by itself more power means more visibility and intrusiveness, it would also add pressure for a corresponding expansion of the pan-European democratic process – through Europe-wide referendums, directly elected Commission presidents or similar measures. But this would carry significant risks in its own right. For one thing, more democracy means still more visibility and intrusiveness. For another, once one rejects the assumption that communal sentiments and a shared public sphere arise as a mere reflex to democratic institutions and practices, the expansion of the latter in the absence of the former could turn transnational democracy into a force for division rather than cohesion (Cederman 2001a; Chapter 1 above).

To conclude this chapter two further observations are relevant. Both tie in well with the broader social constructivist framework outlined at the beginning of this study and they help qualify – though not obliterate – the central argument outlined so far. Moreover, from the Union's perspective they give somewhat more cause for optimism regarding its chances of retaining popular support in the long-term.

First, one central assumption of this study was that political practices and institutions are not self-legitimising. Democracy does not become legitimate simply by holding elections, and political institutions and hierarchies do not acquire legitimacy by just 'being there'. Instead, political legitimacy results from a complex interplay involving the 'top-down' creation and dissemination of symbolic categories and 'bottom-up' communicative and deliberative processes, which leads to these categories becoming internalised and self-sustaining. Yet as was also suggested, 'purpose built' policies in areas such as culture and education are not the only activities with a symbolic impact. Other policies in other policy areas – indeed, ultimately all policies in all conceivable policy areas – can serve as vehicles for political symbolism, regardless of whether this stems from actual symbolic intent.

This is an important point, and it has led some political anthropologists to attribute to political power a kind of self-legitimising quality. Power needs legitimacy, but the very act of exercising (and obeying) it has an inevitable 'dramatic' – or 'theatrical' – dimension, and thereby helps generate symbolic representations which help foster its internalisation and the development of corresponding political identities (Balandier 1980). In an EU context, the rituals and media attention surrounding the regular European summits (which in part is consciously orchestrated, but which also reflects the fact that these summits are occasions where powerful leaders meet to take important decisions) is an example of such 'auto-symbolism'.

A similar logic applies to other aspects of European integration. For example, the fact that all Europeans vote simultaneously for a common parliament once every five years helps to entrench the concept of 'pan-European democracy' in the minds of at least some of those who do, observe and talk about the voting. Similarly a (however faintly developed) European corporate 'entity process' is both reflected in and reinforced by the fact that even the most ardent 'anti-Europeans' tend to frame their arguments in terms of 'Europe' doing this or that. In the end, what all this bears out is the broader postulate that social practice and social 'substance' mutually reinforce each other. Doing something and thinking and talking about it solidifies its existence, thus further reinforcing the social practices linked to it, and so on. This is the 'performative' function of discourse and the constitutive and 'structuring' effect of social practice and agency that inspires, in various forms, most constructivist approaches to the social world.

But what does all this mean for political legitimacy in the EU? On the one hand, it may enhance it in so far as it allows EU-related institutions and practices to be symbolically signified, transmitted and internalised even in the absence of conscious 'top-down' symbolic policies. But on the other hand, it may also aggravate the problem. For as suggested in Chapter 1, by becoming more visible and more 'talked about', political institutions augment their need for legitimacy in the first place. Herein lies one of the most intriguing paradoxes of political symbolism: to be effective in legitimising political practices and institutions it must make them more visible; but this increases the need for their legitimisation still further.

The second observation is connected to this and flows from another key postulate of social constructivism. Some of the most interesting recent work on European integration explores how the EU acts back upon its member states and continuously impels their re-definition and 're-imagination'. Underpinning some of these accounts is a type of 'identity incorporation' model that differs from more conventional 'multi-level' identity renderings. As national self-definitions adjust to participation in the European integration process, 'Europe' becomes gradually incorporated into the national identity equation proper: 'Irish *and* European' becomes 'Irish *as* European' and to some extent the two melt into one (see Hayward 2002). This is a subtle difference to more conventional 'multilevel' identity accounts, but one with profound implications. For in this scenario, the 'meaning of Europe' is nationally defined and thus continues to diverge from one national context to the next. By extension, generating a sense of belonging to 'Europe' and support for the EU becomes part and parcel of national identity maintenance and an objective of national political symbolisms. By shaping representations of 'Europe' to fit in with those of the member states they at the same time fit the member states into the EU.

Such a process is compatible with the 'auto-symbolism' dynamic outlined above, and the two can unfold alongside each other. On the one hand, by virtue of its very existence and functioning the EU has a symbolic effect on its citizens, becoming more 'real' to them as it develops and penetrates into their everyday lives. But, on the other hand, perceptions of Europe are mediated by the different national contexts in which these citizens live, giving rise to different nationally defined 'Europes' and ways of 'being European'. The member states remain the most important symbolic and deliberative spaces, and national rather than supranational elites continue to be the central symbolic actors.

Conceptually, this 'incorporation' model is not easy to grasp. It is 'second level' in that the meaning of 'Europe' and of 'being European' is nationally defined and varies from one society to the next. But it is also 'third-level' in that it still entails notions of 'Europe' as a real existing entity and community with aims, needs and meanings attached to it. Yet in this rendering there are various nationally defined European 'entity processes' rather than a single all subsuming one. By extension, there are still multiple 'levels' of identification, but the boundary between them is fluid and the symbolic content and meaning of the outermost – European – layer fluctuates from one member state to the next.

In many ways this is not a new argument: 'Europe' has always meant different things in different member states and the EU has helped shape national re-definition processes ever since its founding (Marcussen, Risse, Engelmann-Martin, Knopf and Roscher 1999). Moreover, the example of some culturally fragmented domestic systems as discussed earlier is once more relevant here: the Swiss state probably survived in part precisely because it allows its member societies to define their 'Swissness' in different ways, shaped by their different cultural and historical contexts.

Even so, important dangers lurk in all this. If for its member populations 'Europe' becomes little more than a projection of their national values onto a larger plane, the resulting discrepancies between the different national 'Europes' could provoke friction (Risse in press). Perhaps this serves as yet another sign of caution that 'talking about Europe' across national boundaries might not inevitably generate shared political loyalties and communal sentiments in the process. Rather, for the different member societies it may bring into sharper relief the contrasts between their respective 'Europes', thereby weakening their perception of integration as a shared overarching project.

Against this backdrop, the Union and the member states face three main challenges. First, they must limit the Union's authority, visibility and intrusiveness to a level where it can be incorporated into national symbolic processes without overpowering them. The second challenge is to subject European integration to more intense democratic and deliberative processes first and foremost *inside* the member states. This could help generate – inevitably national – answers to some of the central questions of 'purpose' and 'meaning' that have overshadowed the European project since its inception yet that have remained underproblematised in many national discourses on Europe, only to resurface and haunt the European project in recent years. Finally, the different nationally defined 'Europes' emerging from this must be reconciled into a more or less coherent overarching political framework. This 'Europe' will then of course feed back into the different national identity equations and the various 'Europes' they contain. In this rendering, then, 'being national' and 'being European' are in permanent negotiation, and tensions between them could lurk all around. But ultimately they may also come to sustain each other, constituting a peculiar form of post-national identity mix.

Theoretically, such a scenario is less tidy and less elegant than the various 'Russian dolls', 'concentric circles of allegiance' and 'multi-level identities' models that seek to construct 'Europe' as an outermost identity layer featuring invariant symbolic content and meaning for all its citizens. Practically, it demands more subtlety and produces more ambiguity and fluidity than a more centralised approach to European identity construction roughly modelled after state- and nation-building projects in centuries past, at least in form and method if not necessarily in content and intensity. Yet as this study has shown, the latter has remained politically unacceptable to national elites and culturally indigestible to broader publics, and there is little to suggest that

this will change soon. In the meantime, a gradual incorporation of – nationally produced and therefore idiosyncratic and mutually divergent –
'European content' into the domestic political symbolisms of the member
states might well be the most viable source of political legitimacy for the
European Union.

Notes

1 As was argued, even for Deutsch himself the impact of interaction on mutual perceptions is ambiguous, and here, too, the constructivist claim that material processes do
not have inexorable ideational consequences is relevant. Finally, there remains the
question of whether it was the democratisation of Western Europe after 1945 rather
than a growing level of interaction between its societies that most laid the foundations
for the West European security community and thus for European integration.
2 Admittedly, a causal link between the two attitudes is not self-evident: a belief that the
EU is economically beneficial may be conditioned by a greater liking of the EU in the
first place, rather than vice versa (see Theiler 2004a).

REFERENCES

Note: In 1993 the erstwhile 'Commission of the European Communities' was renamed 'European Commission'. Below I use the name 'Commission' to designate the authorship of Commission documents up to 1993 as well as after.

'A People's Europe: Report from the *ad hoc* Committee' (1985), *Bulletin of the EC*, Supplement No. 7.

Abbott, Andrew (1995), 'Things of boundaries', *Social Inquiry*, 62: 857–882.

Abercrombie, Nicholas and Bryan Turner (1978), 'The dominant ideology thesis', *British Journal of Sociology*, 29: 149–170.

Adler, Emanuel (1997), 'Seizing the middle ground: Constructivism in world politics', *European Journal of International Relations*, 3: 319–363.

Adler, Emanuel and Michael Barnett, eds (1998), *Security Communities*, Cambridge, Cambridge University Press.

Altermatt, Urs, Catherine Bosshart-Pfluger and Albert Tanner (1998), *Die Konstruktion einer Nation: Nation und Nationalisierung in der Schweiz, 18.-20. Jahrhundert*, Zürich, Chronos Verlag.

Anderson, Benedict (1991), *Imagined Communities: Reflections on the Origin and Spread of Nationalism*, London, Verso.

'Audiovisual Eureka' (1999), available on the Internet at www.aveureka.be /homepage.htm (accessed January 1999).

Auer, Stefan (2004), *Liberal Nationalism in Central Europe*, London, Routledge.

Balandier, Georges (1980), *Le pouvoir sur scènes*, Paris, Baland.

Bamber, David (1998), 'EU scraps children's comic that promotes single currency', *Sunday Telegraph*, 18 October (Internet edition).

Baras, Jean-Pol (1989), *Gagner l'Europe culturelle*, Brussels, Labor.

Barth, Fredrik (1969), 'Introduction', in *Ethnic Groups and Boundaries: The Social Organization of Culture Difference*, ed. Fredrik Barth. Boston, Little, Brown and Company.

Beetham, David and Christopher Lord (2001), 'Legitimizing the EU: Is there a "post-parliamentary basis" for its legitimation?', *Journal of Common Market Studies*, 39: 443–462.

Bekemans, Léonce and Athanassios Balodimos (1992), 'Etude concernant les modifications apportées par le Traité sur l'Union Politique en ce qui concerne l'éducation, la formation professionnelle et la culture', College of Europe, Bruges, Mimeograph.

Bell, Gordon, ed. (1995), *Educating European Citizens: Citizenship Values and the European Dimension*, London, Fulton.

Bendix, Regina (1992), 'National sentiment in the enactment and discourse of Swiss political ritual', *American Ethnologist*, 19: 768–790.

Benzoni, Maria and Michel Dumoulin (1999), 'L'identité européenne, enjeu de politiques culturelles et d'information?' Paper prepared for the Colloque 'Les identités européennes au XXème siècle', Paris, 30 September–2 October.

Berger, Peter and Thomas Luckmann (1991), *The Social Construction of Reality: A Treatise in the Sociology of Knowledge*, London, Penguin.

Billig, Michael (1995), *Banal Nationalism*, London, Sage.

Blackledge, Robert (1991), 'Großbritannien', in *Politische Bildung in Europa: Die europäische Dimension in der politischen Bildung*, ed. Will Cremer and Otto Schmuck, Bonn, Bundeszentrale für Politische Bildung.

Blanke, Hermann-Josef (1994), *Europa auf dem Weg zu einer Bildungs- und Kulturgemeinschaft*, Cologne, Carl Heymanns Verlag.

Borneman, John and Nick Fowler (1997), 'Europeanization', *Annual Review of Anthropology*, 26: 487–514.

Bourdieu, Pierre (1995), *Outline of a Theory of Practice*, Cambridge, Cambridge University Press.

Bourdieu, Pierre (1994), *Raisons pratiques: sur la théorie de l'action*, Paris, Éditions du Seuil.

Bourdieu, Pierre (1980), 'L'identité et la represésentation: éléments pour une réflexion critique sur l'idée de région', *Actes de la recherche en sciences sociales*, 35: 63–72.

Bourdieu, Pierre (1971), 'Systems of education and systems of thought', in *Knowledge and Control: New Directions for the Sociology of Education*, ed. M. F. D. Young, London, Collier-Macmillan.

Brock, C. and W. Tulasiewicz, eds (1994), *Education in a Single Europe*, London, Routledge.

Brubaker, Rogers (1999), 'The Manichaen myth: Rethinking the distinction between "civic" and "ethnic" nationalism', in *Nation and National Identity: The European Experience in Perspective*, ed. Hanspeter Kriesi, Klaus Armingeon, Hannes Siegrist and Andreas Wimmer, Chur/Zürich, Rüegger.

Brubaker, Rogers (1996), *Nationalism Reframed: Nationhood and the National Question in the New Europe*, Cambridge, Cambridge University Press.
Brubaker, Rogers and Frederick Cooper (2000), 'Beyond "identity"', *Theory and Society*, 29: 1–47.
Bulletin of the EC (1994, No. 10), point 1.2.132.
Bulletin of the EC (1993, No. 10), point 1.2.176.
Bulletin of the EC (1992, No. 3), point 1.2.221.
Bulletin of the EC (1992, No. 1–2), point 1.3.263.
Bulletin of the EC (1991, No. 6), point 1.2.107.
Bulletin of the EC (1990, No. 11), point 1.3.193.
Bulletin of the EC (1990, No. 11), point 1.3.12.
Bulletin of the EC (1990, No. 7–8), point 1.3.304.
Bulletin of the EC (1990, No. 3), point 1.1.190.
Bulletin of the EC (1989, No. 2), point 2.1.84.
Bulletin of the EC (1987, No. 3), point 3.4.1 et seq.
Bulletin of the EC (1986, No. 4), point 2.1.81.
Bulletin of the EC (1986, No. 2), point 2.1.89.
Bulletin of the EC (1985, No. 12), point 2.1.125.
Bulletin of the EC (1985, No. 5), point 2.1.59 et seq.
Bulletin of the EC (1984, No. 6), point 1.1.9 (subheading 6).
Bulletin of the EC (1976, No. 11), point 2501
Bulletin of the EC (1972, No. 10): 15–16.
Calhoun, Craig (1997), *Nationalism*, Minneapolis, University of Minnesota Press.
Cederman, Lars-Erik (2001a), 'Nationalism and bounded integration: What it would take to construct a European demos', *European Journal of International Relations*, 7: 139–174.
Cederman, Lars-Erik (2001b), 'Political boundaries and identity trade-offs', in *Constructing Europe's Identity: The External Dimension*, ed. Lars-Erik Cederman, Boulder, Lynne Rienner.
Cederman, Lars-Erik and Christopher Daase (2003), 'Endogenizing corporate identities: The next step in constructivist IR theory', *European Journal of International Relations*, 9: 5–35.
Cederman, Lars-Erik and Peter Kraus (2002), 'Transnational communication and the European demos', Paper prepared for presentation at the SSRC-sponsored workshop on 'Cooperation and Conflict in a Connected World'. New York City, 28 February 2002.
Chekel, Jeffrey (2002), *Persuasion in International Institutions*, Oslo, ARENA Working Paper No. 02/14.
Chekel, Jeffrey (1999), 'Social construction and integration', *Journal of European Public Policy*, 6: 545–560.
Chekel, Jeffrey (1998), 'The constructivist turn in international relations theory', *World Politics*, 50: 324–348.
Christiansen, Thomas, Knud Erik Jørgensen and Antje Wiener (1999), 'The

social construction of Europe', *Journal of European Public Policy*, 6: 528–544.

Chryssochoou, Dimitris N. (1994), 'Democracy and symbiosis in the European Community: Towards a confederal consociation?', *West European Politics*, 17: 1–14.

Citron, Suzanne (1991), *Le mythe national: l'histoire de France en question*, Paris, Éditions Ouvrières.

Coakley, John (1992), 'The social origins of nationalist movements: A review', in *The Social Origins of Nationalist Movements: The Contemporary West European Experience*, ed. John Coakley, London, Sage.

Cohen, Abner (1969), 'Political anthropology: The analysis of the symbolism of power relations', *Man*, 4: 215–235.

Cohen, Anthony P. (1989), *The Symbolic Construction of Community*, London, Routledge.

Collins, Richard (2002), *Media and Identity in Contemporary Europe*, Bristol, Intellect.

Collins, Richard (1995), 'Reflections across the Atlantic: Contrasts and complementaries in broadcasting policy in Canada and the European Community in the 1990s', *Canadian Journal of Communication* 20 (online edition), available on the Internet at http://www.cjc.online.ca/viewarticle.php?id=315 (accessed November 2004).

Collins, Richard (1994a), *Broadcasting and Audiovisual Policy in the European Single Market*, London, John Libbey.

Collins, Richard (1994b), 'Unity in diversity? The European single market in broadcasting and audiovisual, 1982–92', *Journal of Common Market Studies*, 32: 89–110.

Collins, Richard (1993a), *Audiovisual and Broadcasting Policy in the European Community*, London, University of North London Press.

Collins, Richard (1993b), 'Public service broadcasting by satellite: Eurikon and Europa', *Screen*, 34: 162–175.

Collins, Richard (1990), *Television: Policy and Culture*, London, Unwin Hyman.

Collins, Richard (1989), 'The language of advantage: satellite television in western Europe', *Media, Culture and Society*, 11: 351–371.

Commission (2004a), 'Commission Report to the European Parliament, the Council and the Committee on the Regions ... on the implementation of the Community programmes Kaleidoscope, Ariane and Raphael', COM 2004, 33 final.

Commission (2004b), 'See Europe in Brussels', available on the Internet at www.europa.eu.int/en/comm/dg10/infcom/visits/cec5.html (accessed March 2004).

Commission (2004c), 'European integration in university studies', available on the Internet at europa.eu.int/comm/education/programmes/ajm /ajm/index_en.html (accessed May 2004).

Commission (2004d), *Impact of School Partnerships (Socrates II/Comenius 1 2000–2006: Mid-Term Evaluation)*, Brussels, European Commission.

Commission (2004e), 'Netdays 2004', available on the Internet at http://europa.eu.int/comm/education/programmes/netdays/index_en. html (accessed April 2004).

Commission (2003a), *Designing the Future Programme of Cultural Cooperation for the European Union After 2006,* Brussels, European Commission.

Commission (2003b), 'Muddles and misunderstandings', available on the Internet at www.europa.eu.int/en/comm/dg10/em/m01.html (accessed June 2003).

Commission (2003c), 'Europe by Satellite', available on the Internet at www.europa.eu.int/ comm/ebs/index_en.html (accessed June 2003).

Commission (2003d), *Cinema, TV and Radio in the EU: Data 1980–2002,* Luxembourg, OOPEC 2003.

Commission (2003e), '"Education & Training 2010": The success of the Lisbon Strategy hinges on urgent reforms' (Draft joint interim report on the implementation of the detailed work programme on the follow-up of the objectives of education and training systems in Europe), COM 2003, 685 final.

Commission (2003f), 'Proposal for a European Parliament & Council Decision establishing a Community action programme to promote bodies active at European level and support specific activities in the field of Education and training'), COM 2003, 273 final.

Commission (2002a), *Education and Training in Europe: Diverse Systems, Shared Goals for 2010,* Luxembourg, OOPEC.

Commission (2002b), 'Erasmus student mobility 1987/88–2002/03', available on the Internet at www.europa.eu.int/comm/education/programmes /socrates/erasmus/statisti/ stat15.pdf (accessed March 2004).

Commission (2001a), 'Cultural Cooperation in Europe Forum 2001', Brussels, Directorate-General for Education and Culture.

Commission (2001b), 'Communication from the Commission to the Council, European Parliament, Economic and Social Committee, the Committee on the Regions on a new framework for co-opeation on activities concerning the information and communication policy of the European Union', COM 2001, 354 final.

Commission (2001c), 'Communication from the Commission to the Council, the European Parliament, the Economic and Social Committee and the Committee of the Regions on certain Legal Aspects Relating to Cinematographic and other Audiovisual works', COM 2001, 534 final.

Commission (1999a), Cultural Networks', available on the Internet at www.europa.eu.int/en/comm/dg10/culture/en/action/network_en.html (accessed January 1999).

Commission (1999b), 'Information and Communication', available on the

Internet at www.europa.eu.int/en/comm/dg10/infcom.html (accessed January 1999).

Commission (1999c), 'Principles and guidelines for the Community's audio-visual policy in the digital age', COM 1999, 657 final.

Commission (1998a), 'Euromyths & misunderstandings', available on the Internet at www.cec.org.uk/myths/index.htm (accessed November 1998).

Commission (1998b), 'Learning about the euro at school', available on the Internet at www.europa.eu.int/en/comm/dg22/euro/dem3-en.html (accessed November 1998).

Commission (1998c), 'Commission Recommendation of 23 April 1998 on dialogue, monitoring and information to facilitate the transition to the euro', available on the Internet at www.europa.eu.int/euro/html/sommaire-dossier5.html?lang=5&dossier= 149&nav=5 (accessed August 1998).

Commission (1998d), 'Groupe de travail "l'education et l'euro"', available on the Internet at www.europa.eu.int/en/comm/dg22/euro/projet.html (accessed November 1998).

Commission (1998e) *The Raspberry Ice Cream War: A Comic for Young People on a Peaceful Europe without Frontiers*, Luxembourg, OOPEC.

Commission (1998f), 'Learning for active citizenship: A significant challenge in building a Europe of knowledge', available on the Internet at www.europa.eu.int/en/ comm/dg22/citizen/index.html (accessed December 1998).

Commission (1997a), '1997 Action aimed at young people: Call for proposals', *OJEC* No. C47: 9–10.

Commission (1997b), 'The European Film Industry Under Analysis: Second Information Report 1997', available on the Internet at http://europa.eu.int/comm/avpolicy/legis/key_doc/cine97_e.htm (accessed January 2005).

Commission (1997c), 'Commission green paper on the convergence of the telecommunications, media and information-technology sectors, and the implications for regulation – Towards an information-society approach', COM 97, 623 final.

Commission (1997d), 'Socrates: The Community action programme in the field of education: Report on the results achieved in 1995 and 1996 ...', COM 97, 99 final.

Commission (1997e), 'Towards a Europe of knowledge', COM 97, 563 final.

Commission (1996a), 'Opinion of the Commission ... on the European Parliament's amendments to the Council's common position regarding the proposal for a European Parliament and Council decision establishing a Community action programme in the field of cultural heritage: The Raphael programme', COM 96, 627 final.

Commission (1996b), *Educational Multimedia: First Elements of Reflection*, Brussels, European Commission.

Commission (1996c), *Learning in the Information Society: Action Plan for a European Education Initiative (1996–98)* (Communication to the European Parliament, the Council, the Economic and Social Committee and the Committee of the Regions), Brussels, European Commission.

Commission (1996d), 'Education – training – research: The obstacles to transnational mobility', *Bulletin of the EC*, Supplement No. 5.

Commission (1995a), 'European Community action in support of culture' (Communication from the Commission to the European Parliament and the Council of the European Union), COM 95, 110 final.

Commission (1995b), 'Proposal for a European Parliament and Council Decision establishing a Community action programme in the field of cultural heritage (Raphael)', COM 95, 110 final.

Commission (1995c), 'Opinion of the Commission ... on the European Parliament's amendments to the Council's common position regarding the proposal for a European Parliament and Council decision establishing a programme to support artistic and cultural activities having a European dimension ("Kaleidoscope")', COM 95, 659 final.

Commission (1995d), 'Proposal for a Council Decision establishing a European guarantee fund to promote cinema and television production', COM 95, 546 final.

Commission (1995e), 'White paper on education and training – teaching and learning – towards the learning society', COM 95, 590 final.

Commission (1994a), 'European Community action in support of culture' (Communication from the Commission to the European Parliament and the Council of the European Union; Proposal for a European Parliament and Council Decision establishing a programme to support artistic and cultural activities having a European dimension Kaleidoscope 2000 [presented by the Commission]; Proposal for a European Parliament and Council Decision establishing a support programme in the field of books and reading Ariane [presented by the Commission]), COM 94, 356 final.

Commission (1994b), *Information, Communication, Openness: Background Report*, Luxembourg, OOPEC.

Commission (1994c), 'Strategy options to strengthen the European programme industry in the context of audiovisual policy of the European Union' (Green Paper), COM 94, 96 final.

Commission (1994d), 'Europe's way to the information society: An action plan (Communication from the Commission to the Council and the European Parliament and to the Economic and Social Committee and the Committee of Regions)', COM 94, 347 final.

Commission (1993a), 'Green paper on the European dimension in Education', COM 93, 457 final.

Commission (1993b), 'White paper on growth, competitiveness, and employment: The challenges and ways forward into the 21st century', COM 93, 700 final.

Commission (1992a), *XXVIth General Report on the Activities of the European Communities*, Luxembourg, OOPEC.

Commission (1992b), 'New prospects for Community cultural action' (Communication from the Commission to the Council, the European Parliament and the Economic and Social Committee), COM 92, 149 final.

Commission (1992c), 'Report on the Community's involvement in the 1992 Olympic Games' (Communication from the Commission to the Council and the European Parliament), COM 92, 575 final.

Commission (1992d), 'Youth information action plan' (Communication from the Commission to the Council and the European Parliament), COM 92, 297 final.

Commission (1991a), *Memorandum on Higher Education in the European Community*, Brussels, Task Force on Human Resources, Education, Training, Youth.

Commission (1991b), *Memorandum on Open Distance Learning in the European Community*, Brussels, Task Force on Human Resources, Education, Training, Youth.

Commission (1990a), 'Young people in the European Community' (Memorandum from the Commission to the Council and the European Parliament), COM 90, 469 final.

Commission (1990b), 'European literary prize – Organisational rules', *OJEC*, No. C35: 7.

Commission (1990c), 'European translation prize – Organisational rules', *OJEC*, No. C35: 8.

Commission (1988a), 'The European Community and culture', *European File* No. 10.

Commission (1988b), 'Towards a large European audio-visual market', *European File* No. 4.

Commission (1987a), 'European identity: Symbols and sport', *European File* No. 6.

Commission (1987b), 'A fresh boost for culture in the European Community' (Commission Communication to the Council and Parliament transmitted in December 1987), *Bulletin of the EC*, Supplement No. 4.

Commission (1986), 'Action programme for the European audio-visual media products industry', COM 86, 255 final.

Commission (1985a), 'Proposal for a council regulation on a Community aid scheme for non-documentary cinema and television co-productions,' COM 85, 174 final.

Commission (1985b), 'Amended proposal for a Council regulation (EEC) on a Community aid scheme for non-documentary cinema and television co-productions', COM 85, 800 final.

Commission (1983), 'Realities and tendencies in European television: Perspectives and options' (Report from the Commission to the European Parliament), COM 83, 229 final.

Commission (1978), 'Educational activities with a European content: The study of the European Community in schools' (Communication from the Commission to the Council), COM 78, 241 final.

Commission (1977), 'Community action in the cultural sector' (Commission Communication to the Council submitted on 22 November 1977), *Bulletin of the EC*, Supplement No. 6.

Commission (1974a), 'Education in the European Community', *Bulletin of the EC*, Supplement No. 3.

Commission (1974b), 'Draft resolution of the Council of the European Communities and of the conference of Ministers of Education meeting within the Council for cooperation in the field of education', *OJEC* No. C58: 20–21.

Commission (1973), 'For a Community policy in education', *Bulletin of the EC*, Supplement No. 10.

Commission (1972 [1968]), 'Declaration by the European Commission on the occasion of the achievement of the Customs Union on 1 July 1968', in *European Integration*, ed. Michael Hodges, Harmondsworth, Penguin Books.

'Communication on Audiovisual Eureka' (2003), Issued by the 54th meeting of the Coordinators' Committee of Audiovisual Eureka, Brussels 18 February 2003, available on the Internet at www.mediadesk. at/TCgi_Images/mediadesk/20030225153538_1.doc (accessed May 2004).

Connor, Walker (1972), 'Nation-building or nation-destroying?', *World Politics*, 24: 319–355.

Council (2000) 'Council Decision of 20 December 2000 on the implementation of a programme to encourage the development, distribution and promotion of European Audiovisual works (MEDIA Plus – Development, Distribution and Promotion) (2001–2005), *OJEC*, L13: 35–43.

Council (1995), 'Council Decision of 22 December 1995 on the implementation of a training programme for professionals in the European audiovisual programme industry (Media II – Training)', *OJEC*, No. L321: 33.

Council (1994), 'Conclusions of the Council of 10 November 1994 on the Commission communication concerning European Community action in support of culture', *OJEC*, No. C348: 1–2.

Council (1991a), Resolution of the Council and the Ministers for culture meeting within the Council of 7 June 1991 on the training of arts administrators', *OJEC*, No. C188: 1–2.

Council (1991b), 'Resolution of the Council and the Ministers for culture meeting within the Council of 7 June 1991 on the development of the theatre in Europe', *OJEC*, No. C188: 3–4.

Council (1989), 'Council Decision of 28 July 1989 establishing an action programme to promote foreign language competence in the European Community (LINGUA)', *OJEC*, No. L239: 24–32.

Council (1988a), 'Council Decision of 16 June 1988 adopting an action programme for the promotion of youth exchanges in the Community – "Youth for Europe" programme', *OJEC*, No. L158: 42–46.

Council (1988b), 'Resolution of the Council and the Ministers of Education Meeting within the Council on the European dimension in education of 24 May 1988', *OJEC*, No. C177: 5–7.

Council (1987a), 'Resolution of the Council and of the Ministers responsible for Cultural Affairs, meeting within the Council of 9 November 1987 on the promotion of translation of important works of European culture', *OJEC*, No. C309: 3.

Council (1987b [1985]), 'Conclusions of the Council and of the Ministers for Education meeting within the Council of 27 September 1985 on the enhanced treatment of the European dimension in education', in *European Educational Policy Statements*, 3rd edition, Luxembourg, OOPEC.

Council (1987c), 'Council Decision of 15 June 1987 adopting the European Community Action Scheme for the Mobility of University Students (ERASMUS)', *OJEC*, No. L166: 20–24.

Council (1976), 'Resolution of the Council and of the ministers of education, meeting within the Council of 9 February 1976 comprising an action programme in the field of education', *OJEC*, No. C38: 1–5.

Council (1963), 'Décision du Conseil du 2 avril 1963 sur l'établissement des principes généraux pour la mise en oeuvre d'une politique commune de formation professionelle', *Journal Officiel des Communautés Européennes*, No. 63: 1338–1341.

Council of Europe (2004), 'Eurimages', available on the Internet at www.coe.int/T/E/Cultural_Co-operation/Eurimages (accessed March 2004).

Council of Europe (2003), 'Education for democratic Citizenship: 2001–2004: Activity report for 2003', DGIV/EDU/CIT (2003) 32 rev 3.

Council of Europe (1988), 'Resolution (88) 15 setting up a European support fund for the co-production and distribution of creative cinematographic and audiovisual works ("Eurimages")', Strasbourg, Council of Europe.

Cremer, Will and Otto Schmuck, eds (1991), *Politische Bildung in Europa: Die europäische Dimension in der politischen Bildung*, Bonn, Bundeszentrale für Politische Bildung.

Cronin, Mike (1999), *Sport and Nationalism in Ireland: Gaelic Games, Soccer and Irish Identity since 1884*, Dublin, Four Courts Press.

Davies, Norman (1996), *Europe: A History*, Oxford, Oxford University Press.

Davis, Eric (1996), 'The museum and the politics of social control in modern Iraq', in *Commemorations: The Politics of National Identity*, ed. John R. Gillis, Princeton, Princeton University Press.

de Rougemont, Denis (1985), *The Meaning of Europe*, London, Sidgwick and Jackson.

de Sélys, Gérard (1996), 'La machine de propagande de la Commission', *Le Monde Diplomatique*, June: 8–9.

de Witte, B. (1987), 'Building Europe's image and identity', in *Europe from a Cultural Perspective: Historiography and Perceptions,* ed. A. Rijksbaron, W. H. Roobol and Weinglas, The Hague, Nijgh & Van Ditmar Universitair.

'Declaration on European identity' (1973), in *Bulletin of the EC,* No. 12, point 2501.

Delahaye, Yves (1979), *L'Europe sous les mots: le texte et la déchirure,* Paris, Payot.

Delanty, Gerard (1995), *Inventing Europe: Idea, Identity, Reality,* London, Macmillan.

Delors, Jacques (1985), 'Speech by Mr Delors', *Bulletin of the EC,* No. 9, point 1.1.1.

Delouche, Frédéric, ed. (1993), *Illustrated History of Europe: A Unique Guide to Europe's Common Heritage,* London, Weidenfeld and Nicolson.

Deutsch, Karl W., Sidney A. Burrell, Robert A. Kann, Maurice Lee Jr., Martin Lichterman, Raymond E. Lindgren, Francis L. Loewenheim and Richard W. Van Wagenen (1957), *Political Community and the North Atlantic Area,* Princeton, Princeton University Press.

Deutsch, Karl W. (1954), *Political Community at the International Level: Problems of Definition and Measurement,* Garden City, Doubleday.

Dill, Richard W. (1989), 'Europa-TV – zu Tode geliebt', in *Europäisches Fernsehen – American-Blend? Fernsehmedien zwischen Amerikanisierung und Europäisierung,* ed. Winand Gellner, Berlin, Vistas.

Doran, Patrick F. (1991), 'Irland', in *Politische Bildung in Europa: Die europäische Dimension in der politischen Bildung,* ed. Will Cremer and Otto Schmuck, Bonn, Bundeszentrale für Politische Bildung 1991.

Dörner, Andreas (1996), *Politischer Mythos und symbolische Politik: Der Hermannmythos: Zur Entstehung des Nationalbewusstseins der Deutschen,* Reinbek bei Hamburg, Rowohlt.

'Draft European Act' (1981), *Bulletin of the EC,* No. 11, point 3.4.1.

Durkheim, Emile (1922), *Éducation et sociologie,* Paris, Librairie Félix Alcan.

Duroselle, Jean Baptiste (1990), *Europe: A History of its Peoples,* London, Viking.

Edelman, Murray (1967), *The Symbolic Uses of Politics,* Urbana, University of Illinois Press.

Emirbayer, Mustafa (1997), 'Manifesto for a relational sociology', *American Journal of Sociology,* 103: 281–317.

Etzioni, Amitai (1968), *The Active Society: A Theory of Societal and Political Processes,* New York, The Free Press.

Etzioni, Amitai (1965), *Political Unification: A Comparative Study of Leaders and Forces,* New York, Holt, Rinehart & Winston.

Eurobarometer (2002), *Europeans' Participation in Cultural Activities: A Eurobarometer Survey Carried Out at the Request of the European Commission (Eurostat).*

Eurobarometer (1973 *et seq.*), Brussels, European Commission.

European Audiovisual Observatory (2003), 'European cinema attendance stagnates as local films fail to travel', available on the Internet at www.obs.coe.int/about/oea/pr/mif2003.html (accessed May 2004).

European Audiovisual Observatory (2002), 'The Imbalance of trade in films and television programmes between North America and Europe continues to deteriorate', available on the Internet at www.obs.coe.int/about/oea/pr/desequilibre.html (accessed May 2004).

European Broadcasting Union (2003), 'Euronews', available on the Internet at www.ebu.ch/news/press_archive/2003_and_prev/press_news_2003_90_euronews.php (accessed November 2003).

European Council (1985), 'European Council Milan 28 and 29 June 1985: Conclusions', *Bulletin of the EC*, Supplement No. 7.

European Cultural Foundation and European Institute for the Media (1988), *Europe 2000: What Kind of Television?* (Report of the European Television Task Force), Manchester, The European Institute for the Media.

European Parliament (2001), 'Report on cultural cooperation in the European Union – Committee on Culture, Youth, Education, the Media and Sport, Rapporteur: Giorgio Ruffolo' (2000/2323(INI)), available on the Internet at www.budobs.org/Ruffolo%20report.pdf (accessed April 2003).

European Parliament (1995), 'Resolution on the establishment of a European civilian service', *OJEC*, No. C269: 232–233.

European Parliament (1988), 'Resolution on the Commission proposals for action to promote European culture', *OJEC*, No. C122 1988: 38.

European Parliament (1985), 'Resolution embodying the opinion of the European Parliament on the proposal from the Commission of the European Communities to the Council for a Regulation on a Community aid scheme for non-documentary cinema and television co-productions', *OJEC* No. C288: 30–31.

European Parliament (1984), *Draft Treaty Establishing the European Union*, Luxembourg, European Parliament Publications and Briefings Division.

European Parliament (1983), 'Resolution on the promotion of film-making in the Community countries', *OJEC*, No. C307: 16–19.

European Parliament (1982a), 'Report drawn up on behalf of the Committee on Youth, Culture, Education, Information and Sport on radio and television broadcasting in the European Community', *EP Doc.*, No. 1–1013.

European Parliament (1982b), 'Resolution on radio and television broadcasting in the European Community', *OJEC*, No. C87: 110–112.

European Parliament (1980), 'Motion for a resolution on radio and television broadcasting in the European Community', *EP Doc.*, No. 1–409.

European Parliament (1979), 'Resolution embodying the opinion of the European Parliament on the communication from the Commission of the European Communities to the Council concerning Community action in the cultural sector', *OJEC*, No. C39: 50–51.

European Parliament and Council (2001), 'Decision No 161/2001/EC of the European Parliament and of the Council of 19 January 2001 on the implementation of a training programme for professionals in the European audiovisual programme industry (MEDIA TRAINING) (2001–2005), *OJEC*, No. L26: 1–9.

European Parliament and Council (2000a), 'Decision No. 508/2000/EC of the European Parliament and of the Council of 14 February 2000 establishing the Culture 2000 programme', *OJEC*, No. L63: 1–9.

European Parliament and Council (2000b), 'Decision No. 1031/2000/EC … of 13 April 2000 establishing the "Youth" Community action programme, *OJEC*, No. L117: 1–10.

European Parliament and Council (2000c), 'Decision No. 1934/200/EC of the European Parliament and of the Council of 17 July 2000 on the European Year of Languages 2001', *OJEC*, No. L232: 1–5.

European Parliament and Council (2000d), 'Decision No. 253/2000/EC of the European Parliament and of the Council … establishing the second phase of the Community action programme in the field of education "socrates"', *OJEC*, No. L28: 1–15.

European Parliament and Council (1997), 'Directive 97/36/EC of the European Parliament and of the Council of 30 June 1997 amending Council Directive 89/552/EEC on the coordination of certain provisions laid down by law, regulation or administrative action in Member States concerning the pursuit of television broadcasting activities', *OJEC*, No. L202: 60–71.

European Parliament and Council (1995), 'Decision No. 818/95/EC of the European Parliament and of the Council of 14 March 1995 adopting the third phase of the "Youth for Europe" programme', *OJEC*, No. L 87: 1–9.

European schoolnet, available on the Internet at www.eun.org/eun.org2 /eun/en/index_eun.html (accessed April 2004).

European youth portal, available on the Internet at www.europa.eu.int /youth/ (accessed June 2004).

Eurydice, available on the Internet at www.eurydice.org (accessed June 2004).

Eurydice (1996), 'Thematic Bibliography: The European Dimension in Education', available on the Internet at www.eurydice.org/Documents /Bibliographie/Dimension/en/FrameSet.htm (accessed April 2001).

Faroux, Anne-Laurence (1993), 'Politiques culturelles et intégration européenne: propos sur un système dichotomique', doctoral thesis, European University Institute.

Farquharson, John E. and Stephen C. Holt (1975), *Europe from Below: An Assessment of Franco-German Popular Contacts*, London, George Allen & Unwin.

Field, Frank (1998), *European Dimensions: Education, Training and the European Union*, London, Jessica Kingsley Publishers.

Fine, Robert and Will Smith (2003), 'Jürgen Habermas's theory of cosmopolitanism', *Constellations* 10: 469–487.

Finnemore, Martha (1996), 'Norms, culture, and world politics: Insights from sociology's institutionalism', *International Organization*, 50: 325–348.

Firth, Raymond (1973), *Symbols: Public and Private*, London, Allen & Unwin.

Flouris, George (1995), 'Greece: The image of Europe in the curriculum of the Greek elementary school', in *Educating European Citizens: Citizenship Values and the European Dimension*, ed. Gordon Bell, London, Fulton.

Fritsch, Anke (1998), *Europäische Bildungspolitik nach Maastricht – Zwischen Kontinuität und neuen Dimensionen: Eine Untersuchung am Beispiel der Programme ERASMUS/SOKRATES und LEONARDO*, Frankfurt, Peter Lang.

Gaserow, Vera (1997), '2,5 Euro: Wieviel ist den dette?' *Die Zeit*, 20: 65.

Geertz, Clifford (1973), *The Interpretation of Cultures: Selected Essays*, London, Fontana Press.

Gellner, Ernest (1983), *Nations and Nationalism*, Oxford, Basil Blackwell.

General Budget of the European Union for the Financial Year 2002, Luxembourg, OOPEC.

General Report on the Activities of the European Communities (1973 *et seq.*), Luxembourg, OOPEC (Internet edition available at www.europa.eu.int).

George, Stephen (1991), *Politics and Policy in the European Community* (2nd edition), Oxford, Oxford University Press.

Giddens, Anthony (1984), *The Constitution of Society: Outline of a Theory of Structuration*, Cambridge, Polity Press.

Gikopoulos, G. and A. Kakavoulis (1991), 'Griechenland', in *Politische Bildung in Europa: Die europäische Dimension in der politischen Bildung*, ed. Will Cremer and Otto Schmuck, Bonn, Bundeszentrale für Politische Bildung.

Gillis, John R., ed. (1996), *Commemorations: The Politics of National Identity*, Princeton, Princeton University Press.

Goodson, Ivor F. (1995), *The Making of the Curriculum: Collected Essays* (2nd edition), Washington DC, The Falmer Press.

Green, Andy (1990), *Education and State Formation: The Rise of Education Systems in England, France and the USA*, London, Macmillan.

Guibernau, Montserrat (1996), *Nationalisms: The Nation-state and Nationalism in the Twentieth Century*, Cambridge, Polity Press.

Guzzini, Stefano (2000), 'A reconstruction of constructivism in International Relations', *European Journal of International Relations*, 6: 147–182.

Haas, Ernst B. (1970), 'The study of regional integration: Reflections on the joy and anguish of pretheorizing', *International Organization*, 24: 607–646.

Haas, Ernst B. (1967), 'The uniting of Europe and the uniting of Latin America', *Journal of Common Market Studies*, 5: 315–343.

Haas, Ernst B. (1964), *Beyond the Nation-state: Functionalism and International Organization*, Stanford, Stanford University Press.

Haas, Ernst B. (1961), 'International integration: The European and the universal process', *International Organization*, 15: 366–392.

Haas, Ernst B. (1958), *The uniting of Europe: Political, Social and Economic Forces 1950–1957*, Stanford, Stanford University Press.

Haas, Peter (1992), 'Knowledge, power and international policy coordination', *International Organization*, 46: 1–35.

Habermas, Jürgen (1991), 'Citizenship and national identity: Some reflections on the future of Europe', *Praxis International*, 12: 1–19.

Habermas, Jürgen (1984), *The Theory of Communicative Action: Reason and the Rationalization of Society* (Vol. 1), Boston, Beacon Press.

Habermas, Jürgen (1976), *Legitimation Crisis*, London, Heinemann.

Hackl, Elsa (2001), 'Towards a European Area of Higher Education: Change and Convergence in European Higher Education', Florence, European University Institute Working Paper No. 2001/09.

Haigh, Gerald (1998), 'Viva Socrates!' *Times Educational Supplement*, 27 February (Internet edition).

Hall, Stuart (1980), 'Encoding/decoding', in *Culture, Media, Language: Working Papers in Cultural Studies 1972–79*, ed. Stuart Hall, Dorothy Hobson, A. Lowe and Paul Willis, London, Hutchinson.

Handler, Richard (1996), 'Is "identity" a useful cross-cultural concept?', in *Commemorations: The Politics of National Identity*, ed. John R. Gillis, Princeton, Princeton University Press.

Harding, Gareth (2003), 'Europe: Teaching through comic books' (United Press International), available on the Internet at www.theyesmen.org/articles/captaineuroarticlewashpost.html (accessed March 2004).

Harrison, R. J. (1990), 'Neo-functionalism', in *Frameworks for International Co-operation*, ed. A. J. R Groom and Paul Taylor, London, Pinter.

Havel, Vaclav (1985), 'The Power of the Powerless', in *The Power of the Powerless: Citizens Against the State in Central-Eastern Europe*, ed. John Keane, Armonk, NY, M. E. Sharpe.

Hayward, Katy (2002), 'Ireland Reimagined: Nationalism in a European Context', PhD dissertation, University College Dublin.

Held, David (1988), *Political Theory and the Modern State: Essays on State, Power and Democracy*, Cambridge, Polity Press.

Hettling, Manfred (1998), 'Geschichtlichkeit: Zwerge auf den Schultern von Riesen', in *Eine kleine Geschichte der Schweiz: Der Bundesstaat und seine Traditionen*, ed. Manfred Hettling, Mario König, Martin Schaffner, Andreas Suter and Jakob Tanner Frankfurt, Suhrkamp.

Hettling, Manfred (1997), 'Erlebnisraum und Ritual: Die Geschichte des 19. März 1848 im Jahrhundert bis 1948', *Historische Anthropologie*, 5: 417–434.

Hickel, Raymond (1991), 'Frankreich', in *Politische Bildung in Europa: Die europäische Dimension in der politischen Bildung*, ed. Will Cremer and Otto Schmuck, Bonn, Bundeszentrale für Politische Bildung.

Hix, Simon (1994), 'Approaches to the study of the EC: The challenge to Comparative Politics', *West European Politics*, 17: 1–30.

Hobsbawm, Eric (1994), *Nations and Nationalism since 1780: Programme, Myth, Reality*, Cambridge, Cambridge University Press.

Hobsbawm, Eric (1993a), 'Introduction', in *The Invention of Tradition*, ed. Eric Hobsbawm and Terence Ranger, Cambridge, Cambridge University Press.

Hobsbawm, Eric (1993b), 'Mass-producing traditions: Europe, 1870–1914', in *The Invention of Tradition*, ed. Eric Hobsbawm and Terence Ranger, Cambridge, Cambridge University Press.

Hogg, Michael and Dominic Abrams (1988), *Social Identifications: A Social Psychology of Intergroup Relations and Group Processes*, London, Routledge.

Hölzle, Claudia (1994), *Bildungspolitik in der Europäischen Gemeinschaft: Die Angleichungsproblematik von Bildungssystemen in der Europäischen Gemeinschaft am Beispiel Spaniens*, Cologne, Bohlau Verlag.

Hopkins, Ken, Miles Howarth and Joanna Le Métais (1994), *Into the Heart of Europe: The Education Dimension*, Slough, National Foundation for Educational Research.

Hörner, Wolfgang (1996), 'Einführung: Bildungssysteme in Europa – Überlegungen zu einer vergleichenden Betrachtung', in *Bildungssysteme in Europa: Entwicklung und Struktur des Bildungswesens in zehn Ländern: Deutschland, England, Frankreich, Italien, Niederlande, Polen, Russland, Schweden, Spanien, Türkei*, ed. Oskar Anweiler, Günter Brinkmann and Friedrich Kuebart, Einheim and Basel, Beltz Verlag.

Hoskins, Colin and Rolf Mirus (1988), 'Reasons for the US dominance of the international trade in television programmes', *Media, Culture and Society*, 10: 499–515.

Houlihan, Barrie (1999), 'Sport, national identity and public policy', *Nations & Nationalism*, 3: 113–137.

Howe, Paul (1995), 'A community of Europeans: The requisite underpinnings', *Journal of Common Market Studies*, 33: 27–46.

Inglehart, Ronald (1991), 'Trust between nations: Primordial ties, societal learning and economic development', in *Eurobarometer: The Dynamics of European Public Opinion: Essays in Honour of Jacques-René Rabier*, ed. Karlheinz Reif and Ronald Inglehart, London, Macmillan.

Jackson, Thaddeus Patrick and Daniel H. Nexon (1999), 'Relations before states: Substance, process and the study of world politics', *European Journal of International Relations*, 5: 291–332.

Janssen, Bernd (1994), 'Bildungspolitik', in *Jahrbuch der europäischen Integration 1993/94*, Bonn, Europa Union Verlag.

Janssen, Bernd, ed. (1993), *La dimension européenne pour enseignants: Rapport de la deuxième conference sur la dimension européenne dans l'enseignement et dans l'education*, Bonn, Europa Union Verlag.

Janssen, Bernd (1992), 'Bildungspolitik', in *Jahrbuch der europäischen Integration 1991/92*, Bonn, Europa Union Verlag.

Janssen, Bernd (1990), *Die europäische Dimension in Unterricht und*

Erziehung: Zur Entschliessung empfohlen, zur Entschliessung angenommen?, Bonn, Europa Union Verlag.

Janssen, Bernd (1989), 'Bildungs- und Kulturpolitik', in *Jahrbuch der europäischen Integration 1988/89*, Bonn, Europa Union Verlag.

Janssen, Bernd (1987), 'Bildungs- und Kulturpolitik', in *Jahrbuch der europäischen Integration 1986/87*, Bonn, Europa Union Verlag.

Janssen, Bernd (1986), 'Bildungs- und Kulturpolitik', in *Jahrbuch der europäischen Integration 1985*, Bonn, Europa Union Verlag.

Janssen, Bernd (1985), 'Das Europa der Bürger – der "kleine Bruder" im Abseits: Zur Arbeit des Adonnino-Ausschusses', *Integration*, 8: 165–173.

Janssen, Bernd (1982), 'Bildungs- und Kulturpolitik', in *Jahrbuch der europäischen Integration 1981*, Bonn, Europa Union Verlag.

Janssen, Bernd (1981), 'Bildungs- und Kulturpolitik', in *Jahrbuch der europäischen Integration 1980*, Bonn, Europa Union Verlag.

'Joint declaration on Audiovisual Eureka' (1990), in Matto Maggiore, *Audiovisual Production and the Single Market*, Luxembourg, Commission of the EC, Appendix V.

Jupille, Joseph, James A. Caporaso and Jeffrey T. Checkel (2002), 'Integrating Institutions: Theory, Method, and the Study of the European Union', Oslo, Arena Working Paper No. WP 02/27.

Kaelble, Hartmut (1987), *Auf dem Weg zu einer europäischen Gesellschaft: Eine Sozialgeschichte Westeuropas 1880–1980*, Munich, Beck.

Kaeser, Marc-Antoine (1998), 'Helvètes ou Lacustres? La jeune Conféderation suisse à la recherche d' ancêtres opérationnels', in *Die Konstruktion einer Nation: Nation und Nationalisierung in der Schweiz, 18.-20. Jahrhundert*, ed. Urs Altermatt, Catherine Bosshart-Pfluger and Albert Tanner, Zürich, Chronos Verlag.

Karolina-Burger-Realschule, available on the Internet at www.kbrs.bildung-rp.de/comen3_e.htm (accessed April 2004).

Kertzer, David (1988), *Rituals, Politics, and Power*, New Haven, Yale University Press.

Kledal, Birger and Svend Lauridsen (1991), 'Dänemark', in *Politische Bildung in Europa: Die europäische Dimension in der politischen Bildung*, ed. Will Cremer and Otto Schmuck, Bonn, Bundeszentrale für Politische Bildung.

Kostakopoulou, Theodora (1997), 'Why a "community of Europeans" could be a community of exclusion: A reply to Howe', *Journal of Common Market Studies*, 35: 301–8.

Krosnick, Jon A. (1988), 'Attitude importance in social evaluation: A study of policy preferences, presidential candidate evaluation and voting behavior', *Journal of Personality and Social Psychology*, 53: 505–14.

Kurzer, Paulette (2001), *Markets and Moral Regulation: Cultural Change in the European Union*, Cambridge, Cambridge University Press.

Laffan, Brigid (1996), 'The politics of identity and political order in Europe', *Journal of Common Market Studies*, 34: 81–102.

Lange, André and Jean-Luc Renaud (1989), *The Future of the European Audiovisual Industry*, Manchester, The European Institute for the Media.

Laponce, Jean (1988), *Languages and their Territorries*, Toronto, University of Toronto Press.

Letze, Otto (1986), 'Deutsch-Französischer Jugendaustausch: Organisation und Interaktion', doctoral dissertation, University of Tübingen.

Liebes, Tamar and Elihu Katz (1989), 'On the critical abilities of television viewers', in *Remote Control: Television, Audiences, and Cultural Power*, ed. Ellen Seiter, Hans Borchers, Gabriele Kreutzner and Eva-Marie Warth, London, Routledge.

Lijphart, Arend (1977), *Democracy in Plural Societies: A Comparative Exploration*, New Haven, Yale University Press.

Lijphart, Arend (1968), 'Consociational democracy', *World Politics*, 21: 207–225.

Lindberg, Leon N. (1963), *The Political Dynamics of European Economic Integration*, Stanford, Stanford University Press.

Lindberg, Leon N. and Stuart A. Scheingold (1970), *Europe's Would-be Polity: Patterns of Change in the European Community*, Englewood Cliffs, Prentice Hall.

Loth, Wilfried (1991), *Der Weg nach Europa: Geschichte der europäischen Integration 1939–1957*, Göttingen, Vandenhoeck & Ruprecht.

Maaß, Kurt-Jürgen (1978), *Die Bildungspolitik der Europäischen Gemeinschaft*, Bonn, Raabe.

Maggiore, Matto (1990), *Audiovisual Production and the Single Market*, Luxembourg, Commission of the EC.

Mann, Michael (1970), 'The social cohesion of liberal democracy', *American Sociological Review*, 35: 423–439.

Marcussen, Martin, Thomas Risse, Daniela Engelmann-Martin, Hans Joachim Knopf and Klaus Roscher (1999), 'Constructing Europe: The evolution of French, British and German nation-state identities', *Journal of European Public Policy*, 7: 261–289.

Massart-Piérard, Françoise (1986), 'Limites et enjeux d'une politique culturelle pour la Communauté Européenne', *Revue du Marché Commun*, 293.

McLaren, Robert I. (1985), 'Mitranian Functionalism: Possible or impossible?', *Review of International Studies*, 11: 139–152.

McQuail, Denis and Sven Windahl (1993), *Communication Models for the Study of Mass Communications* (2nd edition), Harlow, Longman.

'MEDIA II: Development and training' (Draft text as amended by the EP). *OJEC* No. C166: 178–200.

McRae, Kenneth (1983), *Conflict and Compromise in Multilingual Societies*, Waterloo, Wilfrid Laurier University Press.

Meyer, John W. (1977), 'The effects of education as an institution', *American Journal of Sociology*, 83: 55–77.

180

REFERENCES

Meyer, John W., John Boli, George M. Thomas and Francisco O. Ramirez
(1997), 'World society and the nation-state', *American Journal of Sociology*,
103: 144–81.
Ministers responsible for Cultural Affairs (1986a), 'Resolution of the
Ministers responsible for Cultural Affairs meeting within the Council of 17
February 1986 on the establishment of transnational cultural itineraries',
OJEC, No. C44: 2.
Ministers responsible for Cultural Affairs (1986b), 'Resolution of the
Ministers responsible for Cultural Affairs, meeting within the Council of
13 November 1986 on the European cinema and television year (1988)',
OJEC, No. C320: 4.
Ministers with responsibility for Cultural Affairs (1986a), 'Resolution of the
Ministers with responsibility for Cultural Affairs, meeting within the
Council of 13 November 1986 on the protection of Europe's architecture
heritage', *OJEC*, No. C320: 1.
Ministers with responsibility for Cultural Affairs (1986b), 'Resolution of the
Ministers with responsibility for Cultural Affairs, meeting within the
Council of 13 November 1986 on business sponsorship of cultural activi-
ties', *OJEC*, No. C320: 2.
Ministers with responsibility for Cultural Affairs (1986c), 'Resolution of the
Ministers with responsibility for Cultural Affairs, meeting within the
Council of 13 November 1986 on the conservation of works of art and arte-
facts', *OJEC*, No. C320: 3.
Mitrany, David (1966), *A Working Peace System*, Chicago, Quadrangle Books.
Moravcsik, Andrew (1999), 'Is something rotten in the state of Denmark?
"Constructivism and European Integration"', *Journal of European Public
Policy*, 6: 669–681.
Morley, David (1992), *Television, Audiences and Cultural Studies*, London,
Routledge.
Morley, David and Kevin Robins (1989), 'Spaces of identity: Communications
technologies and the reconfiguration of Europe', *Screen*, 30: 10–34.
Morrell, F. (1996), *Continent Isolated: A Study of the European Dimension in
the National School Curriculum in England*, London, Federal Trust for
Education and Research.
Mosse, George L. (1991), *The Nationalization of the Masses: Political
Symbolism and Mass Movements in Germany from the Napoleonic wars
through the Third Reich*, Ithaca, Cornell University Press.
Müller-Solger, Hermann, Armin Czysz, Petra Leonhard and Ulrich Pfaff
1993, *Bildung und Europa: Die EG-Fördermaßnahmen*, Bonn, Economica
Verlag.
Myeurope, available on the Internet at www.eun.org/eun.org2/eun
/index_myeurope.cfm (accessed April 2004).
Neave, Guy (1984), *The EEC and Education*, Stoke-on-Trent, Trentham
Books.

Negrine, Ralph and Stylianos Papathanassopoulous (1990), *The Internationalization of Television*, London, Pinter Publishers.

Netdays 2002: Summary of Results, available on the Internet at www.netdayseurope.org/library/Documents/Results_EN.doc (accessed May 2004).

Netdays Europe, available on the Internet at www.netdayseurope.org (accessed April 2004).

Neville-Jones, Pauline (1983), 'The Genscher-Colombo proposals on European Union', *Common Market Law Review*, 20: 657–699.

Nicholas, Joseph (1991), Letter to the editor, *The Guardian*, October 25: 22.

Noam, Eli (1991), *Television in Europe*, New York, Oxford University Press.

Nundy, Julian (1992), 'History leaves Britain behind', *The Independent on Sunday*, 19 January: 15.

Obradovic, Daniela (1996), 'Policy legitimacy and the European Union', *Journal of Common Market Studies*, 34: 191–221.

Onuf, Nicholas (1989), *World of our Making: Rules and Rule in Social Theory and International Relations*, Columbia, SC, University of South Carolina Press.

Otala, Leenamaija (1992), *European Approaches to Lifelong Learning: Trends in Industry Practices and Industry-university Cooperation in Adult Education and Training*, Geneva, The CRE-ERT European University-Industry Forum.

Oxford English Dictionary, (1989) (2nd edition), Oxford, Clarendon Press.

Palacio-Villa, Miguel (1991), 'Spanien', in *Politische Bildung in Europa: Die europäische Dimension in der politischen Bildung*, ed. Will Cremer and Otto Schmuck, Bonn, Bundeszentrale für Politische Bildung.

'PartBase' (2004), available on the Internet at www. partbase.eupro.se (accessed May 2004).

Patman, Jan Jindy (1999), 'Nationalism and after', *Review of International Studies*, 24: 149–164.

Peege, Friedrich-Karl (1973), 'Die wirtschafts- und sozialpolitischen Aspekte der gemeinsamen Berufsbildungspolitik in der EWG', doctoral dissertation, University of Mainz.

Pentland, Charles (1973), *International Theory and European Integration*, New York, The Free Press.

Percheron, Annick (1985), 'La socialisation politique: défense et illustration', in *Traité de science politique* (Vol. 3), ed. Madeleine Grawitz and Jean Leca, Paris, Presses Universitaires de France

Perriaux, Anne-Sophie (1990), 'La Communauté Économique Européenne, les États et la culture 1957–1987', *Revue de Synthèse*, 4: 271–287.

Piaget, Jean and Anne-Marie Weil (1951), 'The development in children of the idea of the homeland and of relations with other countries', *International Social Science Bulletin*, 3: 561–576.

Plas, Hans (1991), 'Niederlande', in *Politische Bildung in Europa: Die europäische Dimension in der politischen Bildung*, ed. Will Cremer and Otto

Schmuck, Bonn, Bundeszentrale für Politische Bildung.

Polaczek, Dietmar (1982), 'Lehrstück über Europa', *Frankfurter Allgemeine Zeitung*, 22 September: 25.

Poulot, Dominique (1997), *Musée, nation, patrimoine, 1789–1815*, Paris, Gallimard.

Puchala, Donald (1981), 'Integration Theory and the study of international relations', in *From National Development to Global Community: Essays in Honor of Karl W. Deutsch*, ed. Richard L. Merritt and Bruce M. Russett, London, George Allan & Unwin.

Ravault, René Jean (1986), 'Défense de l'identité culturelle par les réseaux traditionnels de "Coerséduction"', *International Political Science Review*, 7: 251–280.

Reading, Viviane (2004), 'The Future of European Audiovisual Policy', Westminster Media Forum London, 22 April 2004, available at the Internet at www.europa.eu.int/rapid/start/cgi/guesten.ksh?p_action.gettxt =gt&doc=SPEECH/04/192|0|RAPID&lg=EN&display=   (accessed   May 2004).

Reif, Karlheinz and Ronald Inglehart, eds (1991), *Eurobarometer – The Dynamics of European Public Opinion: Essays in Honour of Jacques-René Rabier*, London, Macmillan.

Renner, Günter and Wolfgang Sander (1991), 'Bundesrepublik Deutschland', in *Politische Bildung in Europa: Die europäische Dimension in der politischen Bildung*, ed. Will Cremer and Otto Schmuck, Bonn, Bundeszentrale für Politische Bildung.

'Report on European Union' (1976), *Bulletin of the EC*, Supplement No. 1.

Ringmar, Eric (1996), 'On the ontological status of the state', *European Journal of International Relations*, 2: 439–466.

Risse, Thomas (in press) 'European institutions and identity change: What have we learned?', in *Identities in Europe and the Institutions of the European Union*, ed. Richard Herrmann, Marilynn Brewer and Thomas Risse, Lanham, MD, Rowman & Littlefield.

Ross, George (1995), *Jacques Delors and European Integration*, Oxford, Oxford University Press.

Rübsamen, Dieter (1978), 'Möglichkeiten und Grenzen supranationaler Europäischer Kultur- und Bildungspolitik', *Bildung und Erziehung*, 31: 238–273.

Ryba, Raymond (1992), 'Toward a European dimension in education: Intention and reality in European Community policy and practice', *Comparative Education Review*, 36: 10–24.

Ryngaert, Johan (1987), 'Le Conseil "mixte" culture: un événement vite redimensionné', *Rivista di Studi Politici Internazionali*, 216: 581–590.

Sandell, Terry (1996), 'Cultural issues, debates and programmes', in *The European Union Handbook*, ed. Philippe Barbour, Chicago, Fitzroy Dearborn Publishers.

Sandholtz, Wayne and John Zysman (1989), '1992: Recasting the European bargain', *World Politics*, 42: 95–128.

Scharpf, Fritz W. (1998), 'Demokratie in der transnationalen Politik', in *Politik der Globalisierung*, ed. Ulrich Beck, Frankfurt am Main, Suhrkamp Verlag.

Schlesinger, Philip (1997), 'From cultural defence to political culture: Media, politics and collective identity in the European Union', *Media, Culture & Society*, 19: 369–391.

Schlesinger, Philip (1996), 'From cultural protection to political culture? Media Policy and the European Union', paper prepared for the Europaeum conference on 'Defining and projecting Europe's identity: Issues and trade-offs', Geneva, 20–22 March.

Schmid, Carol L. (1981), *Conflict and Consensus in Switzerland*, Berkeley, University of California Press.

Schmitter, Philippe C. (1996), 'Examining the present Euro-polity with the help of past theories', in Gary Marks, Fritz W. Scharpf, Philippe C. Schmitter and Wolfgang Streeck, *Governance in the European Union*, London, Sage.

Schmitz-Wenzel, Hermann (1980), 'Einführung', in *Bildungspolitik in der Europäischen Gemeinschaft*, ed. Hermann Schmitz-Wenzel, Baden-Baden, Nomos Verlagsgesellschaft.

Sciarini, Pascal, Simon Hug and Cédric Dupont (2001), 'Example, exception or both? Swiss national identity in perspective', in *Constructing Europe's Identity: The External Dimension*, ed. Lars-Erik Cederman, Boulder, Lynne Rienner.

Searle, John (1995), *The Construction of Social Reality*, London, Penguin.

Shaw, Joe (1999), 'From the margins to the centre: Education and training law and policy', in *The Evolution of EU Law*, ed. P. Craig and G. De Búrca, Oxford, Oxford University Press.

Shils, Edward and Michael Young (1975), 'The meaning of the coronation', in *Center and Periphery: Essays in Macrosociology*, ed. Edward Shils, Chicago, University of Chicago Press.

Shore, Chris (2000), *Building Europe: The Cultural Politics of European Integration*, London, Routledge.

Shore, Chris (1996), 'Transcending the nation-state? The European Commission and the (re)-discovery of Europe', *Journal of Historical Sociology*, 9: 473–496.

Shore, Chris (1993), 'Inventing the "people's Europe": Critical approaches to European Community "cultural policy"', *Man*, 28: 779–800.

Simmel, Georg (1955), *Conflict and the Web of Group-Affiliations*, New York, The Free Press.

Smith, Anthony D. (1992), 'National identity and the idea of European unity', *International Affairs*, 68: 55–76.

Smith, Anthony D. (1991), *National Identity*, London, Penguin.

Social Europe (1989), Supplement No. 8.

Social Europe (1988), Supplement No. 5.

Social Europe (1987), Supplement No. 3.

'Solemn Declaration on European Union' (1983), *Bulletin of the EC*, No. 6, point 1.6.1.

Soysal, Yasemin (1994), *The Limits of Citizenship: Migrants and Postnational Membership in Europe*, Chicago, University of Chicago Press.

Spillman, Lyn (1997), *Nation and Commemoration: Creating National Identities in the United States and Australia*, Cambridge, Cambridge University Press.

Spiteri, Sharon (2004), 'EU accused of pooling money for propaganda purpose', available on the Internet at www.euobserver.com/index .phtml?sid=9&aid=6739 (accessed September 2004).

Stewart, Cathy and Julian Laird (1994), *The European Media Industry: Fragmentation and Convergence in Broadcasting and Publishing*, London, Financial Times Business Information.

Tait, Alan (1996), 'Open and distance learning policy in the European Union, 1985–1995', *Higher Education Policy*, 9: 221–238.

Tajfel, Henri (1981), *Human Groups and Social Categories: Studies in Social Psychology*, Cambridge, Cambridge University Press.

Taylor, Paul (1991), 'The European Community and the state: Assumptions, theories and propositions', *Review of International Studies*, 17: 109–125.

Thaa, Winfried (2001), '"Lean citizenship": The fading away of the political in transnational democracy', *European Journal of International Relations*, 7: 503–523.

Theiler, Tobias (2004a), 'The origins of Euroscepticism in German-speaking Switzerland', *European Journal of Political Research*, 43: 635–656.

Theiler, Tobias (2004b), 'Culture and European integration (review article)', *Journal of European Public Policy*, 10: 841–848.

Theiler, Tobias (2003), 'Societal security and social psychology', *Review of International Studies*, 29: 249–268.

Theiler, Tobias (2001), 'Why the European Union failed to Europeanize audiovisual policy', in *Constructing Europe's Identity: The External Dimension*, ed. Lars-Erik Cederman, Boulder, Lynne Rienner.

Theiler, Tobias (1999a), 'International integration and national beliefs: A psychological basis for consociationalism as a model of political unification', *Nationalism & Ethnic Politics*, 5: 46–81.

Theiler, Tobias (1999b), 'Viewers into Europeans? How the European Union tried to Europeanize the audiovisual sector, and why it failed', *Canadian Journal of Communication*, 24: 557–587.

Tindemans, Leo (1976), 'Text of Mr Leo Tindemans' letter to his European Council colleagues sent on 29 December 1975', *Bulletin of the EC*, Supplement No. 1.

Tracey, Michael (1988), 'Popular culture and the economics of global television', *Intermedia*, 16: 9–25.

Tranholm-Mikkelsen, Jeppe (1991), 'Neo-functionalism: Obstinate or obsolete? A reappraisal in the light of the new dynamism of the EC', *Millennium*, 20: 1–22.

Treaties establishing the European Communities; Treaties Amending these Treaties; Documents Concerning the Accession (1973), Luxembourg, OOPEC.

UK Parliament Hansard, written answers for 11 Nov. 1999, pt. 6.

UK Parliament Hansard, written answers for 28 Oct. 1998, pt. 4.

Wacquant, Loïc J. D. (1996), 'Towards a social praxeology: The structure and logic of Bourdieu's sociology', in *An Invitation to Reflexive Sociology*, ed. Pierre Bourdieu and Loïc J. D. Wacquant, Cambridge, Polity Press.

Wallace, William (1990), *The Transformation of Western Europe*, London, Pinter Publishers.

Wæver, Ole (1996), 'European security identities', *Journal of Common Market Studies*, 34: 103–132.

Wæver, Ole, Barry Buzan, Morten Kelstrup and Pierre Lemaitre (1993), *Identity, Migration and the New Security Agenda in Europe*, London, Pinter.

Weber, Eugene (1976), *Peasants into Frenchmen: The Modernization of Rural France, 1870–1914*, Stanford, Stanford University Press.

Wedell, George (1986), 'The establishment of the Common Market for broadcasting in Western Europe', *International Political Science Review*, 7: 281–297.

Weiler, J. H. H. (1996), 'Legitimacy and Democracy of Union Governance: The 1996 Intergovernmental Agenda and Beyond', Oslo, ARENA Working Paper No. 22.

Wellens, K. C. and G. M. Borchardt (1989), 'Soft law in European Community law', *European Law Review*, October: 267–321.

Wendt, Alexander (1999), *Social Theory of International Politics*, Cambridge, Cambridge University Press.

Wendt, Alexander (1992), 'Anarchy is what states make of it: The social construction of power politics', *International Organization*, 46: 391–407.

Winter, Klaus (1980), *Das Europäische Bildungswesen im Prozeß seiner Internationalisierung: Eine vergleichende Analyse unter besonderer Berücksichtigung der Reformansätze in der Lehrerausbildung*, Weinheim and Basel, Beltz Verlag.

Witte, Barthold C. (1991), 'Kulturpolitik', in *Jahrbuch der europäischen Integration 1990/91*, Bonn, Europa Union Verlag.

Zabusky, Stacia E. (1995), *Launching Europe: An Ethnography of European Cooperation in Space Science*, Princeton, Princeton University Press.

Zamoyski, Adam (1988), 'Just an historic case of Euro-fudge', *Sunday Telegraph*, November 6: 13.

Zimmer, Jochen (1989), 'Europäisches Fernsehen: Programme, Probleme und Perspektiven', in *Europäisches Fernsehen – American-Blend? Fernsehmedien zwischen Amerikanisierung und Europäisierung*, ed. Winand Gellner, Berlin, Vistas.

INDEX

Note: 'n' after a page reference indicates a note on that page.